for Steve -

ARCTIC WILD

In honor of the "wolf spirit"
"you've so readily shared
with me..." I love you
and hope we can both
stay close to our own
wild, free spirits

love you always,

Jennifer ♡

X-mas
'91
Namaste,
my friend
...lovers, companions, homeowners etc etc....!

ARCTIC WILD

by Lois Crisler ILLUSTRATED

HarperPerennial

A Division of HarperCollins*Publishers*

91 92 93 94 95 C W 10 9 8 7 6 5 4 3 2 1

TO THE WOLVES OF THE ARCTIC TUNDRA

AND TO THOSE PEOPLE WHO WILL ACT TO PRESERVE

LIFE AND HABITAT FOR THEM

Contents

Illustrations follow pages 78 and 174.

From my memories of Lois Crisler two stand out most vividly. One is the occasion of our first meeting, sometime in the early fifties, in Boulder, Colorado. She and her husband Herb (or Cris, as she called him) had come down from their cabin home in the Tarryall Mountains to join me at the hotel for lunch. I remember them at table: the soft-spoken statuesque woman with magnificent braids of hair wound around her head, and the man, sturdy and of lesser stature, with a jolly ruddy face and bright bright eyes framed by dark hair and beard. In those days any beard set a man apart, and Herb Crisler's was notably luxuriant.

It was a time of snow, we were a mile high and they had come from still higher, colder altitudes. To a publisher out of New York a pre-luncheon drink seemed called for—a routine and meager courtesy. The Crislers greeted the suggestion with pleased amazement, as something unheard-of but delightfully imaginative. They chose, I believe, a glass of muscatel.

Over lunch, a friendly and easy time, our talk turned to the Crislers' family of wolves, dog-wolves, dogs—and to Alatna who reigned over them all, one of the five wild wolves they had brought to Colorado from a remote section of the Brooks Range in Alaska. Lois invited me to go back to Crag Cabin with them that afternoon—a distance of perhaps thirty or forty miles. I could stay overnight, she said, and sleep in Alatna's bed in Cris's greenhouse. I have always regretted that I had to decline —for reasons that seemed urgent at the time and certainly not because of any distaste for the sleeping arrangements. Such an aura of confidence and authority was generated by the Crislers when they spoke of their animals that I feel sure I would not have flinched had they proposed that Alatna share her bed with me. They were that impressive.

Before this meeting Lois and I had corresponded at considerable length. A partial manuscript of *Arctic Wild* had passed through my hands on its way to the trustees of the Eugene F. Saxton Memorial Foundation, who awarded Lois a fellowship to see the project to completion. Subsequently I became her editor when Harper's put the book under contract. I recall in particular a letter I received from her acknowledging a check for an advance against royalties. Her thanks for a sum that today seems shockingly modest were accompanied by a list of the luxury items the check had purchased. Chief among them were a choice carcass for the animals' consumption and a supply of toilet paper. As the Crislers had foreseen when they elected to take the wolves out of Alaska, the animals housed in the monstrous pen at Crag Cabin were to keep them forever poor.

Arctic Wild was published in 1958, to wide acclaim. This was before the publication of *Silent Spring*, before there was an "ecological movement" drawing public attention to the dangers threatening humankind through careless disregard of wilderness areas and their creatures.

It was almost by accident that Lois and Herb Crisler became intimately involved with wolves during their eighteen-month stay in the Far North, which is the subject of the book. They had gone to the Arctic, on an assignment from Walt Disney, to photograph caribou in migration—which led to a study of all the related wild life of the region. Wolves, they had to conclude from their observations, were essential to the well-being of caribou herds as they shepherded out the ailing, crippled, inferior animals. And the Crislers' experience of two families of young wolves they raised from puppyhood forced them to the belief that popular myths have slandered one of the earth's most interesting and ingratiating creatures, that wolves—unlike dogs and men—are "gentle-hearted"; they are "just not feisty, fighting animals." At the end of their stay in the Arctic, Lois could write: "Wolves have what it takes to live together in peace." It was a fact that had grown upon them slowly. "In a reasonable world," she asserted, "these peaceful predators would be the most cherished object of study by our race, trying to unlearn war. Why then do people hate wolves and seek to exterminate them?…It takes a psychiatrist to say."

It is this sort of informed comment, born of direct, clear-eyed observation, that makes *Arctic Wild* as relevant and exciting an experience today as it was fifteen years ago—as it will be for years to come. It is very possibly more timely now than it was when it first appeared, for the reason that ground has been broken by the Crislers themselves, by Rachel Carson and others who preceded and succeeded them. People outside as well as inside scientific circles are aware of what is happening to the quality of life on earth. They are more ready to listen, and to heed.

Lois, before most of us were alerted, feared the encroachments civilization was making, and *Arctic Wild* is an eloquent cry of warning. "We believe that the last frail wonderful webs of wilderness now vanishing from Earth are of some infinite value, a value only sensed and very deep—and liable to perish and be lost in this day. Wilderness without its animals is dead. Animals without wilderness are a closed book." And: "Wilderness is a quality gone from human environment. Tameness is the air one breathes in civilization. People suppose wildness is ferocity. It is something far more serious than that. It is independence—a life commitment to shouldering up one's own self."

I said that I have two vivid memories of Lois. The second has to do with a visit she made to me in Connecticut in 1966, when the writing of *Captive Wild* was in progress. I met her at the Old Saybrook station as she arrived by train from Rachel Carson's summer home in Maine, and I see her coming toward me on the platform—a commanding figure, erect, unhurried. It was a troubled period in her life following the break-up of her marriage, full of fears and uncertainties. Some things she could talk about but one sensed many things withheld. The days she spent with me were a time of curious quiet as she rested, observed and stored away impressions to be recalled in letters years later: the tree with the odd root system that reminded her of a similar formation in a Western forest; the mongrel neighbor dog Zeke, "shining, assured, coming over to call, so confidently"; "the woman with the baby, the grave young girl who has by now outgrown the playhouse she was sure you would like to clamber to see." Beneath the quiet much was stirring.

One hesitates to attempt description of a person as private and complex as I felt Lois to be. Her friend and literary agent, Marie Rodell, calls to mind "the strange eyes, the erect walk, the tremulous smile, and all the shyness and fear and gentleness." To some of us—who have, for sure, never "brushed eyes" with a wolf—Lois's eyes had something of the quality of Alatna's, described as "the famous, impersonal wolf attentiveness." Did it come of having lived with vast spaces, of having secret knowledge of worlds within worlds beyond distant hills? The shyness and gentleness, I am confident, were born in part of long practice in avoiding intrusion upon any living creature. That she knew fear is certain. Not fear of the wilderness but rather of strictures imposed by civilization. People in masses could terrify her, and so could the thought of a future lacking money to ensure independence. Yet overriding fear was a kind of courage it is difficult to understand or assess—courage to endure physical hardships few of us can conceive of, and the courage to stand up to her life commitments when every door seemed closed, every choice intolerable. A woman of sophisticated intelligence and fierce pride, an artist in her command of language and her whole approach to life (ballet was one of her passions), Lois had a singular innocence that was very appealing. "Well, I declare," she would say in response to some trivial bit of information outside her field of knowledge. She consistently undervalued herself, her deference was flattering.

In a letter received while she was working on *Captive Wild* she wrote: "I dare not say it in the book, but I have a sense of holiness about wild nature, in spite of its sometimes dreadful aspects....I want to find some way of expressing this feeling acceptably." I think she did. The message rings clear in both her books, and in *Arctic Wild* it carries a note of joyous participation.

Lois's death in early June, 1971, came without sharp warning and by her wish was kept a private matter. It is good to remember that in the last years she had the independence she cherished and found genuine contentment near friends she counted as family on the edge of the Olympic wilderness of Washington State—in "the most pleasing place I've had, a three-room house with a big, tranquil, bare living room looking through five wide windows into madronas and firs." For companions there were a "humble" black tomcat and a "fearless" squirrel—"very small and vanishing touches of the wild, but I enjoy them."

ELIZABETH LAWRENCE KALASHNIKOFF

Deep River, Connecticut
January, 1973

Foreword

The Arctic is the last great wilderness of North America. On the rolling tundra or among the ridges and promontories of the Brooks Range one may still find complete isolation from the world as most of us know it. For a year and a half Lois Crisler and her husband, Herb, lived in that remote land, filming the arctic wildlife for one of the major Hollywood studios. This book is Lois's journal. But it is much more than a narrative of the Crislers and of what they did. It is an account of the country and of the animals that populate the arctic landscape. To write a penetrating book about a landscape one must be in love with it. Lois Crisler is manifestly in love with the tundra. Her writing skillfully portrays the joys and the sorrows, the intimacies and ecstasies of one who has lived with and who understands the Arctic in all its moods.

There are many ways to view a landscape. Some observers see principally the scenery, in a topographic sense. In retrospection they call to mind the sweeping vistas, the dizzy heights or the changing light effects. A charming example of such a view of the Brooks Range is Robert Marshall's recent book, *Arctic Wilderness* (University of California Press, 1956. Others will tend to describe an area in terms of plant life. I have a good friend who almost invariably begins an account of an outdoor adventure with a word picture of the vegetation—to her a hillside may be a "white curtain of daisies framed in dark pines"; or an alpine meadow is "a blue table of lupine with a clump of pale willows as a centerpiece." To Lois Crisler a landscape is characterized by the animals that live there. In recalling a scene she will remember most vividly the distant weaving line of a band of trotting caribou, or the saucy tail-jerking of sik-sik squirrels among the rocks. Not that Lois overlooks the scenery, or the vegetation, or the colors in the sky. But these are all settings and backdrops for the animals. Such a view of the arctic landscape is particularly gratifying to a vertebrate zoologist like myself. Furthermore it is highly informative. I have read few accounts of the northland that portray so vividly and faithfully the characters and behaviorisms of the native birds and mammals. Best of all are the observations of caribou and wolves and their complex interrelations in the perpetual struggle for existence.

Caribou are the dominant grazing animals of the North; wolves are their only important predators. To meet year-round forage requirements the caribou migrate enormous distances from season to season, summering on the tundra as far north as the arctic coast and wintering in the more southerly timber zones where branching lichens are available for winter food. Wolves follow the great herds most of the year, extracting a constant toll of victims from the migrants. The Crislers had an unusual opportunity to watch day after day the contest of wits and speed and courage between the hunters and the hunted. Most of the caribou that were caught proved to be weak or sick. Time and again healthy animals—even young calves—were seen to outrun the wolves. It has often been stated, but rarely demonstrated, that predation does in fact result in elimination of the unfit in a prey population. Lois Crisler's written record of her observations lends credence to this concept and raises again the question of the biological wisdom of killing wolves to "protect" caribou.

The Crislers' observations of wolves went beyond merely watching them chase caribou. In each of the two summers of their stay, they raised a litter of wolf pups taken from wild parents. A substantial part of this book is comprised of Lois's intensely interesting observations of these captives. In fact this volume probably includes the most meticulous and complete description of wolf mannerisms and behavior that has been written. It calls to mind the writings of Konrad Lorenz of Austria on the behavior of various breeds of dogs (*Man Meets Dog*, Houghton Mifflin Company, 1955) in which he contrasts the behavior patterns of breeds derived from the wolf and those descending from the jackal. The Crisler account of wolf personality will be good source material for the behaviorists.

This factual appraisal of the Crisler manuscript falls far short of being a just evaluation of the book, whose charm lies not in the scientific value of its facts but in the delightful manner of its writing.

A. STARKER LEOPOLD

Professor of Zoology, University of California

1 *On the Trail of the Caribou*

━━━━━━━━━━━━━━━━━━━━━━━━━━━━━━━

Andy Anderson, the arctic bush pilot at Bettles Field in Alaska, could have said, in answer to my nagging questions, "Mrs. Crisler, God alone knows the answers to the things you are asking. You and your husband will gamble your lives and I will gamble mine to help you. But I cannot answer your questions. If you and Cris go through with what you intend, you're going to learn some of the answers. But you won't be able to tell them to anybody else. And you'll learn with tears and glory, fear and love, this land; so that all your life— provided you live—its great freedom will haunt you with longing. You'll pray to get out and cry because you can't come back."

Outwardly Andy was silent. In the face of the Arctic, which was unknown to Cris and me, and in the face of those northernmost mountains on the North American mainland, the Brooks Range, largely unknown to anybody, I kept lugging my ignorant, earnest questions to Andy, sure that if he only would he could answer. He looked at me without smiling, he was taciturn, he wasted valuable question-and-answer time, between his continual flights, sitting with a magazine, reading.

A few simple basic facts were all I wanted, so we wouldn't waste our time and money. When will breakup come this year? How long will it last? Breakup is the period of four to six weeks during which the thawing ice is unsafe for plane landings. Before it, ski planes can land almost anywhere, on lake or tundra. After it, float planes can land on lakes and rivers. But during breakup there is no safe natural landing place.

Above all, what would be the best place to spend breakup, immobilized as far as plane transportation was concerned, where we could be reasonably sure of finding caribou? We were going into the Brooks Range to make a motion-picture record of the lives of caribou and if possible of their wild shepherds, the wolves.

This would not be our first experience in filming wild animals in their habitat. Ever since our marriage, twelve years before, we had photographed in wilderness areas in the States and shown the pictures on national lecture circuits. But those pictures had been filmed in habitat we knew and lived in. Now we were to take pictures in unfamiliar terrain for theater distribution.

In one swift week we had left our log cabin in the Tarryall Mountains of Colorado; conferred in Hollywood with the men contracting for Cris's exposed film; flown to Fairbanks, the northernmost city in Alaska; and then, in an unheated DC-3 with a red-nostriled stewardess, and with our familiar dunnage roped to upturned seats across the aisle from us, we had flown on northward to Bettles Field. It was merely an airstrip in spruce wilderness on the Koyukuk River, just north of the Arctic Circle, humanized only by a few CAA buildings at one end, Eskimo shacks at the other, and the handsome unfinished box of the roadhouse alongside.

Early this morning, in the generous but confusing laissez-faire of the roadhouse, I had prepared breakfast for Andy and Cris. Then the men, each with a parka under one arm, maps or dunnage in the other hand, walked out to the plane. The snow was frozen and slick. But on the runway only white streaks remained on the brown earth. A plane on skis could not land here much longer.

The red wing light burned like a jewel. Andy and Cris shoved the tail around by hand. The plane went up the field and came sprinting down, the skis plowing out like toothpicks stuck on a potato. It was airborne as it passed me. The straight black line of the wings tilted a little in the wind as the plane rose away against the sunrise over the Brooks Range. The men were gone to search for caribou.

To my surprise when Andy returned a few hours later he was alone. He had set Cris down on a bare white mountain shoulder, a few miles ahead of a dark file of four hundred caribou, plodding northwestward over the snow on their annual spring migration to the north side of the Brooks Range for the summer. He had equipped Cris from the emergency supplies a bush pilot must carry: sleeping bag; tent—it could not be set up though, because there were no tent poles to be cut on that naked mountain; a fire pot, which is a kind of blowtorch for warming the airplane engine—it burns a gallon of gas an hour; two gallons of gas; and rice and pancake flour, which Cris fancied he could cook on the blowtorch.

Andy said I was to join Cris two days later, at the lake nearest to him, where Andy could pick us up after breakup. I was to bring supplies for over breakup.

But how would I get them? There was no time to send to Fairbanks; the DC-3 came up only twice a week on its way north to Point Barrow. Cris had brought along some dry groceries, but far from enough for over breakup. When we left the States we had not even known to what part of Alaska we would come. Our assignment was simply to photograph wild animals. In Fairbanks, Cris had made a quick decision to try for caribou. But when we came here to Bettles Field we had not known whether we would work out from here, stay here at all, or try some entirely different place.

People think of an expedition into remote wilderness as something like a big military affair planned long ahead by many helpers, or else as a safari with guides who know the country and the equipment it calls for, and where to look for the animals. Guides, professional or merely hopeful, had indeed offered themselves to us, at twenty-five dollars a day, having no idea of how close we would require to get to the animals—Cris's test question was, "At what distance would you shoot a grizzly I was photographing if it started toward me?"—nor the least intention of sharing the labor of backpacking if it came to that. We could not afford guides; this was not to be a short trip.

It was very hard to get helpful information. The problems of photographing wild animals are very different from those of getting to see or shoot them. In our own country we knew where to look for the various animals at various seasons. What we needed here was Cris's opposite number, someone who knew the local animals as Cris knew those in the Olympics or Rockies.

Alaska is, of course, a whole set of totally different terrains. Equipment for one is not useful for another. We had brought our old, cherished equipment for rainy country and arid country, and it had served us very well the previous year, when we had photographed in the temperate-zone parts of Alaska—the Katmai, the Kenai and Mount McKinley National Park. But equipment for cold country we did not have, nor time to get it after Cris decided to go at once for caribou. However, it was spring and should soon warm up.

Even the flying itself was not so simple as one might suppose. Either the weather was wrong or, if good, the bush pilot had to make his mail runs. Then when he was ready to take us, the hundred-hour checkup on the plane might be due and a mechanic must be flown up from Fairbanks to work all day and, if we were urgent, sit up all night to break in the overhauled engine so we could fly the next morning.

Yet another consideration was that a Cessna could not carry much weight in addition to passengers—only about what three packhorses could carry. We had the initial weight of Cris's photographic outfit. We had to carry our clothing, housing, food, fuel and tools. This meant we would do without, skimp, trusting to improvise and make do.

Andy gave us far more than piloting. He gave his interest in our project. Right now he took me to his private supplies and let me choose what I wanted.

On April 21, 1953, he and I flew calmly up the wide, white, spruce-clad valley of the John River, winding into the heart of the Brooks Range. I did not dream that like Cris I was to meet the arctic wilderness alone. We did not speak; the engine noise discouraged talking. Andy drove along the air like a farmer in a Ford, glancing with quiet pleasure at the white mountain prows on either side of the river. Once he skimmed around a sunlit crag apparently for the sheer joy of doing it. I watched the snow beneath us for tracks. At intervals we passed over beaded tangles of them, each hoof or paw puncture full of shadow now, at seven in the morning.

After an hour Andy banked west and climbed. We left the valley and entered country he had never flown over. The map was spread on my knees for him to consult, matching terrain and map at a hundred ten miles an hour. We had left trees behind. We were flying between treeless mountains robed in white velvet, slashed with perpendicular azure shadows. Faint dimpling shadows on the pure snow near the plane marked creeks lying still in the pattern of summer ease.

Now I really began to apply myself. We were heading into the country where I was to be set down. Would it be live or dead? Below us flew white birds. But there were no animal tracks on the snow.

I watched with fierce intensity for more than tracks. Andy spoke through the engine noise: "This is the way you will walk out if you have to."

I nodded. "I know."

A glance at the map on my knees, then out at the white mountains. Above all, landmarks. From the ground would I see that pyramid mountain? South here. West again. The divide? Yes, passable, easy.

Tulialek Lake below us was baby-blue ice riffled with snow, like white artificial leather. We hit it with a crash that tore off the tail-ski bolt. The riffles were a foot high and frozen like rocks. Andy tested the wing struts. Unbroken. We set my dunnage on the ice, found pliers and wire, and Andy hitched on the tail ski.

"I'll be as careful of it as I can," he promised. "I'll be back with Cris in two hours."

Then I was alone in deep silence. Probably the only other human beings in the Range itself, from the Bering Sea to Canada, and from Point Barrow to Bettles Field, were the half-dozen Eskimo families at Anaktuvuk Pass at the head of the John River, seventy-five miles across the mountains as the raven flies. Eskimos are not scattered all over the Alaskan Arctic; they are concentrated along the coast, where the jobs or villages are. Indeed, the Eskimo population has always centered along the coast because of the food supply there, in the form of oceanic mammals.

Now I could eat with anxiety my intense words when we landed: "This is a hell of a country to spend breakup in! Not a track in fifty miles!" I had sensed instantly that Andy's picture of me as a lady had altered. No matter! He would tell Cris my words—bare, like a fiat, without modification. No chance to talk things over, if this; if that. I might find I had made the decision on where *not* to spend breakup in one impulsive outburst.

But pleasure like quiet ice water flowed over the narrow channel of that distress. I had a lot to do. The sun beat on the lake in this shadeless country. Already in places shallow water stood on the blue ice. I spread a tarp and moved things onto it—boxes, sleeping bags, tools, tent rolls. I explored for our possible camp site.

I avoided looking at my watch. When I did, there was a quarter of an hour to go yet.

Of course the plane did not come. I still had plenty to do but now I faced the future. If that tail ski had given way in landing or in taking off— They had little in the way of supplies. Would Andy be able to get Umiat by radio? Umiat, the only habitation from Bettles to Point Barrow, was a dot of a military establishment, a dozen men or so, a hundred miles to the north of me. I knew Andy could not get Bettles, south of the Range. Would it be two days before they were found? Had Andy included setting me down here in his flight plan? I was ashamed of that thought.

I looked at the silent dark assembly of boxes on the blue ice. I had enough. But—the men?

Then came a pang of pure fear for myself—needless but there. Alone in the Arctic. And a stranger pang, the pure feeling of loneliness. I don't think I had ever felt that before.

At two P.M. the noise was not the noise of the wind, engine-roaring over the boxes. It was the plane. The plane disappeared against the mottled rock and snow of the mountainside. Then nearer than I expected, lower too, it was coming in level over the far end of the lake.

Cris's dark bearded face showed at the window, his arm stuck out, something fell—a note weighted by an empty oil can. "Going to Bettles. Back for you tonight or tomorrow. Lots of love, Cris."

The words were something—the information. But that seemed like nothing. The men were safe! Nothing else mattered. I could stay here alone for a month, it made no difference. It didn't matter about our getting pictures.

There was a lot to do. I loved doing it. The tarp was leaking. It took me until four o'clock to backpack everything off the ice with my packboard to a cove of thawed tundra at the foot of a snow wall by the lake. My cheeks flamed, between sun and wind and blazing snow. I put on my old hunting mask of green netting, formerly used to veil my pink face when approaching wild animals. There was plenty of drinking water on the lake now—flat pools. When a cloud interfered with the sun, the wind was liquid ice.

At the cove I sorted the dunnage into what to ditch, what must go and what I hoped could go. I supposed Andy could not take off with the weight he had landed with.

An odd noise near me, like a coffee grinder, made me look up. On top of the snow wall stood a pure-white bird against the pale-blue sky, a rock ptarmigan in "stockings" of white feathers. There was a speck of ruby by each eye. It turned its slender head, "grinding" meditatively, considering me. I guessed that the cove was its evening resort.

Life outdoors is not one of idleness. I was busy until after eight o'clock. It took me longer to put up the tent—a waist-high mountain tent, one of two tents we had brought—than if I could have used pegs; but I could not drive pegs into the frozen ground. After an anxious minute I remembered what to do. I anchored the tent ropes around heavy dunnage—the few rocks in the cove were frozen immovable. Also I weighted the bottom of the tent walls so they would not flap against me in the night. I fixed everything outside so the wind could not tip it over and startle me. I did not want to be startled.

There was nothing to fear except the one chance in a million of a grizzly, out from hibernation, strolling by. A wolf would consider a long time before tackling a layout like mine. But a grizzly might not hesitate. I thought of my sole weapon, a hatchet, and of a grizzly's thick skull. There would be little I could do. I dismissed the topic.

I made an unpleasant discovery. A hat-sized hollow by the tent had filled with water. The ground was getting squashy. I had figured that snow wall too smartly. The warm afternoon's melt from it was seeping irresistibly down through the tundra. I tried to trench it away from the tent. Lichens and moss flew, huckleberry roots gave. Then there was the ice, as solid as stone; an inch down, the floor. I could bash it a little—it chipped frost-color—but I could not trench it.

The freeze would have to stop that water soak pretty soon. Parka, boots and pants off, I crawled into the twilight of my tent and into the sleeping bag filling its floor. I thought the tent would lash all night. Actually, almost the minute I sacked in, the wind stilled; a lace handkerchief would hardly have flapped. Whenever I awoke in the arctic twilight, the silence was illimitable.

There was a gruff noise outside. I yanked open the tied end of the tent at my head and peered out. Just the snow wall and my boxes, sitting quietly on the tundra below it. About three A.M. there were a lot of gruff noises. Then under me began gurgles—big slow gurgles like the last water guggling from a tub. Something was happening to the melt water, causing all the noises.

Ptarmigan liked my cove. They did not sack in themselves until after ten o'clock. By three-thirty the world invited them again and they cruised around talking. I listened, half sleepy, half electric, as if I lay on a wide shore of strangeness and pleasure.

They were great talkers. They gave forth a whole battery of odd little noises. A put-put-p-p-p, accelerating, seemed to be the basic pattern. They could turn that out sweet and cheerful, or like a mechanical toy, or speed it to a rattlesnake purr. Or croak like a frog. Then there was the coffee-grinder noise. All were meditative little noises, never twice the same, and all uttered in the ptarmigan voice, very individual, quite low-pitched—like a girl talking bass, quaint.

They uttered sweet noises, too—sweet chickenlike inquiries and croonings. This meant nothing special to me at the time. It would be a year yet before I realized I had heard their courtship voices, used once a year, for a few days only.

In the morning I was untroubled to find myself under a white fog. Once I thought I heard a plane far off. I did not know that in a year you could count on your fingers all the planes seen or remotely heard in this country. I did not dream this was Andy, trying desperately to get me out because this was the last possible day he could take a ski plane off Bettles Field, and only a ski plane could land here until after breakup. The melt had been unexpectedly rapid the day I landed here. If Andy failed I might well be stuck here alone for several weeks.

Tranquilly I sat on a box, combing my hair. The sun was burning out the fog. My knee toward the vague sun felt warm, my cheek toward the west cold. So still, so utterly still. I breathed deep and enjoyed it. Suddenly I realized why. The air was fragrant. Hardly to be noticed, but present, was a very faint, delicate sweetness of arctic "hay"—dried grass tufts, dead huckleberry leaves and gray and yellow lichens.

Above the snow wall rose the one familiar feature in this new world—the blue that goes all around the planet, pale here but refined from the least trace of impurity. A raven went over, gargling a comment at seeing me: "Yowk, yowk. Ook. Oork." The lake ice split like thunder every minute or two.

"I want—" I thought aimlessly. Then, without intending it, I began to center down, as the Quakers say. Now to shed off the wants, the troubled, distorted wants—for fresh vegetables to eat instead of lima beans and rice; for letters from friends; for my own tool-and-craft kitchen at home. These were fila- ments dragging my heart back toward civilization. "Pull them out," I thought. "What *do* I want?" My answer was instant. "To be where 'the people that walk on four legs' are. For the rest I can pick myself up, get off the couch of uncorseted slackness. Tauten my muscles and take the direction of the desire under the desires."

Involuntarily I was squaring away for the summer's work. What I did not know was that ahead was not a summer but eighteen months in the Arctic, fourteen of them alone with Cris in the Brooks Range.

There was a pulse in the air that was not even a noise yet. The plane was coming! For the second time this day Andy had flown clear up here from Bettles Field.

To my surprise he loaded all the dunnage except the wooden boxes of Blazo cans. He would not have taken those even if he could—they formed too valuable an emergency cache in this remote place. The riffles on the lake had softened and shrunk since yesterday. Our take-off was not too rough.

Even as I scrambled from the plane at Bettles Field, the mechanics, Frank Tobuk and "Canuck," knelt to remove the skis and change over to wheels for summer. We could not fly north of the Range from Bettles Field again until after breakup.

Why had Cris given up camping at Tulialek? The caribou, he found, had mostly passed through, going westward. West we too must go. We should be lucky if we could locate and get ahead of any one of the large arctic herds of caribou. (There were said to be five in Alaska.)

It is hard for anyone in civilization to imagine our problem. It is the very gospel of civilization that someone knows the answer to everything. It makes you lean for support. Now we had to stake our whole work on unknowns, and nobody at all could guide us.

We did not know caribou, yet we had to make a major decision about them at once, before the start of breakup trapped us south of the Range. That is, we had to pick a camp spot for over breakup; and it had to be ahead of the caribou but where they intended to pass, or spring would be wasted for Cris. The two most valuable times of year for a wild-animal photographer are spring and fall, the times of babies and of mating. It was just one more complication that the spot had to be near a lake where we could be picked up by a float plane after breakup.

Andy solved our first problem, getting onto skis again. He flew us west along the south side of the Range to the village of Kobuk. We landed on wheels on a thawed gravel bar in front of the village, and carried our dunnage across to a frozen lake back of it. Here John Cross of Kotzebue picked us up in a ski plane based on Bering Sea ice.

First Andy and then John flew Cris north into the Range, scouting for the caribou. Andy returned to Bettles. There was a troubled period of desperate haste and baffled waits. Whereever we camped, the caribou had already passed through, always going westward. Once we abandoned gear in a sudden take-off ahead of fog. That shocked me. A degree of human expendability was part of our work and we gave it no thought, but to abandon matériel!

At last we landed at Kotzebue. We were as far west as we could go. Cris picked by map a lake north of the Range; John was to fly him there in the morning. But a new difficulty arose. Even as we had landed here at Kotzebue, a bush pilot and his passenger crashed in a white-out along the Bering Sea coast. John was acting station manager and must remain until the fog should clear and the bodies could be brought out.

We had lost our race, it seemed. We were stuck here for over breakup. John Cross reassured us. "The ice here is sloppy but it won't go out for a couple of weeks yet. And north of the Range it's winter yet."

On May 1, John flew Cris to his chosen lake. Two days later, with a second Cessna load, I followed, piloted by Tommy Richards, part-Eskimo bush pilot.

2 Prisoners of the Arctic

My flight toward Cris's camp was a flight back into winter. First over brown pond country; glints of light on water followed us in a wave, like specks of light seen through an old tarp. Next, over zebra stripings of snow. And then over the unphotogenic jumble of low mountains patched by thaw. But when we crossed to the north side of the Range, we entered a world almost white.

Below us on the silver shine were small scattered bands of caribou. Outlying caribou reared and ran to join their bands as we passed over. This country was alive!

Ahead in the vast whiteness appeared that unmistakable thing, the black dot of human geometry, Cris's camp. It pleased me when Tommy said, as we tilted over it to land on the lake, "Cris has a good camp."

Tommy broadcast our landing. He could no longer get Kotzebue. "But someone might hear; that happens sometimes," he said.

Cris, looking dark, hooded and rugged, came up happily and began without social preamble, even as we climbed from the plane. "Six hundred caribou passed yesterday. Going *east!*" So we were ahead of them, near the turn-around area of the westernmost caribou, I surmised. Cris proceeded. "And I saw two wolves and a fox. The wolves got away but I got a little of the fox."

"I like it here!" said I. Tommy looked surprised.

While he wrapped tarps around his engine, I went up the bank to Cris's camp and made coffee for him. It was so easy to do that it made me smile to myself. Cris had carved shelves in the blue-white snow and on them were my cooking things, arrayed in homely order. The gas stove hummed with a low blue flame under a kettle of melting snow.

Vaguely disturbing was the fact that there were ice crystals in the cup when Tommy handed it back to me. Also that the low white ridge across the lake, perhaps a mile away, was faintly hazed, though the day was sunny.

Tommy left and we were alone at last, where there were animals and Cris could begin his work. We were farther from other humans than we had ever been before. We were on the northwest front of the Brooks Range, near the head of the Colville River, where the last ripples of the De Long Mountains subside toward the deadly arctic slope, going north to the Arctic Ocean. The lake was cradled in low ridges, the highest one, Noluk Mountain, just south of camp.

Camp was on a shelf halfway up a drift built out from the east bank of the lake. As busy and intent as two squirrels we backpacked my dunnage from the lake and pitched the umbrella tent beside the mountain tent Cris had been using. We took the latter for a storeroom and made all snug and convenient in the larger tent.

That night it snowed. Powder snow drove on an east wind that shook the tent and whipped the taut canvas in my face as I lay in the sleeping bag in the crotch of floor and wall.

We lay it out the next day. Until now we had hardly looked the Arctic in the face. With unconscious arrogance, wrapped in the heat and smoke of our little project, we had thought of the Arctic chiefly as the field for Cris's work.

The storm continued. When it was not snowing, there was still a ground blizzard. Cris's shelves, also the roofless toilet carved in snow, drifted over. Cris dug them out once, then let them go. There was no lee from the storm on personal errands outdoors. We moved supplies from the mountain tent into the umbrella tent and struck the former to keep it from ripping under the weight of drifts.

The umbrella tent was living room, dining room, kitchen, bedroom, storeroom, camera room, laundry and bath. It was eight by eight at the floor but the usable space was not that large. The tent slanted to a peak; the center pole and branching crossbars obstructed the standing room. Half the floor was filled by the arctic sleeping robes, two bags zipped into one huge bag, lavishly lined with wool blankets that had deep overlaps around the neck. But we could not enjoy the length of the bag because of cartons and sacks stowed at each end, nor the full width because of the center pole.

Luxurious as the sleeping robes were, they could not have kept us warm laid directly on the canvas floor lying on snow. We spread a couple of gray-furred reindeer hides under the bag, also plastic air mattresses. The latter added no warmth—on the contrary—but gave comfort desirable when one is to sleep on the ground not for weeks but for months.

The other half of the floor was our living space. A board

along the wall, raised a foot off the floor, held the stove and utensils. Between it and the head of the bed was jammed a carton of apricots, sugar and flour, which squashed with use into a comfortable seat, except that one had to lean forward from the slant of the wall.

Obstructing the remainder of the floor was a small luxury, a one-burner gasoline stove, set for safety in an opened five-gallon Blazo can. Cris had brought it for a possible bivouac camp later on. He lighted it every morning and evening for half an hour of illusory warmth. We had no Blazo to spare for heating; the Blazo was to come on a charter flight two weeks from now.

A dark armor of ice soon coated the inside of the tent. On the rare still mornings I awoke to find frost tassels three inches long hanging from the sloping canvas close over my face. My skimpy borrowed caribou-fawn parka was old and shedding. Hairs floated from my arms at the least movement. The floor was soon a squalid mat of ice and hair.

One's every movement was half frustrated. Even when alone in the tent I could never stand quite upright, even by snaking my head between sock-and-towel-hung crossbars. Always before in camping, though we had lived hard, we had enjoyed space, privacy, liberty—and a margin of safety. All outdoors had been the annex to tarp lean-to or tent. Now we had squalor and discomfort.

Wryly, Cris remarked, "Camping down south on the Yukon in hip-deep snow last spring was palatial luxury compared with this."

Daily I had one sure pleasure—breakfast. Cris prepared it, not to pamper me but because, as he mildly explained, "I don't like fur pancakes."

He had a routine. He had me stay in bed and out of the way. First he dried his socks and warmed his boots over the one-burner. Warming his footgear was a small luxury he indulged himself in at any camp—wisely so here. My own feet, stuck hurriedly into icy boots, were often cold all day. I wore rubber shoepacks, chosen for after breakup. Cris had the same and also canvas mukluks. Adequate arctic clothing was still months ahead of us.

I guarded my eyes from Cris's elbows while he dressed. Then, very neatly and dexterously, he prepared breakfast. He melted ice and washed his hands. He handed me the hot damp cloth to freshen up with. While more ice melted, he dry-mixed the hotcake flour. We had worked out a high-**protein recipe that gives the most** appetizing way of using powdered eggs.

Here is the recipe. Half a cup each of powdered eggs, powdered whole milk, wheat germ and whole wheat flour. A dash of cornmeal for texture. Salt, sugar, baking powder, melted canned butter and water. These hotcakes did not fail us, leaving us strengthless halfway through the morning's work. And they were delicious, so we thought.

Next Cris prepared our greatest luxury, a quart of hot powdered whole milk. I sat up, leaning sidewise to dodge the wall, and received my pint aluminum cup of the delicious stuff.

By now water was thawed to mix the hotcakes. Cris fried canned bacon, then hotcakes. He tossed me a little plastic sack of brown sugar to sprinkle on my cakes. Then he served my breakfast—two plate-sized hotcakes crowned with a mound of melting butter and a curl of browned bacon. He baked his own cakes next. And then—at last!—he heated water for my cup of powdered coffee.

We already realized we did not have enough food, and we were rationing some things. In our two plane loads there had not been weight to spare for another pound. But at least this one meal each day was filling and good. I looked forward to it. I prized its small extra tidbits, the bacon, butter, coffee.

All this time Cris had crouched on his heels or roosted on the edge of the bed, leaning toward the stove. Now he went outdoors and there was room for me to get up. I melted ice and washed the dishes. I set the pan aside for a little while, then lifted out the frozen dishwater and stacked it by the door to go out whenever the door was opened.

We were reluctant about opening the door. The zipper, iced by the trifling steam of breath and cooking, slipped off its track and held perilously at the slide only. Cris would work the slide patiently until he closed the gap. Usually we zipped open only the bottom of the door and crawled under.

Day after day the storm continued. Powder snow drove by from endless arctic wastes to the east in a ground blizzard that punished the eyes, burned an exposed wrist like fire and built hummocks under the tent floor. It drifted into the tent through the worthless zipper, covering the camera sacks and the cartons and the lower half of the bed.

The tent was drifting under. It looked as if we would have to move camp out onto the glare ice. In our ignorance of the Arctic, we had brought no shovel or saw. A hand saw is one of the most useful tools in the Arctic. With it you can cut snow blocks to make windbreaks, igloos or other temporary shelters.

Cris is a skilled axman. Given tree and ax he can make anything—from a house to the maul and wedges for splitting the tree. "Come back to the trees, boy," implored Old John Larson on the Yukon, in a penciled letter we received later. "You're safe there."

But Cris was resourceful. He contrived a shovel. Using the midget saw on his pocket knife, he haggled a piece of plywood into a blade and sheathed its edge with an opened five-pound powdered-milk can. He fastened on a stick for handle. It was not a bad shovel. He shoveled snow all one day and part of each day afterward. We did not have to move camp.

Out on the lake the everlasting streamers of snow riffled across the blue glare ice like locks of wind-driven hair. I knelt on the lake and chipped ice for water, using a heavy pocket knife. A hatchet was one more tool we had supposed we would not need. The chips of ice scooted away on the glare until I had a hollow that would hold them from the wind. I scooped them into the pail with mittened hands. We melted ice instead of snow because when you melt a pail of ice you have almost a pail of water, but when you melt a pail of this dry snow you have only a little water in the bottom of the pail.

Whenever the storm slackened, Cris pushed out to learn the country.

"I'm just going over to look at that caribou carcass on the lake," he said one afternoon. Four carcasses lay on or near the lake on our arrival here.

Actually he crossed the lake and climbed the ridges to the north, looking toward the Colville River. He was already out of sight when I first crawled out to look for him.

Fog came in over the lake between camp and the nearest ridge. The wind drove hard. Would Cris lose his direction coming home? He is a superb outdoorsman but, I felt, over-confident sometimes. Anxiously I thought of what John Cross had said about arctic flying. "It's a cat-and-mouse game in this country. You're all right as long as you remember who's mouse." I thought that could apply to walking too.

About six in the evening I felt assurance that all was well and that Cris was coming. I went out with confidence to look. The darling black speck actually was there, out on the lake under the dim fog. It lengthened a little, wobbling toward me. (The drifts made uneven walking.)

I set out to meet it, my heart laughing. Ahead of me, Cris

emerged from the dim fog into the dim sun. He was gilded. His old brown clothes were gold-tinged. The snow, driven in taffylike striations, was more azure with the long low shadows than white.

I hugged Cris—old thin leather jacket, snow-whitened beard —and turned to walk home with him. He said, "See that glitter in the air?"

"Yes. It's specks but they go by so fast they look like splinters."

"Tinsel!" Cris corrected. How safety and beauty are tangled. With Cris safe I could see the beauty.

We sacked in as soon as we had eaten supper, in order to save Blazo. It was intensely cold but Cris had rearranged the sleeping robes, a small adjustment that made the difference between warmth and cold. All day I would be half cold. "Get up and be cold," I thought each morning. But the sleeping robes were warm. They even gave the illusion of warmth the minute one got into them, still icy cold.

Deliberately this evening I "traveled." I rehearsed our automobile trips in the warm South. Cris helped—perhaps he was glad to; he slowed my pace, remembered details better than I did, routes, sometimes even motels. California, east Texas, Louisiana, Florida. Then the supreme, delicious heat—Key West. We had walked, our first night there, until midnight. It was too hot to sleep. On porches behind vines sat invisible people, murmuring to one another. Rough palm fronds brushed our hands along the narrow sidewalks.

I reached almost frantically from one memory to another— always of the South—not to drop back for a moment into the storm, the hundreds of miles of unsurvivable wastes of speeding snow, from which we were protected only by the taut lashing canvas, the zipper. Death, really, if that failed.

Our gear was pitiful. Skill didn't count too much here. Only what one had made the difference between life and death.

If each of us had had a good parka, I should have felt more confidence.

Pleasantly but soberly Cris remarked, "John Cross said any man that got into a plane to fly it without the fear of God in his heart wouldn't last long. I say anyone that comes into the Arctic to camp alone in winter conditions without the fear of God in his heart won't last long either."

I saw the weak points in our frail line of defense—our thin, clumsy clothes, the pencil-slender generator on the gasoline stove, the pocket knife, the balky zipper. Behind these there was nothing to fall back on, no second line of defense.

Slowly my apprehensiveness dwindled as day went after day harmlessly. At first I was aware only of the sea of deathly white cold for hundreds of miles around. Now I saw our islet of safety.

Not for lack of will but for lack of weight, I had brought no reading matter. Luckily however, our mail had caught up with us at Kotzebue just before I left. In it were two *New Yorkers* and a *Christian Century*. Also I had brought a tiny New Testament. Oddly enough, that was no good to read here. It seemed so terribly social wherever I opened it. There could be no man-to-man experience here. The serious thoughtful *Christian Century* was no good either.

But the *New Yorkers!* Those were the reading for the arctic wilderness. By the eleventh day of the storm I had still not squandered them by reading them through. There was so much in each. An ad showing a California house. An ad I loved, it looked down a steep street in San Francisco toward Market. Coming up the hill were a cable car and an automobile—with people in them! And a few pedestrians. You could see their faces. Again and again I turned to that ad.

By far the most precious part of the magazine was "Goings on About Town." I read each theater announcement carefully, noting curtain time, which side of Broadway the theater was on, etc. I decided on plays for a joyous weekend, including matinees on Wednesday, Thursday and Saturday, and on Friday night Beatrice Lillie. Then the dine-and-dance places. The articles I saved, to read aloud to Cris in the evenings after we were sacked in.

I was reading a *New Yorker* profile one evening, when the wind laid and Cris scrambled up. He put on mukluks, shoved the rock-hard drift from the sagging door, worked the zipper and started out for a couple of pails of ice.

He turned back, holding the door open for me to see out. "Look, Lois."

The lake was gray-white, drifted, shining under the low, mist-flared sun. No horizon, just white dimness. Stillness. Utter. Entire. I felt a mixture of faint fear—because I was cold and there was no recourse—and exultation because of the uncanny glory and strangeness. It was the face of the Arctic.

3 The Living Arctic

There was a miraculous fact about this deadly white wilderness: it was alive! Animals lived here. And found food.

Trapped in the dark little tent, it was only by luck we saw them. Cris had souped up the tent for the southern parts of Alaska the previous year with two additions, one for williwaws in the Katmai, the other for mosquitoes: a webbing belt around the middle, set with grommets for extra guy ropes, and a zippered mosquito-netting door. Now we wished we had put in frostproof peepholes so we could watch, perhaps film, what passed us during the storm.

Two wolves, for instance. We did not see them but found their tracks in soft drifts. Probably the same pair Cris had seen on first arriving here.

The first animal we did see was the rarest of them all. He had business on the lake, so he stayed around a long time on each visit. He was a very busy, businesslike animal, a wolverine. About every two days he made a tour of the four caribou carcasses around the lake, always in the same order, beginning with the one nearest camp. He lingered at each but traveled fast to the next, using a lopsided gallop. By now they were mere skeletons, but the wolverine could afford to overlook no bet.

This was our first glimpse of the terrible conservingness of the arctic animals. Our own lives seemed to me a bit on the marginal side here. But the wolverine's life *was* marginal.

The first time I saw him I hesitated to tell Cris; I thought I'd had an optical illusion. I saw this small dark animal speeding over the drifted snow on the east end of the lake and hurried for the binoculars. In a moment I was back but the animal had vanished. And there was no place to have gone. For miles around the whiteness lay wide open. Later I found what had happened. The carcass had sunk into the snow, as dark objects do, and the hollow hid the small wolverine.

His smallness astonished me. From the hair-raising stories about wolverines I had assumed they were the size of tigers and twice as ferocious. Cris assured me this was an adult and that adult wolverines weighed only thirty pounds or so.

Small as this size seems to a human, it gives the wolverine a curious distinction. He has the middle size in the whole range of animals, from least shrew to whale.

I crouched alone in the tent one morning, washing the

aluminum camp kit. On the green canvas by the bed wavered
a pattern made by racing snow outdoors in the dim sunlight.
On the floor beside me lay a snowdrift partly covering the
bed. Nubbles of snow clung to the canvas overhead, in spite
of the ceaseless shudder and flap of the tent.

Faintly from without came my name, distorted on the
wind. I crawled under the door and forced my eyes to look
east into the ground blizzard. Cris was on the spit above camp,
bent at the scope sight of his camera. It pointed upward at
the ridge southeast of camp. Up there small dark figures
were breaking over the skyline. Caribou!

They lobbed down to a wind-bared patch and nibbled.
Then they started down the steep loose snow toward the
spit. They broke into a run and came tearing downward. A
gore-shaped whorl of snow drove down with them, avalanch-
ing or wind-riding. They swept out onto the spit and came
toward us, dimmed now by the wildly driving snow. One
black-looking shape saw us and stood attentive for a while.
None of the others did. They were eating! They pawed the
snow and nibbled the herbage they uncovered. (The word
caribou derives from the Algonquian for "shoveler," the
pawer of snow.) And they had enough fun and spirit to have
made that downward rush. A feeling of wonder and love
came over me. "The strange, wonderful, incredible beasts!" I
thought.

Cris brought the camera down into camp, where the snow
was trampled blue and squealing between quivering arms of
drifts. He pitched the tripod firmly and hooded the camera.
It must be always ready. Besides, even if there had been room
for it to stand in the tent, the lens would have fogged when
brought outdoors.

With dignity—quaint, no doubt, but happy—I gave Cris
an accolade: "Your choice of Noluk is justified."

He said honestly, "I lost some footage." Though winterized, the camera had all but stuck because of cold. Cris had speeded it to sixty-four frames per second in order to get a speed of twenty-four frames. When it broke loose and ran freely, he had not heard it, in the confusion of the storm. From there on the film would be overexposed. "I must have got some stuff before that happened," he consoled me.

From then on we found more caribou tracks every time we went outdoors. They were barely dented in the hard snow and sprinkled with black pellets and dotted with urine marks and small digs for food.

Cris started outdoors, as usual, after breakfast one gray still morning, but bent back to the door and said in a low voice, "Caribou coming right past—thick!" I dressed and scrambled outdoors.

They were coming around the end of the spit in a thick column half a dozen wide, the biggest mass of caribou we had yet seen. Gray bodies with white collars. Slender legs all ticking along as if the column were one millipede. The rustle of snow, bodies touching, breathing. Now and then a caribou on the near side of the flow halted to stare at us a minute, then walked on.

It was baffling. It looked as if the answers to all our questions about caribou must lie almost in touching distance. What are their little ways and habits? What are the great patterns of the migrations, trailed and projected unseen? The gray fur bodies streamed by. I looked with a baffled intensity felt only once before, when John Cross had asked me, a stranger to flying and the Arctic, "What is the direction and velocity of the wind?" And I had stared frantically out my window in the Cessna at the white wilderness below, all my faculties mobilized but helpless. He had meant me to observe the cloud shadow racing over a lake; it was a clue. But which items were the clues now?

But we did observe one caribou way. They were going

west, like most of the caribou these days. But they circled clear around the north side of the lake. Not one hoof touched glare ice. So! Caribou feared ice.

On the west side of the lake, straight across from camp, they scattered on the slope to dig and eat, looking strangely like a throng of picnickers on a winter beach.

Now came an "emerald" of wilderness experience. Cris had gone to shoveling snow. I stood by the tent door watching the last two dozen caribou filing around the north bank. Suddenly they began to run. Then they halted and turned to look back the way they had come. I looked too.

"Cris!" I called softly. We both watched. A small dark-and-streaked animal was running straight at the waiting caribou. Our wolverine!

"Why, the foolish thing!" I said, with a clean leap for a usual conclusion. "He can't do anything with them."

Then we laughed. The wolverine was walloping steadily past the line of legs. The caribou pivoted their heads down, around and up to watch him. He left them flat-footed, staring after him, as he loped on toward the second carcass on his beat. Living caribou idled near but he never gave them a tumble. He worried the skeleton diligently for five minutes, then headed at a gallop for the next.

I thought of that old Eskimo dance song Hannah, Andy's wife, had told us about: "The Busy Little Wolverine." "I like the wolverine," said Hannah gravely. "He's so brave and strong and busy." At any rate busy! It would be expecting too many "emeralds" to hope to see for ourselves whether he was also brave and strong. City people, receiving only the collections of emeralds in pictures or words, underrate them. Only wilderness people know how rare they are. To see the interaction of two of the larger species of animals in the wilds is rare indeed.

The next day we were deceived into thinking spring had

come. It was sunny and still. I took a bath that was unexpectedly frigid. Cris erected a crosspole and sunned the sleeping robes.

I told him plainly that his next project was foolish. He made a tool of angle iron, sharpened and fastened to a pole, and jabbed a neat well in the blue lake ice, two feet square and five deep. It actually filled with seep water and I was thankful enough to dip, not chip, for water.

That evening he started a third project and made a ramshackle shovel so I could help. We shoveled off the hard windrows of snow on the glare ice, preparing a runway for Tommy, due to charter in with Blazo on May 17.

I stepped gingerly on the glare, mindful of a maxim of wilderness morality. Billy Everett, an eighty-year-old wilderness man of the Olympics, had uttered it quietly and resolutely as he and I waited while Cris anchored a rope for us to descend a cliff. "It's not right to get hurt in the wilderness. It makes trouble for people."

On the morning of the seventeenth we awakened to a painful disappointment. For the first time since our arrival here, the lake was socked in. Then a small miracle happened. At a quarter of twelve the sky blew clear. At twelve, Tommy bristled briskly across the ridge to the south and touched down on our runway, surprised to hear of our fog.

He sat on the edge of the sleeping robe, nursing a cup of my scarce coffee. On this charter we could have had all the food Kotzebue afforded, but we should have had to order it when Tommy flew me here. At that time I, at least, did not know how short our supplies were.

Tommy had brought Blazo—now we could burn it for warmth—and also a wonderful present, a carton of magazines, some old, some new, the finest he could buy in Kotzebue. His choice was a tribute to our taste—*Popular Mechanics*, not *Confessions*.

A few caribou were loitering on the far side of the lake, pale on the sunny snow, and Tommy said, half in earnest, "I ought to kill you one."

I half wished he would. But we were here of our own choice, we had come by plane, it was up to us to bring our food. Living off the country in this age of the world is an anachronism, except in real, unavoidable emergency.

Anxious about the fog, I went out to look. It was coming in fast on the east wind. Tommy, unperturbed, looked west through the open door. Presently he looked again. He set his coffee cup carefully on the floor. "I'd better be going." He ran for the plane. "See you next July," he said and closed the door. He roared away through the last rathole of blue to the northwest, circled unseen overhead, and the roar died to the southwest.

It turned cold again, but now it was often foggy and still. The well froze. The everlasting bang and whip of the tent were silenced. The birds were silenced too; they had chirped for a day or so. "They're laying it out like us," said Cris.

I felt a touch of claustrophobia. The longing to do something, to be out in an interacting environment furthering some project was like a dull heavy object pushed against my chest. This was time-no-time. Not even time of waiting. All movement of change was stilled, except for the slow flap of dimmer light over the Arctic, graying down for three or four hours at "night," then lightening. "That Greek philosopher who said there is no change was right," I thought. Our piece of the world was locked. Moveless. Gone into deep freeze. And we, small creatures of change, unconscious as a rule of the perpetual flow of change, like showery cascades through which we habitually darted, became conscious now of what we were adapted for, and famished for change.

Yet these days were like the last of a phase. During this phase, these weeks here, nothing had been demanded of me. Ahead, though I could not know it, were to be demands almost beyond my strength. To my surprise, I rather hated to see this phase go.

4   *Arctic Spring*

On the night before May 23 it rained! Water ran in on the tent floor.

In the morning Cris threw back the tent door. Long rolls of cloud lay in a blue sky above brown-patched hills. Birds sang, ducks and geese talked. "Kyook! Kyook!" Piercing calls an octave higher, "HEE-yoo!"

"Everything came north at midnight," said Cris. "The geese came with the rain. Little birds with new cries came. I thought I heard gulls."

We left the tent flap open during breakfast. The air was mild and polished with bird songs. Outdoors you could look without thinking about it in any direction. The fight it had been even yesterday to look east! The snow was warm and soft. Yesterday you could no more have broken a piece with your hands than gouged a chunk of steel.

We had a sense of prosperity and potentiality. I saw it in Cris's eyes and bearing. The exhilaration and expectancy!

Freed! A margin! We had a margin again. Tirelessly we reiterated, "Do you remember what it was like this time last
week!"

These were some of the stages in our liberation. When we
could first air the sleeping robes. First bathe. First dip a pail
of water. First zip open the tent door freely and step in and
out instead of crawling. Biggest first for me—when I could
discard my shedding fawn parka, put on instead my faded
blue poplin summer parka and scrape the squalid mat of hair
and ice from the floor. That happened this day. From now
on we seldom had to fish caribou hair from the hot milk.

Another big first. Taking off my wool undershirt and long
johns at night. They had dragged heavily askew in the jumble of wool blankets and I had longed for the clean neat
rollable body in slick sheets. (Of course we still had no
sheets.)

The next day there began a unique and totally unexpected
phase of our life. Cris moved camp from the softening snow
shelf up onto the spit, which was nearly bare of snow. In
the next day or two he added a "veranda." It was a floor
walled with tarps and later, when mosquitoes came, to be
roofed with a tarp.

But it was not the new camp that was unique; it was the
site. We found ourselves in the very midst of a colony of
nesting Alaska-Lapland longspurs, and they treated us like
caribou. That is a happiness all but unknown any longer, to
be accepted fearlessly by wild creatures. To a city person it
may seem like a slight thing. It wasn't. If you stay in the
wilderness a long time, you get to feeling like a pariah: every
living thing shuns you. The shadow of human cruelty covers
Earth. Unnoticed, it darkens the spirits of humans themselves.

The longspurs rushed between us. They hopped a yard
from our feet as we moved quietly about our work.

And they sang. The females were silent—except for a hair-raising screech if you stepped on the tussock in whose side they had a nest. The males sang from the highest elevations available on the tundra. These amounted to little, so they climbed the sky and sang, like skylarks, on the wing.

The male would beat up hard to fifty or a hundred feet, rarely two hundred. At the top of his climb he spread his wings and glided diagonally to the tundra, singing as he came. He was a pure dot of life, victorious and total, gliding on his small triangle of wings with as much skill and control in his class as a man-o'-war bird in a grander class.

He ended his glide a couple of feet from his mate, who had waited quivering. Usually she received his advances at once. But sometimes she waited without a quiver until just as he reached her, then nonchalantly rose and flitted off.

His song was a skylark warble, so fast and complicated it sounded like a duet. Sometimes it was! At almost any minute during the warmth of the day I could look up and see one or two longspurs somewhere close over the tundra, winging up to make their glides. They repeated their song on the way down. There was many a moment of pure delight for a human when that song, more beautiful when close, broke out at the level of one's ear as the bird passed, six feet away. If the east wind drove him toward the blank white of the lake, he descended fast; he did not sing on a spoiled glide. And each time a bird sang, it gave one a fresh sense of pleasure and well-being.

The male of the pair that nested back of the tent was the richest bird on the spit: he had the height of the tent and veranda frame to sing from. The wind pushed him and he sang as he toppled from post to crossbar. It blew his soft body feathers forward and he sang. He sat on the tent-peak nail, eight feet from my face as I baked hotcakes on the veranda, and he sang.

Cris had contrived a table for the stove, so I cooked standing instead of crouching. We even had a wash bench. We bathed in the sunshine on the veranda, sheltered from the wind, standing in an opened Blazo can and using warmed water lavishly from another one on the bench.

We could no longer get out to the well on the lake ice because a moat of water was deepening around the shore. But a creek had opened back of the spit, at present tearing wildly anywhere over the tundra until its bed in the gully should thaw.

Arctic spring is a torrent of events that speed you along like rapids. The grass must have had its green catkins all but ready; they foamed into yellow stamens. The dark-rose color faded from those big single pussywillows that stand, each solitary on its finger-high "tree." A spider showed up the day after our big liberation day. The few flies were copulating. As yet, no mosquitoes.

"This is a little paradise time in the Arctic now," said Cris, "between the cold and the mosquitoes."

Things moved fast with the longspurs. A hollow shaped in the side of a tussock one day; lined with white feathers—ptarmigan, probably—the next; an egg the next. Five eggs and she was setting. Now we heard a new call. If we neared a nest the male uttered an infinitely mournful, minor flute call, the nest warning, "Tsit PEER!"

We stepped warily; the stricken screech of the female if you stepped on the tussock above her nest! We posted nearby nests with stakes.

Worse evils than feet threatened them. Foxes beat a trail along the bank between tent and lake. A weasel used it. He whipped erect to gaze at us; we "froze." His outstanding ears framed a face so dark you could hardly make out his dark eyes. His belly was a stripe of the most sheerly beautiful fur I ever saw—lemon-colored. He leaped onward, a grace note, a trill, the slender arch of his body always reminding me of something else, something in musical notation. Into a parka-squirrel hole and out, leaping. Then lifted instantaneously to hind feet to observe us again. The longspurs were no fighters but once in a while they ganged up and scared him a little.

Events of spring were vital, not sweet. One night I was awakened by a terrific sloshing, accompanied by formless, unremitting cries as of a person with a speech impediment trying to talk. I went outdoors. It was the old squaw ducks. Two males and a female had previously moved onto a patch of open water where the creek emptied into the lake, surrounded by blue-white ice.

The males were fighting. One pulled himself up out of the water at a forty-five-degree angle and pursued the other. The female stayed near at first, then went over to the ice. Body humped murderously, pintail dragging, the pursuer walked across the top of the water, slap, slap, slap with each splay foot. The two squared away. There was a dash of white water, a turmoil with parts of bodies out. Then the clinch. One male held the other under water until my diaphragm ached with wanting it to get air. It fought. Its head was up for a moment. Then it was trampled under.

That was a bad night for me; I excoriated myself afterward for days. I should have wakened Cris to film the fight. Now, walking back in the low gold sunlight toward the sleeping tent, I compounded my error. My eye was caught by movement across a small gully in front of the tent. It was two blond foxes, as dead a hay color as the grass. But they were tan on tan, a monotone, not photogenic. Besides, they were doing nothing, just idling around.

I would not waken Cris for this. But dutifully I unhooded the camera and recorded a few feet myself.

Suddenly the situation flashed into something memorably photogenic. The foxes trotted over to the top of the bank.

Both bank and lake shore were still white. One fox skidded down the steep snow and crouched cat-teasingly on the shore, looking up at the other. It plunged down, hit the first fox, and they rolled and tumbled. Then one fox broke away and dashed to the top of the bank again, expressly to rollick down a second time.

Soundlessly they played, casting long blue shadows. Every least snow crust had a long blue shadow.

I flopped the unwieldy machine around, focused and pressed the button. Nothing happened. "Busted!" I thought furiously. "The damn thing's busted." Gliding at last, too late, for Cris, I realized: it was run down. The foxes glanced at me and trotted away along the white shore.

Both the duck fight and the fox play had been "nuggets." A nugget is action, not a mere portrait. And it is action occurring in such a way that it can be photographed. Cris counts three nuggets a season a fair average. In one night I had lost two.

Courting, fighting, breeding, blooming—the torrent of vitality stormed on. The first flowers bloomed up among the rocks on the southwest tips of the ridges—rose-colored flowers and lavender anemones. "They have their parkas on," observed Cris. Their stems were furry. Showy mounds of yellow glacial geum, also furry-stemmed, bloomed on the tundra.

But these were as nothing compared with a lone cluster of yellow flowerets I came to on a naked ridge. It crouched in scalloped fans of white lichen. It was an inch high and two across and to me it glowed like a neon light. I rose from looking at it and gazed far around. For the first time I realized, with surprise, that in a month these miles of tan monotone would tinge with green.

There was one unforgettable evening. Evenings were the good time of day. All day the tundra would be big, plain, hot, vacant and dead. And quavering terribly with heat waves. But at evening it came alive and promising. The light was big and warm and gracious.

We were eating supper on the veranda and I had just started to call Cris's attention to five caribou trotting near, pearly-looking in the low sunlight, when he stopped me with a soft exclamation. "There they are! The birds that sound like the wind."

Two dark parasitic jaegers flashed out over the white lake and performed a courting flight. They flew almost wing tip to wing tip, one leading, the other following. They flew fast. Their sharp dihedral wings were made for fast flight and maneuverability and this was the consummate flying of their skilled lives. They dipped almost to the ice, flashed in V turns, rose, pitched down. We almost gasped at the perfection, the daring. They were like two wonderful skaters—one leading, the other responding—skating with wild daring and skill in three dimensions instead of two. They made the star skating of an ice revue seem laborious and timid.

A third jaeger appeared and the flinging dance was over. Each bird was on his own. There were growling mews. Cris laughed. "They don't like that third character cutting in!"

He cut in again as I washed the dishes. The mated jaegers sat now in the bright low sunlight across the gully, calm, cuddly, staying close together. She nestled; he stood breast beside her back. They turned their heads in a way that made me smile. She turned hers right, he turned his right. She turned hers left, he turned his. A strange environment to them here? Or were they equally cautious and regardful by the ocean? At each longspur song, each duck squall, the jaegers turned their heads alertly, as if the bird-song air were full of meaning.

The third jaeger joined them, impelled to seek the company of his own kind here on the tundra, the long journey to which would otherwise be meaningless to him. Instantly the beaks of the mated pair opened: "Myow!"—a thin, reedy cry. The third jaeger gave up and flew off. The pair settled calmly again, watching, being together.

As if motionless, the semi-palmated sandpiper hung above the shore, chirring faster than tongue could imitate. "The bird with marbles in its throat," Cris called it. The Eskimos have an onomatopoetic name for it, "liva-liva."

Bird songs laced the air. A longspur rose and began his glide. Glorious, looking down at the tundra, he swept downward, a fleet flake of sunlit white, balancing in perfect control, singing as he came. Another longspur was rising to my right. "Our" male, on the veranda post, sang. These males had all been nestlings, probably, on this very spit of tundra by the lake, and their fathers, too, had sung in the big calm evenings.

I heard the coffee-grinder noise overhead and a ptarmigan alighted near the veranda. But at the same moment two longspurs alighted near and the startled ptarmigan rose before he settled. There was a clatter and a rush past my knees. The ptarmigan swept through the veranda and alighted on the crosspole just above my face. I froze, then sank a little so I could get a good look at those Egyptian-looking scarlet "eyebrows" of his and dramatically lengthened, soot-black eye and beak. His back was a marble curve against the blue; his white "fur" leggings were wonderfully soft-looking.

I turned my head silently to see Cris, who had stolen up from the lake; his ruddy sunburned face smiled in the dark beard at me and the bird both. Amused, we waited upon the next move of the unself-conscious bird. It lifted and ruffled its plumage, deepening each feather with a light blue shadow.

Then Cris, so often to my vexation yet amusement the observer first, the photographer only as an afterthought, uncovered the camera and actually got a frame filler before the bird left.

This very night happened to be our nearest to seeing the midnight sun. Usually clouds came up at night. But when we awoke at two A.M., there was a cheerful gold blur at the center of the north wall of the tent. Congratulating us on this event unexpected in our lives—for never had we dreamed of camping in the Arctic—Cris murmured the trite words with innocent pleasure: "The land of the midnight sun!"

It was true: we—Cris and Lois!—were right here. The slight feeling of elation woke me wide up. Just as well. Cris dozed through what happened next but I could not have done so. It was the ptarmigan.

For the next two hours he made our tent peak his headquarters, sitting still awhile with an occasional low hint of the coffee-grinder noise, a mere thread of a purr; and also occasionally dropping one more dry cylinder of excrement with a thud on the taut canvas. Then launching off with a flap-whir of wings and a full-blown "coffee-grinder." After ten or fifteen minutes back he came with the same noise. My restless turning below him did not disturb him in the least, except maybe to elicit one more low growl of the "coffee-grinder."

I did not feel sleepy. Nothing could have been more jolly and inviting than this pleasant low sunshine beamed cheerfully, with low candlepower, at our green tent. Vitality was all around me. This was a moment of pause between two hurrying cycles: wintry conditions were over; in a day or two we would start the hardest backpacking trip of my life—one I felt was a bit hazardous.

At a moment like this it was inevitable to think, not of wilderness, but of what will destroy it—civilization. There is a secret tension between love and despair in anyone nowadays who goes into wilderness with his eyes open. No carefree love of the planet is now possible.

This was the first "great" wilderness I had ever been in. Yet all our married life we had lived in "wilderness," first in the Olympics in Washington State and then in the Colorado Rockies. But it was captive wilderness. This was free. It sounds obvious but is known to few: free wilderness gives you the experience of freedom. I could not know freedom consciously yet, though I felt it. It is a vital experience totally different from anything experienced in civilization; it has to grow on you. A starving child does not instantly experience bounding health after one good meal.

Great wilderness has two characteristics: remoteness, and the presence of wild animals in something like pristine variety and numbers. Remoteness cannot be imitated in cheap materials; and wilderness without animals is mere scenery.

It looks as if two movements are gaining their peak now: the power to wipe out our environment; the power to love it. Possibly the power to leave Earth will overtake both of the other powers, and the decision will be postponed to another planet. It is a love-or-death theme that makes the love-death theme of Tristan and Isolde look puerile.

Cris and I just happened to be fitted, physically and psychologically, to live in wilderness. Cris had what it took. He was interested in new country and new animals. He had a natural talent for finding his way in trackless wilds, and enjoyed cultivating it. He had endless skills and ingenuity.

Above all, from my point of view, he had enormous zest. There was nothing he was not willing to do in the way of hard work, and he enjoyed whatever he did. It was a real surprise to me after my sober years of teaching at the university before our marriage. Not a day passed without a belly laugh over some nonsense. He woke up mornings, punning sleepily before his eyes were open. It dazzled me.

The morning after our unforgettable evening, the moment Cris had licked his chops over his final hotcake, up he got and went with appetite to measuring and setting his nails to hold the tarp roof for the veranda. Then he asked if I minded if he put the tarp up. I assented and sat cowering and smiling to myself, eating my own hotcakes while he hammered and things jarred and the paper-crackling tarp hung down against my back.

The roof up, he sat down and smiled at it; ate one of my hotcakes. Then, shoving his arms into his knapsack straps, he stated clearly, "I'm going to hotfoot it straight across the lake to that rocky knoll—there might be a parka squirrel over there—and then come back along this ridge to the southeast and back to camp. I won't be gone long." This meant that he would be gone until two or three o'clock, but not until five or seven. Briskly he kissed me and briskly stepped off.

Telling each other our plans was a wilderness precaution—though often one returned from the direction opposite that announced. Today Cris returned as promised, and the day seemed warmer and less threatening when I saw him coming.

He had found parka squirrels. Their territorial or mating fights were over apparently, but the pretty speckled fur of the males was blood-scabbed where hides had been ripped in the savage fights of spring.

On May 29 something happened that made us wonder: no caribou passed. Until now they had drifted to and fro daily, as if we were near the end of the migration course of this westernmost herd of the Arctic.

Then on May 31 another small event happened that rang clear and decisive—if we had understood it—as the far-off bugle of a great advance: thirteen caribou passed, going westward, and eleven of them were bulls. They were the first mature bulls we had seen in the Arctic.

Neither of these facts seemed to us to have any bearing

on Cris's project which we were about to begin. We were to backpack southward across the Brooks Range to the Noatak River and summer there. Tommy would fly in twice, to carry out his part of the plan, but on the first trip he would not see us. That would be about July 5, when the lake was sure to be ice-free for a landing on floats. He would pick up our base camp and fly it to the Noatak and cache it there, along with our mail and groceries from Kotzebue, "on the north bank of the Noatak, west of the mouth of the Kugururok." He would mark the cache with a rag on a pole, so we could spot it from the mountains as we approached. We were to reach it about July 17.

His second flight would be on July 19, when he would meet us at the cache and fly me out to stock up on supplies for the rest of the summer.

I distrusted the plan. For nearly six weeks we should be creeping through the tumbled Range, unfindable in case of emergency. Also our dependence on hitting that cache was too absolute. When we thought we were within a day's journey from it, Cris intended to discard sleeping bags, stove and tent. There would be no food by that time. It is hard enough to carry food for even ten days when one is handicapped with a camera outfit. Cris's weighed about seventy-five pounds, including film. The trip was to be leisurely, so he could camera-hunt a few days from each bivouac camp.

We must relay because our pack would be heavy. Heavier than if we could have outfitted "outside." The wonder was that we could outfit ourselves at all, here in the wilderness, for a trip like this. The only reason we could do so was that Cris had expected to establish a second camp and camera-hunt between it and base camp. So we did have light sleeping bags, the one-burner stove, the mountain tent—though it leaked and we should have to carry a light tarp to pitch over it.

Food for backpacking was no problem. It was the only kind we had. The worst problem was fuel. Cris expected to travel at an elevation of two to four thousand feet, where we could not depend on finding willows big enough for fuel. We would carry not only the stove—it was much too heavy—but also two cans of Blazo, a gallon to see us to the divide and five to use or discard from there on. We had no other sizes of can to choose from. I came to hate that five-gallon can of Blazo.

Cris expected we would walk twenty-five miles for each five gained.

For two reasons he had given up hope of photographing caribou fawns—his project for spring—near Noluk. First, the cows were drifting both east and west but not staying around; it looked as if they would not fawn here. Long afterward we learned that Tommy, on that day he left us, had seen a large aggregation of caribou about thirty miles southwest of us. Perhaps they fawned there.

Secondly, this country was too gently sloping, it gave no concealment for getting up on the caribou. Cris hoped to meet cows with fawns as we crossed the mountains. Up there, ridges and ravines would give cover.

There was one thread of connection with civilization he would keep: base camp was to remain standing here to fall back on in case of emergency. Not until we had relayed all our stuff to the head of the Kugururok would we speed back light, to close it for Tommy to fly to the Noatak.

So, as we loaded our packboards on June 3, we were not leaving for good. Still this was the start of a venture; each of us marked it in his own way.

In the pure fresh morning, under the shade of the tarp roof on the veranda, I read aloud parts of the eleventh chapter of Hebrews. The mournful, stately, courageous words gave context to our little venture. Those not-so-far-away humans, four thousand years ago, who had been nomads, who had endured hardship, seemed closer to me now than the nice settled people of my childhood. The mists of "niceness" were evaporating from around my life.

I longed for words of heightened awareness to help me feel the invisible dimension of our experience, barely sensed in the midst of our necessary toil. How often in our dozen years of wilderness life had I craved words like that. Had no poet ever backpacked up and camped by his rock-slab cache on the mountain ridge, slept on hard ground by the drop-off till the sun crossed the waves of pale-blue ridges and clouds parted on the glaciers and a bull elk bugled faint and pure from timberline far below?

Nothing I knew, neither music nor poetry, had the right flavor or smell. I wanted wild glory, some strange strain never heard yet, poetry of a million years from now, when we are human instead of adumbrating humanness—something that caught the piercing, close-to-your-being, "personal-impersonal" aspect of nature.

Nearest of all now to what I wanted were bold hard words like the psalmist's: "Yonder is the sea . . . and leviathan, whom thou hast formed to play therein . . . The young lions roar after their prey, and seek their food from God."

Cris's nod to the future was rueful and matter-of-fact. He was out in the sun near the veranda, tightening the lid of the one-gallon Blazo can with a washer cut from cardboard, when suddenly he remarked, "As you get older you get wiser, all right. Trouble is, you're liable to get too durn wise! You remember the hardships you've been through and you don't want to go through'm again."

We shouldered our packs and climbed away from camp, setting our course for the distant headwaters of the Kugururok. As we gained the high tundra, ahead to the south rose the nameless peaks of the Range. To east and west rolled the tan land, empty, formidable, vast.

This was the tundra, the great arctic meadow that flows for thousands of miles along the top of this continent, between Arctic Ocean and arctic mountains and even far up their slopes. It is cut by streams, dotted with ponds and lakes, inhabited by the ever-moving caribou herds, the tundra grizzly, the tundra wolf, and smaller creatures that have chosen the fearsome Arctic to abide in.

The tundra is carpet and table for them all, alike for the prey and the predators. The latter do not live in some other compartment but lay their fur and step their paws on the same mattress and carpet, far-spreading under the pale-blue arctic sky. It is hard for housed humans to understand this houseless, tolerant community of danger.

The tundra is a world out of this world, a thin moss-and-lichen blanket spread over fathomless ice, beneath a sky where in summer the sun does not set and in winter does not rise, and the aurora speeds or drifts in ghostly white across the stars.

The distance walked on tundra is not commensurate with

distances walked in other lands. On tundra one cannot get into a rhythm or swing, or take even two steps together without looking, on account of the tussocks. Those under our feet now were not big, but small, hard and wobbly. One's foot slipped sidewise, slipped back, slipped forward. One's legs got two miles tired for every mile traveled.

Our first arctic backpack camp seemed wild and strange to me. The strangeness began the minute I knelt on the dry sand —a patch Cris had found in boggy tundra—and started to unpack my board. I saw the shadow, heard the wings and knew a bird had alighted on my back. I glanced around and it flew. Cris stood looking at me. "Did you know a snow bunting lighted on your back?"

As soon as Cris had pitched the mountain tent—and even exuberantly lugged up a boulder as boots-off-and-on seat at its door—off he went exploring. Dutifully I cooked the rice.

I felt lonely. Once I saw him small and faraway on the end of a ridge. Like every bush on the tundra, he was gilded on one side, black on the other. The level sun came in under a fog ceiling that cut off the mountaintops, leaving their bases in light-blue shadow.

Against this vast backdrop passed twelve antlered bulls, white in sunlight. They swung by camp with hardly a glance at the tiny layout or me. Going to where? Coming from where?

After supper, instead of sacking in, we went for a walk. I felt an odd stealthiness, as well as delight, as if I were prowling in someone's house.

We came to inhabitants of the "house." A pair of long-tailed jaegers sat side by side on a high bank, black against the night sun. Incredulously, Cris walked to within ten feet of them. Their bright wild eyes looked at him with fearless indifference. We were of the house.

Everything was so interesting I hated to go to sleep that

night. Cris as always fell asleep instantly. But I lay looking out. At Noluk, dark canvas had closed us in. Here the whole end of the little tent was tied wide open. Golden plovers talked. A ptarmigan grated out his bullfrog noise, as Cris called the "coffee-grinder." Even Cris's black-and-gray-lichened boulder by my head looked interesting.

In the morning we left this bivouac, Camp One, in opposite directions, I to bring up the last load from Noluk, Cris to scout ahead for our next camp site. He carried a light load to cache there.

Before setting out he had to make the decision that would hound us daily—take the camera and camera pack and leave them ahead, or leave them here? To carry them both ways was unthinkable. He left them.

I resented the weight of the camera outfit because it seemed needless in this day of light metals. There were even cute nickel trimmings, and Cris had to add to his pack a vial of black paint to keep them from flashing an alert to animals as far as two miles away. Only I can know the labor Cris has performed over the months and years and miles, carrying that camera always at the ready on the tripod over his shoulder except in settled rain or fog—through trailless wilds, along mountainsides where I used both hands but he used one and steadied the camera with the other.

When we met at Camp One that evening his first words dismayed me. "I saw something today that could make us sorry forever after." He told me this story.

"I saw a wolverine going lippety-loppety along the wet grass on the far side of a marsh I was about to cross. I watched him a few minutes, then walked forward. I supposed he would be gone when I got over there. But he stopped and worked at a certain place. I kept walking closer.

"When I was about a hundred yards away, he looked up and saw me, and stood up like a little bear to watch me. And did he run away? He started toward me! Came about twenty-five yards toward me and growled. Came closer and growled some more.

"I was a little worried. You could tell he could put up a mean fight if he wanted to. And then what did he do? He went back to his work, digging at something. I walked to within fifty feet of him and he went on digging. Paid no more attention to me. He had found a little colony of voles. I watched him catch three and eat them. Saw the vole's white belly. Saw it shake itself and wriggle, trying to get out of his mouth."

He added the crowning frustration. "And there were no heat waves."

It would have been the photographic nugget of a lifetime —it was a nugget of wilderness experience at that. So! The "busy little wolverine" was also brave. He did not fear and probably did not know humans.

This caused us a sober wonder whether the grizzlies here were equally uninformed. If so, they might be dangerously brave. There had been no grizzlies around Noluk, but they would be present up here.

The next morning Cris threw me out on the tundra to find his cache at the site of Camp Two. Casually he directed me. Proudly I refrained from asking reassuring amplification. To Cris, the situation informs you, only a fool needs more than a clue. However, he was unusually liberal with words today.

"You go through that pass on the skyline. You can go up that canyon to it—no crags or anything. On the other side of the pass, contour left and hold your elevation. After a while you'll see a ridge running right. The cache is in the side of a peak at the far end of that ridge." He sealed these instructions with the inevitable cachet, "You can't miss it."

Proud of my responsibility but a bit anxious I set out, carrying a heavy pack—the five-gallon can of Blazo and dried foods.

As I neared the foot of the canyon a grizzly was ahead, going my way. I stood unconscious of my pack, watching until he crossed the mouth of the canyon and waddled off. I was unarmed. The far view, which gave me a chance to avoid a grizzly, was my only protection.

As the hours passed I began to wonder anxiously if I could have overlooked a ridge leading right. Then I came to it. I was tired but the ridge was such a paradise that it nullified fatigue. For one thing, it was flat and hard, paved with the shale of eons. I appreciated that footing, after the rough tundra and mountainsides. But its glory was flowers. They were in flat clumps of color, blue, rose, yellow, white. The forget-me-nots were denser and tighter to the ground than any others I had ever seen. Actually I was deadly tired, but I had a kind of enchanted feeling as I picked my steps among the patches along that endless ridge.

At the far end of it I had some worried minutes. I could not find Cris's cache. I climbed up and down and at last blundered onto it. In a damp black niche, brisk and improbable, stood red and white cans of butter, powdered eggs and powdered milk.

The next day I had an odd, solitary adventure. In the morning Cris and I together carried packs to the site of Camp Two. On returning to Camp One for our final night there, we found we had packed all the food ahead, except a starvation supper and breakfast for one person. One of us ought to fall clear back to base camp. There was no question which it would be. Big bulls were passing Camp Two and Cris wanted to get back there early in the morning.

I was still soft. The day's trip had drained me to healthy exhaustion. Now I prepared to go beyond my strength. I collapsed purposefully on the sand for a few minutes—in the sun, for the wind was cold—and accepted two of the four prunes that were here. Then I shouldered my packboard and set out for Noluk, taking along all of Cris's exposed film to date to leave there. Every roll of film we could free ourselves of lightened our load for crossing the mountains. Ounces count in backpacking.

A few hours later I was nearing the lake, but still hidden from it by the high ridge we called Noluk Mountain, when I heard a noise that stopped my heart. A plane was behind the ridge, over base camp. Had Tommy come this soon to remove our camp? If so I was in a predicament. The nearest sleeping bag was at Camp One and the nearest food was hours of walking beyond that, at Camp Two. Of course Tommy might be landing, not taking off. But it was useless to run to try to intercept him. I had a mile to go yet.

A Cessna flew into sight. I tore off my pack and parka and ran stumbling over the hummocks, whirling the parka above my head. The plane flew levelly away toward the south without even a wing dip of recognition. I was unseen. I stood still. A yell of frustration burst from me. The unforeseen noise brought me to self-consciousness. "Scare every caribou in half a mile," I thought sheepishly. I shouldered my packboard and trudged on. It was useless to worry about camp until I rounded the side of the ridge and saw whether it was there or not. Besides, I was preoccupied with that uninhibited yell. Ripping through layers of lifelong "niceness," it had given me a kind of organic surprise.

I contoured in shadow around the edge of the ridge. Ahead in sunlight stood a speck in vastness, our little old tent beside the frozen lake.

The next morning I awoke in white fog. In case Cris too was socked in I carried a pack of food back to Camp One. I emerged from fog as I neared it. The sand was bare in the sunshine, except for a neatly rolled pack standing ready for me to take on to Camp Two.

I would not abandon the food I had brought. I roped both packs to my board, sat down and slipped my arms into the shoulder straps, rolled over onto hands and knees and staggered to my feet. A strap broke as it took the weight. I mended it, shouldered the pack again, and, bending forward to balance the weight, made as good time as usual to Camp Two.

Or rather, to where I supposed it would be. The cache was gone. There was not a trace or sign of human passage on the mountains. Go left or right or up or down? Without setting off my pack I prowled uncertainly. Coming around the end on the ridge, I saw ahead, on a shelf among gray boulders and dryas flowers, the prettiest little camp you could imagine. Cris had the tent pitched taut and trim at the foot of a steep snowfield, overlooking a tundra valley encircled by the Range.

He met me beside the tent. An unexpected feeling took charge of me—pure peevishness. For two days I had done something not often truly accomplished—gone beyond my strength. I sat leaning against my pack without taking it off, to rest a minute before starting supper. Cris's eyes looked tired but gay—his day, too, had been hard. He slipped away and returned, holding his hands cupped.

"Make a big hand," he commanded, smiling. "Both hands!" He opened his and into mine showered iridescent and smoky and double-pointed crystals. "Crown jewels!" he said, pleased. "Tomorrow I'll take you up where I got them and you can pick yourself out all you want."

Irresistibly I giggled. In spite of my best efforts, my peevishness leaked through my fingers. Rocks to backpack across the Range! That was all I needed.

After supper Cris added the following works to those of

his day. First he ascended the little peak above the snowfield to scan the country for caribou. He came back for his camera and started off along the ridge; he had seen a band coming. "They're going to climb that draw at the far end of the ridge and come down over the snow cornice there."

I looked at him in wonder. How did he know which way they would come? Their easiest way would be to circle the base of the ridge, as other bands had done. I dragged after him for a mile, then lay watching. He went on and set up his camera in a dark evening shadow, the only cover there was.

Sure enough the caribou were coming as he had predicted, at first mere sunlit dots far off in the sunlit tan valley below but keeping close to the foot of the mountains. I could hardly spot them with field glasses. Cris had observed them with the naked eye. They deserted the easy way, disappeared while they climbed the draw, then came into sight on the skyline above the snow cornice. They hesitated along it, looking for a way down, then lunged over the brink and wallowed downward. Cris filmed them.

There was something big about the way Cris spent himself. Never bothering to put it in words, he understood you paid for things. What he wanted was big—"I'd like our life to be big and gracious and free," he said once. He paid the same way, magnanimously. He never thought the universe was niggardly or unresponsive. He gave freely of what he had, his strength to work, regardless of whether any return seemed possible. It was his pact with the universe.

When he took me to the crystal ridge, I had a holiday from backpacking: I carried only a knapsack with lunch and wraps. It was to be a day of wonder and disappointment.

I was taking stills of flowers blooming among the crystals when Cris stepped to me and said quietly, "I feel as if I had an appointment and if I rushed I could keep it."

I had seen too much of Cris's hunches about where animals were going to be to disregard this one. I rose at once. Timing is of the essence in a hunch. It is a cogent but diaphanous thing; if you quell its faint impulse you need never try to follow it out somewhat later. It won't work. But if you obey, you sense the timing: "Go a little faster. Not so fast. Steady."

Cris led where he had never been before as if he had a map of his destination. I followed him along a sharp cleaver of black-lichened rocks, some of them kicked tan by recent caribou hoofs. Nothing deterred me from pure enjoyment of easy going except cutting my rubber shoepacks on the sharp rocks. They were the only shoes I had to see me across the Range. I didn't want to wind up a few weeks hence with the soles roped to my feet.

Cris hesitated at a faint, zigzag caribou trail dropping down the side of the ridge; impulsively he followed it. It led us into the pleasantest little valley we had yet come to in the Arctic. Grassy, no hummocks, like a pasture of home except for the sponge of yellow moss under the greening grass. And away through the pass at the head of it coursed a startled wolf, going so fast you could hardly make him out.

Beyond the pleasant meadow we climbed another ridge and at its top paused in wonder. We were in a place we never saw except on this one day but we could never forget it. We called it the Wolf Walk. It was a cleaver along whose crest ran a trail made not by humans—no human trails were in all this land—but by paws of wolves and hoofs of caribou. It was propped up oddly in places by two-foot slabs of rock. Along it lay white crunched caribou bones and bone-cluttered wolf scats.

When did caribou walk this trail? "How would you like to be up here at forty below and the wind blowing?" Cris speculated.

Wide and far on either side, before and behind us, spread the arctic land, unlike anything else we had ever seen. Cones, ridges, rounded rock outcroppings rose dark from the tan tundra below. All smooth-looking, all rounded. "Bland!" I thought in surprise. "That's the word for the Arctic." But the blandness was eerie, for it was one face of danger; one never quite forgot winter.

But we had wasted time. Now we jogged rapidly along the Wolf Walk. A storm was overtaking us. At the north end of the cleaver—a lower cleaver was ahead across a gulch—we stood still under the eave of a cloud breeding rain. Out ahead, twenty miles away, cumulus clouds floored with azure piled remote and calm over sunny lands.

"There they are!" Cris said quietly. "That's what I hurried up here for. And we're too late, it's too dark for color." The light was storm-darkened to f 2.

We watched but Cris never rolled a foot of film. Below us in the dark light on the wild land moved two bands of caribou, about a hundred in each. One band was already ascending the side of the ridge we had come down, beyond the meadow, weaving in files among the dark rock outcroppings.

The other caribou were just entering upon trails freshly dusted by the first band and these trails laced the steep, impossible face of the lower ridge ahead of us. Cris spoke quietly.

"If we had been ten minutes sooner we'd have caught that first band moving on those trails and it would still have been sunlight."

I stood, feeling wretched. Cris spoke again and there was pleasure in his voice. I looked around at him. The pleasure was real. "Aren't they beautiful!" he said. "They're a wonderful animal." He had cast away the moldy nut of failure and was reaching for good cheer as for good fruit.

There was the smell of rain on dry earth. We got into our old featherweight, knee-length parkas—we cherished this apt equipment—and as if in little tents sat out the rain on rock slabs.

Cris eyed the slabs. He got a rock for maul, a rock for wedge and split rock boards, four feet long. "Wouldn't we have a camp though, if these were near enough!"

The sun warmed honey-clover sweetness from all the white dots of candytuft bobbing on the bare rocks. We speeded back toward camp. Nearing it a few hours later we found ourselves suddenly in one of nature's wild, "personal-impersonal" moments.

We were hurrying along a ridge ahead of another rainstorm. The sun shone level in our faces over black mountains ahead. We glanced back to see if we could make it to camp without putting on rain parkas again, and stopped in our tracks.

Almost on our heels stood one leg of a wide, soft, intensely glowing rainbow; it had the deeper iris of mountain rainbows seen against darkness. The arch sprang low over the abyss beside us. Through it showed dimly the dark storm sky and darker peaks.

At camp Cris dived into the tent as the rain hit. I had donned my parka. It streamed with water as I gathered food and stove and thrust them through the door to Cris. Wet-faced and laughing, I followed. That is one of the world's unique pleasures—to lick a storm and make your bed warm in the teeth of the Great Powers.

Cris had rolled the down sleeping bag against the wall. Safe in the five-gallon Blazo can we had brought as windbreak for it sat the one-burner stove, boiling the lima beans I had started at breakfast that morning. Lima beans are my favorite backpacking dinner because they fill you up, yet you don't feel guilty about using up a lot of backpacked weight. We had crisp dried raw onion shreds and, for dessert, tea and walnuts. It was a good meal.

Afterward Cris leaned back against the roll of down and bragged with a straight face. "If I had five years' practice I could keep up with the caribou. I can keep up with them now, but I have to walk twice as far as they do because I have to come to camp to eat and sleep."

This was "cosmic gaiety." Not plain bragging but a special kind of wilderness bragging. The mountain men of the old West must have done it often. You get tired of smallness and hard work. You crave power as you crave a drink of water. Then some exultation of well-being and wild power around you, the great power of wilderness, catches you; you break into cosmic gaiety, pretend you control the uncontrollable. You defy the Great Powers and don't even need words to do so. In the tense gray air on a mountain ridge, as a thunderstorm strides toward you over the plains below, you can catch hands and run laughing as far from your rock overhang as you dare. Farther. Unnoticed mice defying a cosmic Cat. Then flee for the rock and under it as lightning hits and thunder crashes like surf overhead.

The mists now were pulling off the black mountains against the north sun. It was eleven P.M. but the impression was invincible that it was seven of a fine June day.

Cris sunburned in bed that night.

I felt a faint tension about Cris on the days when I relayed and he camera-hunted alone. He would be unfindable if hurt. So I feared.

As I crossed the last ridge into sight of camp one evening and saw a black pencil stub far off on tawny tundra, Cris on his way to camp, I was glad. I had snow melted and supper started when I heard him say hello. I looked around from where I knelt by the stove, on a folded tarp to keep my knees dry. He waved gaily but I saw he was tired: it costs an effort to raise an arm when one's shoulders are bound by the straps of a heavy pack. As usual he carried camera and tripod over his shoulder.

I restrained myself from jumping at him with the main question, any pictures? He sat down in front of the tent, took off shoepacks and socks and asked what I had seen— two bands of bulls, as usual going westward. Then I inquired delicately, "Did you see anything?"

He grinned. "Yes, I got some pretty good pictures. But I walked for them."

We stood at the edge of the drop-off and on the map of the grand terrain, with the aid of field glasses, he showed me his course, confirming my belief that it would be futile to search for him if he ever failed to return. Around us in black shadow and sunlight marched twenty-three nameless peaks of the Range. Rock outcroppings and tundra valleys rolled at their feet. One black dip on the skyline was the pass where next our camp would stand.

After supper Cris told me about his day's nugget.

"I set down my tripod and lay down at a creek to drink. When I raised myself I was kinda startled. A band of bulls was running straight down the hill toward me. Then I thought they were thirsty, traveling and no water, like cattle kept away from water on a hot day—forgetting they depended on snow.

"Instead of coming to the creek they stopped when they got to the foot-high willows along it and began nipping off pussywillows. Those pussywillows were what they were all after and what they all started eating. They didn't stand and eat on one bush at that. A nibble here and a nibble there, meanwhile walking on up the creek."

It sounded like a humble item to add to our growing hoard of caribou information but it had greatness in it. Invisible but beautiful as a fine equation is the interstructuring of the ways of these arctic deer and the fragile arctic flora.

"I think caribou must be the most considerate boarders nature ever set a table for," Cris concluded.

My days were monotonous—there is no monotony like that of toiling a step at a time with a load over vast treeless land where you can actually see your goal hours ahead of you. But daily there was some new kind of flower in bloom, once the small wonder I never forgot, of knee-high plants in bud in the shelter of the very crest of a pass in this high land where most plant life crouched low.

I had fun with the caribou. I supposed this was how it was on the tundra—you always found bands of bulls going westward. In a band of say a dozen big bulls there would be a couple of year-old fawns. These fawns amused me. When the band lay down, the fawns lay heads high, calm and stately like the big bulls.

More and more "teen-agers" were coming along with the bands of bulls and a custom of theirs amused me too. The big bulls would run from me, but always they paused for that one more look back at what had scared them. It is the famous "caribou vacillation." The teen-agers instantly seized this chance to hurry back toward me and stand watching me intently. Was I the first of my deadly species they had seen in their young travels? Never could they quite satisfy their curiosity. When the big bulls turned to flee, follow they must; they dared not linger.

It gave me a scary amusement when I broke over a ridge and found a band of bulls right below me. They vacillated and veered, generating what Quakers call "the sense of the meeting" about how best to save themselves from my small silent figure. Then they lined out and ran, hoofs thudding, long noses lifted level with backs so that the great antlers sank to their shoulders. The palms of the re-curves floated over their heads like helicopter rotors.

It is quite possible that the most beautiful antlers in the world are the antlers of a bull caribou in black velvet. The velvet sometimes is tawny but it is black that is dramatic. The antlers of a feeding bull soar in a steep black V across his white chest, its tip to the tundra, palms spreading wide above his head. In spite of the re-curve, the antlers ascend higher above the bull than his legs go down below, provided he stands ankle-deep in grass.

I observed details. Cris noted something else. Almost absently one evening he brought it forth, a generalization. "About five or six hundred caribou a day, mostly bulls, have been going west and northwest on a ten-mile front for a week now."

I realized it was true. We were in the midst of some great movement of the caribou.

6   The Caribou Bull Migration

We were ready to start down the Kugururok, but first we had a duty to perform. We had left base camp standing, more as a psychological resource than anything else; we knew in emergency we could fall back on it. That last thread of connection with the outside world must be cut; we must make a fast light trip back to Noluk and close base camp for Tommy to pick up and fly across the mountains to our destination, "west of the mouth of the Kugururok on the north bank of the Noatak." (How slick and clear that sounded.) At Noluk we would enjoy our final base-camp luxuries before reaching the Noatak. In water warmed extravagantly with un-backpacked Blazo, we would wash clothes, bathe. We would have two square meals. The following day we would start back into the mountains, staking all, this time, on Tommy's cache near the mouth of the Kugururok.

We left behind all we could, including much unexposed film. Exposed film would go with us to be left at Noluk. The Leica I cached in a plastic sack under an overhanging rock which long afterward with mounting panic I was to find differed not at all from scores of others.

We returned to the old pretty site of Camp Two, pitched the mountain tent and tarp to leave standing there until we returned, and very early the next morning set out for Noluk.

It was to be a day of surprises. The first was when Cris left the great uplands and, where the unforgettable scroll top of Thunder Mountain carves the sky between two headwaters of the Colville River, led down to the east fork. It was easy country down here.

Easy walking on the sand bars. Willows big enough for fuel. Fish in the deepening stream. And we were down among green leaves. Experimentally we nibbled each kind, found one good kind. We were famished for greenstuff.

Once two grizzlies, on the edge of a plateau above us, noted us and followed along above until they came to the drop-off, where, to our relief, they turned aside and did not descend.

We came to a grim place a couple of miles farther along. It was a grizzly "kill yard." The tundra was powerfully ripped up for fifteen feet across, about the usual diameter of a kill yard. In the center lay a dead caribou, cached under the duff. There was meat on the bones. A grizzly does not cache cleaned bones. The grizzly—or grizzlies, for we had seen up to three of equal size together—may have found the caribou dead or dying. It is true that caribou fear grizzlies, but it seemed unlikely that a grizzly could catch a healthy caribou.

A kill yard is a somber place. There was no danger here for us, but I felt better when we left it.

Flags of change were flying on the tundra. We did not "read" them. Once we met a band of bulls doing an unusual thing, namely coming east instead of going west. Always they had been moving westward except on one peculiar recent day, when they had gone in all directions—north, east, west.

Also we met a band composed not of bulls and a few teen-agers, but made up of eighteen yearling fawns. Only one bull chaperoned them; a young fellow with short thick antlers in black velvet.

These yearlings gratified—nearly—their insatiable desire to view fully our kind of animal. We stood frozen, smiling. They stared; they stared. They stepped toward us in unison as if we were Pied Pipers. A bit calflike and foolish they looked, with their broad noses and the white patch back of the black nostrils. The young bull did not feel thus drawn.

He would have preferred to run away. He stepped along back of the group, passing us by. The youngsters themselves were not without tension: many urinated. The act disclosed that there were both males and females in the band.

It was late evening, the sunlight warm yellow, when from the last low ridge we looked ahead down at our little old base camp by the white lake. As usual I looked for that improbable miracle, a drop of supplies. There was nothing.

The last half mile was the hardest of the day, as I trudged after Cris over rough tussocks, tired beyond tiredness.

Cris glanced back. There was happiness in his eyes. "We got a drop," he said quietly.

I would believe that when I saw evidence. It was there—a white canvas sack near the veranda, narrowly missing a mud pool.

The magnitude of the drop only slowly became apparent. Without even taking off my pack I trudged out to a gunnysack on the spit east of the tent and dragged it in. Cris combed the spit and found three more sacks.

The white sack was marked in black crayon, "Open this first. Read note and telegram. Plane waiting." Involuntarily we glanced at the empty sky, though, as Cris estimated later, the drop must have lain here three or four days.

We slid our packs off. Into my weariness joy was creeping not suddenly but in a rising tide. The previous night, in the mountains, I had been irritable and unsleepy from hunger. Dragging spent as a shoestring along that last ridge toward camp I had pondered what to have for supper together with the one can of beef I knew was here.

Now what indeed to have! Canned tomatoes? Canned corn? Canned dehydrated soup? All had come in the drop. Alas, no protein. But oranges! Four dozen. Half of them smashed, so we could eat them unrationed. And four pounds of uncanned butter. The foxes had not touched it. What fox in its right mind would eat stale grease in cardboard when all over the tundra were nests of downy baby birds! The weather, luckily, had been gray and cool.

It was that now-useless telegram that had occasioned the drop. But how, I wondered, could we have answered it. We learned later on. The pilot scribbles and drops a note, weighted by a roll of toilet paper that streams out and marks the landing point. He gives a question you can answer yes or no, by arm signals specified in the note.

The white sack was crammed with mail. With proud absti-

nence which titillated our pleasure of anticipation, we did our
chores, not even indulging in looking at the names on the letters. Carried water from the creek, now flowing in its bed;
cooked; feasted; heated water and bathed.

Then at last, clean, luxuriously sacked in, noble-feeling
from self-control, we read letters. Half of them only. Half
we reserved for the next day. Cris had declared a holiday.
For one day we would lie over to enjoy our drop.

Cris's plan was knocked sky-high. In the morning it was evi-
dent that we were in the path of a great migration.

It was the caribou bull migration. The bulls we had seen
in the mountains had been only the forerunners.

The bulls were coming not en masse but in waves, a few to
a hundred or so in each wave. They crested on the long low
skyline to the east, passed camp, crested again to the west.
On the sky lines they looked, as Cris said, like a row of cairns.

There was an odd effect between waves, an effect that was
the epitome of wilderness, where there is no past and no future, nothing but what is before your eyes. The effect now
was deadness. The land looked dead, forlorn and utterly deserted. My heart sank when Cris took his camera and went
eastward to find a rock where he could shoot down through
the heat waves—even snow in a crotch of rock looked like a
rushing torrent because of heat waves. I thought of the slender
thread he traced on foot, and of the vastness, illimitable,
empty. How could he hope to find the caribou?

Then the next time I looked, there would be that choppi-
ness on the eastern horizon again, another wave coming. But
always the unknowing: some wave had to be the last.

Cris returned, with seven hundred feet of exposed film, and
refused supper though it was something we could not have
up in the mountains—brown beans, requiring too much backpacked Blazo to cook at high altitudes. He sat on a box in the
open door of the veranda, watching through the defile to the

south. Waves were cresting over there too. "I can eat other times," he said merrily, "but this is wonderful."

Seriously he added, "It *is* wonderful, sitting here in the lap of a big migration." A wave of bulls swung by at the great "migration trot." "That trot!" said Cris. "Going someplace. Choog, choog, choog. You couldn't keep up with it." Hoofs actually were flung ahead of muzzles at times. Yet the bulls weren't hurrying; this was their gait. Now we understood something that had puzzled us back in May, when the cows were passing.

Poor, pregnant, hampered by softening snow, yet they had speeded up voluntarily the minute their hoofs met hard snow. You could see the impulse gathering in their bodies; they broke into a trot, the migration trot we knew now.

It had puzzled us then because in the States the animals that we knew had trotted or run only under special stimulus, of fear or play or mating or a downhill run. But no visible stimulus touched the caribou. The whip that stung them was within, the age-long adaptation of arctic deer to arctic tundra. Speedy travel; light nibbling on the go. It was their way.

So the bulls paused and ate as they traveled, overtaking one another. Theirs was the deer's selectiveness multiplied a thousandfold. They were free from any need to garner each available bite in any one spot. A bite as they went, here one, there one, in the ocean of tundra covered with nourishment.

They had one amazing little way, a characteristic movement in the denser waves. Those at the back suddenly ran through and took the front. Taking turns at first choice of tidbits!

We had witnessed the opposite of these caribou ways once, when we camped and traveled with Eskimo reindeer herders. Those reindeer of theirs had put their heads down and chewed steadily along. If not herded they might have lingered, eating out one spot.

The best reindeer herders, the Lapps, say reindeer should

be rotated. Lichens need from three to forty years to recuperate after a passing of reindeer; on the average, ten years. Lichens grow slowly, only a sixteenth of an inch a year.

No herdsman did the caribou have. Or had they? Was the tumult and drive in their strange nerves entirely uncaused? What ungulates do not overcongregate, yard up, if not driven?

The caribou we watched were part of one of the last remaining great caribou herds of Alaska. Guns, fire and kindness had done for the rest. The caribou story is a story of destruction.

When white men struck Alaska, one or two million caribou roamed the land. There is a critical time of year for wild animals, namely winter. But the caribou in winter fared well, the embryos flourished in the wombs. For the caribou then had a great winter range of taiga—white spruce floored with lichens, the favorite winter food of caribou. When a caribou pawed the snow for food, nine digs out of ten netted it a nourishing bite of lichen. (I have already said that the name caribou comes from the Algonquian for "shoveler.")

White men got at the caribou in three ways. First by carnage, the usual carnage wherever man meets animal—both white men and Eskimos armed with white man's weapons killed. Next and worse by fire. The fires of Alaska have been stupendous. Hordes of reckless miners in the gold rushes slashed and burned the timber. Trappers and prospectors continued the burning. For fifty years, from one million to five million acres burned or reburned annually. Eighty per cent of the original white spruce forest burned. With it went the lichen floor, the caribou winter range.

In the third place, marauding whalers and also men of good will took a hand. The whalers hunted—to extinction for all they cared—the whales and walrus the Eskimos depended on. To sustain their crews both winter and summer, they wiped out land animals, caribou and musk oxen. Theirs was probably the most destructive incursion the Arctic ever sustained until the huge incursion for DEW line—the military Distant Early Warning line; but the latter was still on paper. So hundreds of Eskimos starved, or died of white man's diseases.

And kindly white folk imported reindeer to feed them. Between 1891 and 1902 a total of 1,280 reindeer were imported to start herds for the Eskimos. By 1932 that little population had "exploded"; there were nearly 650,000 reindeer. The inevitable happened.

The reindeer hordes ate out their winter ranges. They starved; their numbers crashed. By 1952 only 26,735 reindeer remained in Alaska. And the old rich lichen ranges were eaten out and gone, for reindeer and caribou alike.

An odd thing happened along the Bering Sea. Perhaps there the lichens never can come back. For instead of becoming a desert, the land became lush and green with sedges and shrubs; lichens cannot get a toehold. It is summer range only.

Luckily neither fire nor reindeer reached the Brooks Range. True arctic tundra does not burn.

We did not leave the following morning. When we rose, we found four hundred caribou in sight, over a hundred of them lying between tent and mountainside, and a wave just cresting to the east.

It was a day of tension. All little concerns were overshadowed by the awe of the great movement of the caribou. Cris filmed a passing fox. I sat on the doorstep of the veranda, reconstructing our wool socks with flannelette; by sheer luck I had this yard of spare cloth. "Our" longspur fed by my feet. Cris carved a wooden bobbin and edged a net for grayling; the net had come in the drop and was too big.

But the cause of our tension was the predicament we were

in. It was a wilderness predicament. We had to make a decision affecting Cris's work and make it only on evidence before our eyes. Cris wanted fawn pictures. Would fawns and cows follow the bull migration? Had those cows that passed going west and repassed going east in May fallen in behind the bull migration?

We had one reason to think they had. Along with the bulls came more and more teen-agers and yearlings. It was reasonable to humans to think mothers might follow the young.

The next morning when Cris got up he said lightly enough, "Guess I'll get up and hypothesize about the caribou." But I knew he was troubled. I exerted my mind to help him.

Lucidly I summed up the possibilities. "Either the cows and fawns are all on ahead. Or they're coming. Or they're bypassing us. Or the fawns aren't born yet."

Cris laughed and hugged me. "That's sticking the old neck out!" Then he said soberly, "The trouble is I don't know what to do. I sure wish I had a plane contact now. Someone to fly over, locate the cows and drop us a note."

Why didn't we read a book and get the answer to our problem? We had indeed read a book and read it like a bible, but it did not "take." On the steamer the previous year, as we first came to Alaska, we had read Dr. Adolph Murie's book, *The Wolves of Mount McKinley*. But you need experience to make it come alive. Then it means to you twenty facts, a whole "surround," for each fact stated.

Reaching Alaska, we had gone outdoors. When we had learned enough to ask the right questions, we were beyond reach of books. And this spring, when Cris had decided on the spur of the moment to try for caribou, we were out on their trail at once, with no time nor place to hunt up books.

In wilderness, one great limb of power is amputated, one humans have forged for themselves and depend on so heavily it is hard to imagine life without it. It is the power of forecasting. We could not forecast. We had to decide our course, go or stay, on the facts before our eyes.

We stayed. Cris said, "We'll wait a week for the cows. Then if they don't come we'll still have time to get across the mountains and down the Kugururok before Tommy is to meet us there."

7   *Caribou Fawns*

The week of waiting was marked by big events of nature but not by the coming of the fawns. The migration petered to a close. Cris estimated that twelve thousand caribou had passed, mostly bulls in velvet.

What dominated the tundra world now was the Big Light. The birds slept in the sunlight when it was low and golden from the north. The snow was gone. This is not what people expect from the Arctic. Far to the south, in the temperate zone, the Alaska range would be loaded all summer with snow and glaciers. But here in the arid Arctic the shallow snow soon melted in the ceaseless sunlight.

My eyes tired. I longed for the gentle darkness and stars of the temperate zone. Never here would men have cried a dawn call to pale sky brightening over high crags. What poetry could be indigenous here? Nothing romantic. Only something grand beyond men's fond dabbling in mystery. Here in the ever-sun one felt the pulse of life itself, beating fast.

Big winds tore at the tent. It throbbed and shook incessantly, though a rope was stretched from every grommet, including those in the webbing belt added around the middle of the tent. It almost scared me to be alone at camp with a gale rising, the lake in whitecaps, and Cris not here to drive the angle irons deeper, tighten the cables, brace the veranda frame.

He returned from camera-hunting up in the sheltered foothills one evening, surprised, I thought, to find how wild it was. But after supper he sacked in and fell asleep at once. I should have thought he would lie awake to see if his handiwork, our shelter, would hold.

But no. In spite of the threshing, shoving, beating, throbbing, jumping, he slept. It must be all right, I thought, and slept too. It alarmed me retroactively when in the morning he said, "I thought any minute we'd be out on the tundra without any shelter."

Just before midnight when Midsummer Day would begin, we were awakened by fierce gusts. Sudden hard slaps shook the tent like the vole in the wolverine's mouth. There was a leaden overcast and one breach in it only, low to the north, through which poured golden sunlight. (Night sun is warmer-colored than day sun.)

Recklessly I prepared an unrationed quart of our scarce powdered milk and we saw the big day in. Cris remarked, "Midnight twilight in Fairbanks is more mysterious than midnight sun here. This is just plain sunshine. About like five P.M. on a sunny June day in the Olympics."

All that day the wind was rough. The veranda shook. The tent walloped. The guy ropes were taut. A shore bird cried in short imperious mews like a scared kitten. The ducks were hushed. Noise. Commotion.

But we were being set free. A big dark-blue "lead," or channel, choppy with whitecaps, opened around the south side of the lake. Whenever I left the tent I heard a new sound —waves sloshing at the shore, the stir and slop and shish of water.

When we went to bed that night the lake was still covered with ice except for the broad and changing leads. In the morning Cris wakened me. With quiet jubilance he said, "The ice is gone. There is no ice."

Breakup was over. A plane could land.

Our week of waiting ended. Heavy with disappointment at seeing no caribou cows, we started back into the mountains to go down the Kugururok to the Noatak.

We were climbing away from camp when, pausing to breathe and look back, we saw an ominous sign. In the vast green tundra the lake lay as we had never seen it before—blue and motionless, reflecting the sky. We did not read the sign.

On the first rimrock behind the south ridge, we set off our packs to rest. A longspur fed toward us among the flowers— lavender, cream, purple, pink. Regretfully I said, "The long-spurs don't sing any more."

At this moment one sang on his glide. Cris said, "There's one singing now," and without changing his voice he continued, "There's a band of caribou over there and they have fawns with them."

We both stood up with our field glasses. The caribou were coming over the skyline to the east—about seventy adults, two thirds of them with fawns. Was this it? Were the cows coming through?

We almost had buck fever. Cris started toward them with his camera but forgot his camera pack. I ran after him with it. He smiled and took it. Returning to my own pack, I found his "brassière," the magazine holder. I hung it around my neck and put on my pack.

When I overtook him he was already filming. I heard the

bark of a baby caribou, a low nasal reedy "Ma!" Brief. There were frequent bass cries. The caribou stood below us on a snow patch, a forest of dark legs and long morning shadows.

They were in trouble. They shook themselves, held their noses to the snow. Half a dozen cows with fawns made off over the vast heat-shimmering uplands toward the southwest. After a quarter of an hour one came back running, as if desperate. This as we knew was the sole snow patch in miles, the sole respite from flies. Botflies, which lay their eggs in a caribou's nostrils, must have been troubling the caribou. Later on, warble flies would torment them. Warble flies lay eggs singly, over back and flanks.

We had observed a pitiful thing on what had proved to be the last day of the migration. We made a sortie that day into the high country. Before we left in the morning, three hundred caribou had passed Noluk. But in the mountains all day we saw only a dozen caribou. They were bulls. Each stood alone on some snowbank on the mountainsides, holding his nostrils to the snow.

He stood that way for minutes at a time. Then he would lie down as if tired out. But in a moment he would scramble to his feet, shake his head downward and hold nose tip to snow again. We found a dead caribou, its nostrils clogged with a mass of reddish dead larvae, probably of the botfly.

Now there was an outcry below us, a high-pitched mewing. Five long-tailed jaegers wheeled past, conducting some kind of fuss. Were they, too, affected by the heat? Everything that happened this day was to be marked by a kind of broken, illegible intensity.

I was painfully disappointed at what Cris said as he started away presently. The cows had left the snow, heading away southwestward toward the mountains, and Cris was starting east to meet others, if others were coming.

"This can't be the cow-fawn migration," he said. "Surely the cows would be taking their fawns nearer the mountains, by a route with more escape from flies."

I started toward base camp but, before I could reach it, two incidents happened, highlighting the intensity and strangeness of the day. A lone young caribou bull saw me and started for me at a gallop, blowing through his nostrils like a horse. Did he take me for a long-lost cousin? I felt wild, like a caribou myself; I wanted to rear and run away. At a certain point the young caribou's certainty was shaken. He ran a few steps away, then stood gazing at me as I walked on.

A remarkable incident came next. I was going down the mountainside. Along the base of it trotted a file of bulls. From this file suddenly one bull detached himself. Without a break in his stride, as if he had just heard the call, he swung at a right angle and started straight up the mountain. The knowledge that act betrayed was awesome. This was the first mountain these bulls would have come to in miles. And it was the terrain for snow. The bull knew it.

I turned back and watched till he found the patch the cows had just left.

At the tent I stood outside, regardless of the heat. Scattered bands and individuals kept coming from the east. Two bulls plunged into the lake and swam. Four bulls came at a dead gallop, fly-crazed. It looked as if something hung from their mouths. As they neared I saw it was their lower jaws, hanging open.

Now occurred a strange, pitiful thing, but I felt no pity. Only wonder, as at some pageant too vast for pity. Sixty great bulls in single file passed between the tent and the mountain in the shimmer of heat waves, going west as were all caribou this day. They were trotting fast. Terribly, relentlessly fast. And following them, galloping to keep in hailing distance, came two cows and a baby fawn. As far as I could follow with my eyes, those two and the fawn labored mightily to keep up, galloping two hundred yards behind the receding bulls.

Cris returned from the east. "There's a fawn over here and I want you to help me. I'm going to bring it to camp."

He had watched it for a couple of hours. It lay alone on the tundra east of the spit. Twice a solitary cow had passed near. Each time the fawn struggled to its long legs and ran, trying desperately to join the cow. Each cow veered frantically, trying to throw it off. One stood on her hind legs and struck at it. The fawn collapsed and lay still. It was exhausted. Had its mother, mistakenly attaching herself to a band of bulls instead of the more leisurely cows, abandoned it?

In the States we should have felt no concern about a lone fawn. Its mother, we knew, would graze near and soon return. But here in the great migrations of the Arctic, it looked as if a mother caught in the dilemma of weakening fawn and vanishing herd must choose, of the two, the herd.

The fawn followed us part way, as fawns will do. We dragged it the rest of the way. Cris tied it in the shade of the tent. I offered it warm milk with a wet flannelette nipple. Tainted by smells of hands and rags, the milk repelled it. But it nuzzled the green moss for spilled milk.

The fawn struggled, caught one big cloven hoof over the tent rope and stood passive, head low, looking straight ahead, experiencing God knows what consciousness of all the alien, forever-meaningless, unproductive, unvital noises, intents and smells around it—helpless at a den of predators. I touched it gently. The fawn made a very slight movement of utter rejection.

It was not cute, not "little," not cuddly. It was intensively adapted for the terrible tundra life. Those long legs *must* keep up with the bulls. "There are no babies in the Arctic," I thought.

Cris looked fondly at the fawn. "When the Norseman comes," he said, "we'll take it with us."

I was silent. The fawn lay dull-eyed as if dying, then struggled again. Cris saw we could not keep it. "The heart goes out of them," he said. "Better to let it die free."

We led it back nearly to where we had found it and set it free. The fawn came alive, bright-eyed. It went off bleating, waiting, for the one creature only, who must come, who would come, surely, for the life that was in him.

At eight that evening there was a gray cloud over the sun, gray light on the tundra. A cow came fast from the west, trotting. She passed, almost brushing sides, a lone bull going in the migration direction and paid no attention to him. Nose down at times as if scenting—hurrying, purposeful, the cow was returning counter-migrationwise.

"She will find him," Cris said. His eyes were shining. I sensed that he had prayed.

After this day we understood that heat is more to be dreaded in the Arctic than the merciful clouds and wind.

Before noon Cris had made his decision. These caribou were only a fluke side-toss from the migration, wherever that moved. But they were enough; Cris had his fawn pictures. We would not walk across the mountains hoping to encounter fawns. We would wait here and fly across with Tommy when he came to pick up our base camp. But we would still summer on the Noatak.

When we went up to the high country it was to strike our gale-shredded bivouac, go up to our high cache and return to Noluk with as much as we could carry.

There is a tension about waiting for a plane in the wilderness. Has the appointment you made so long ago been forgotten? It was nearly seven weeks since that noon in the tent when Tommy had promised to pick up our base camp here "about July 5."

On the bright chill morning of July 2, Cris called me. "Look! The longspurs are banding up."

A whole flight of adult longspurs wheeled together above the spit where they had lived with such intensity these past two months. Were they, like us, preparing to leave?

As our own departure day neared we did not walk far from camp. No one expected us to be here. Tommy might come a day or so early. He could land and take off before we could reach the plane. We pinned a note to our dunnage but a note could blow away or be overlooked. The dunnage, except for a skeleton camp, was neatly stowed in the mountain tent, which Cris had pitched at the mouth of the creek, for ease in loading onto a float plane.

Tommy did not come on the fifth. The sixth was stormy. The lake tossed gray and white-capped. Rain dimmed the air. It would be snowing in the mountains. We gave up hope for yet another day.

There came a distant roar. Out of the storm materialized a black Norseman. It touched the waves and taxied to the mountain tent. Down onto the pontoon climbed the pilot, not Tommy but John Cross, surprised to see two dark figures in wet rain parkas running toward him. Disconcerted too, perhaps, for he had brought along his delightful Eskimo wife for the ride. Luckily a Norseman could easily take the unexpected weight of two more people.

Now, all that had happened in our weeks alone here was as nothing. The tension and blind uncertainty of even an hour ago were of no moment now. In the cold dark cabin of the plane, separated from Cris and John up front by the pile of our dunnage, I sat facing Mrs. Cross. There was a seat along each side wall. The plane rose away. I turned and peered down hungrily, hiding tears, at the camp spit, the ridges we had climbed, the lake I should never see again.

Snow mists hid the uninhabited mountains where we had trudged and camped. We flew along the Range in the snowstorm, hunting a way south. The pass John Cross had come through was whitened out. So were the next two passes.

But from one as we flew by, there flashed to us knowledge and a question that interested us intensely but that we could never follow up. Over the lip of this unknown pass poured fresh caribou trails. Made by the cow migration in May? By the bull migration in June? By that late June return into the mountains? The pass slipped behind us into the gray storm. We crossed southward by another.

A queer sight on the bank of the Noatak River below caught my eye—an aggregation of black poles. For some reason poles had been placed upright away off here in the wilderness!

"Why are those—?" I began. Then I realized. Trees! The last meager spruces struggling northward.

I looked down intently as we neared the spot so long the goal of our efforts, the mouth of the Kugururok. It was a forbidding place. Far around, the land was a black desolation of mud. Green ice, a "glacier," still choked the mouth of the Kugururok, causing it to wander, denuding the land. The mountains here stood far back from the Noatak River.

Mrs. Cross stammered in surprise, "Why! We weren't to set your things down here!" She named as the location for our cache a lake I had never heard of. Apparently Cris's plan had been improved upon at Kotzebue. I was mute with shock. Those twelve thousand bulls in black velvet, I thought, had spared us hungry misery, perhaps had saved our lives.

We were flying straight out toward Kotzebue. Two hours ago we had not doubted we would fly to the Noatak and summer there. But the first note had sounded of the stormy new theme that was to dominate our lives from now on. John Cross, handing us our precious mail sack at Noluk, had said, "There's a message, too. Andy radioed that the Eskimos at Anaktuvuk Pass have four wolf pups for you."

Back in April, without much hope, Cris had asked Andy

to arrange if possible for the capture of a litter of wolves. Now we had no time to lose. Already the message was two weeks old; the Eskimos any day might kill the pups for the bounty of fifty dollars each.

From Kotzebue, Cris chartered straight east to Bettles Field with Andy. I flew commercial to Fairbanks to lay in fresh supplies for the unknown adventure before us.

8   Summer Camp in the Brooks Range

On the night of July 11, I chartered north from Fairbanks, piloted by Dick Morehead. Over dim lands in sub-arctic twilight; over the pallid loops of the Yukon, sprawling out of the east; toward the slowly changing pink, then clear gold, northern horizon and into the sunrise of the Arctic. Ahead rose the Brooks Range.

We touched down on the deserted field at Bettles. As I walked with my suitcase to the sleeping roadhouse, I saw near the door a crude pen of plywood panels tied together and knew the wolves must be there. But I did not go to them for a very good reason. Before I left Fairbanks, I had been told by Dr. John Krog, a Norwegian scientist just back from Anaktuvuk Pass, that my first meeting with the wolves would probably determine their lifelong attitude toward me. It seemed incredible, but I was determined to make that first meeting right if I could.

A bed was ready for me on the davenport in the living room back of the lobby. But I was not to sleep yet. Andy's mother stole from her room to give me a message from Cris. He had flown the afternoon before to a new camp site in the Range, but had purposely left the feeding of the wolves to me, to give me an advantage in my critical first meeting with them. For an hour Mrs. Anderson and I tried to start the huge balky oil range to heat milk. At last I took the milk cold and went out to meet the wolves.

The world was unpeopled, cold and still, the sunlight pinkish. I spoke softly and bent over the pen. Two solemn faces, one black, one gray, looked up at me. Their owners cowered timidly under a torn carton. I started to lower the pan of milk. The gray wolf stepped toward it.

At this moment a voice at my shoulder spoke loudly, "May I look at your wolves?" An Eskimo girl had run over from her quarters. The gray wolf growled and shrank under the carton. Whether Dr. Krog was right or not, there was not to be a day when that wolf did not growl at me. In one second I had been branded with a danger sign. To myself I expressed it in the old term from *The Golden Bough:* my "mana" had become dangerous.

It was two o'clock when I sacked in. At six o'clock, hearing voices outdoors, I rose for the day, to guard the wolves, as Cris's message had warned me to do, from the lethal intentions of the Eskimo children.

I found I must wait until night to fly to join Cris. In summer Andy preferred to fly at night because the turbulence was less.

Near midnight our floats touched a still lake in a mountain-walled pass in the central Brooks Range—the Endicott Mountains. The mountainsides on the west shadowed the lake but those on the east were sunlit, and running down from a dot that was our umbrella tent came a small figure, Cris hurrying to meet us.

We had the plane unloaded when he arrived. Andy produced a surprise. He handed Cris his own 30.06, trimmed with hand-carved ivory. He was lending it voluntarily, for a sobering reason. As he had taken off after setting Cris down here a couple of days before, two different grizzlies had stood up and struck toward the plane. He had brought Cris four cartridges, all he could find.

Now we were armed, for the first time in our twelve years in the wilderness. Even when camera-hunting grizzlies and brownies all the previous summer we had gone entirely unarmed.

Andy's concern touched us. It reminded me of the slightly awesome gifts from two strangers the previous spring. Learning we were to fly bush in the Range, each with bashful courtesy had given us morphine to commit suicide with. Neither mentioned the obvious, that it would save us being eaten alive if injured in a crash. With respectful amusement I had wondered to myself where we should carry the morphine, to get at it if both arms were broken. In little nose-bags perhaps? I had also wondered, but with a bashfulness of my own had refrained from asking, whether Andy was similarly fortified.

That morphine gave our medicine kit range if not body: it consisted now of Band-aids and morphine, our bottle of antiseptic having long since frozen and burst. We also carried adhesive tape to mend tarps and sleeping bags.

Why did we carry so little? The answer strikes at the difference between our outlook and the civilized one. Our unconscious rules for living were different from those in civilization. In civilization there is a vast, overwhelming whimper to be secure, sheltered, cared for. But if you refuse danger too much, you refuse life.

We had been aircraft-warning observers in the highest lookout kept open in the Olympics during the Second World War. It was the first winter after our marriage and I was still city-anxious: I wanted a toboggan to get an injured person out on if necessary. It failed to arrive before we were snowed in for the winter. We used skis and snowshoes to get down the mountain once a month or so for mail. We did not get sick. I was learning.

Every summer after that we backpacked beyond the trails in the high country, carrying a tarp to pitch for shelter, sleeping on the ground as we could not spare weight for air mattresses. Ounces count when the man of the team is weighed down with a camera pack.

We carried food. That was the important thing. And an ax and the lightest possible nest of cans for cooking. Ounces for medicine seemed wasted. We took Band-aids and adhesive tape and they were all we ever needed. Friends presented us with first-aid kits; these stayed at home.

Either you must cover every chance, or trust yourself and go free, not tethered like Gulliver among the Lilliputians by a thousand threads of caution. Of course there is a happy medium. We never sought danger. But one has to draw the line or stay in an armchair. Without a word or a thought we drew it at dragging medical supplies for every contingency on earth around on our backs as we joyfully did our chosen work.

Cris got into trouble once. Alone in the Olympics before our marriage, he stepped heedlessly on a rotten log on a steep slope. It broke, he rolled over a cliff and came to with a broken arm. He set it as well as he could—it had to be re-broken—then dragged up wood, hewed it with his good arm, cooked up a pail of rice and set a pail of water beside it. After that he sacked in and suffered for a few days, but he was quite pleased to have broken only an arm, not a leg or his neck. He drank the rinse water from the pail he mixed his hotcakes in; the accident kept him out so long his supplies ran out.

An early spring bivouac camp.

A permanent camp. Lois and the umbrella tent which was the Crislers' shelter for their first four months in the Arctic.

Cris and his Cine-special, scope sight and tripod, which he carried on his shoulder over countless miles of tundra and mountains. You don't have time to unpack camera and tripod. You have to be ready to start photographing immediately.

Housekeeping on the tundra.

Lady.

Cris starts a howl, which Trigger and Lady join wholeheartedly.

Lois and Trigger. A relaxed yawn shows a genial mood.

Trigger and Lady went with Cris on all his trips, whether for supplies left by the plane, for wood, or camera-hunting.

Lady was an inventor of games. She untied Cris's ear flaps every time she could get to them.

Wolves like high lookout points.

Cris finishes the "crackerbox."

The crackerbox commanded a far-ranging view up two rivers, Easter Creek and the Killik. (This is looking up Easter Creek.)

Cris is an inveterate gardener. Near the crackerbox (at foot of mesa) he planted his arctic garden, irrigated it with snow.

Probably the first radishes ever grown outdoors north of the Brooks Range.

In the summer Lois did the washing down by the river to save backpacking water.

The first fall the Crislers used willow brush along the river for fuel. It had to be backpacked half a mile to the mesa top.

Getting the mail at breakup time.

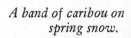
A band of caribou on
spring snow.

The big bulls, caught here in migration trot, are in their prime coat in the fall. (Cris is photographing them.)

The thin line of migrating caribou reached across the tundra and **into** the mountains.

The migration leaves parallel ruts of trails in the tundra.

(left) "Andy" Anderson, arctic bush pilot.

(right) Trigger had to be kept on a chain at Point Barrow, and wasn't very happy about it.

(left) Lois at the forced-draft range in the wanigan at Point Barrow. The frying pan is strictly for photographic purposes, but the kettle is full of melting snow for water.

ERWIN L. VERITY

(right) Trigger did run loose in the wanigan. "How about it? Time to come in?" The cleat was nailed below the window to aid the wolves in climbing out. Claw marks on the door show their efforts.

The den hunt must start from the far side of the river. Cris takes
Jonas across in his homemade boat.

Tootch, the Eskimos' lead dog, and Cris, her new master.

While the men were away on the den hunt, Lois went into the pen and released Scrappie, the wolverine, from its cage. She took this picture to show Cris what had happened in case wolverines were all they are cracked up to be.

The wolverine circles her cautiously . . .

And soon is eating from her hand.

Tootch puts a band of caribou to flight. No caribou will be caught from this band for they are running as a unit, none is falling behind.

Tootch hamstrings and kills a lone "slow" caribou. The wolves do not help and are timid about approaching the caribou.

"What a pity you didn't have epsom salts," I purred, thinking of soaking the arm. (We were courting then.)

"I didn't need them," said Cris, grinning. "I was scared to death and that worked just as well."

It's people outdoors or people indoors. Either "outdoors" with your deep will, or "indoors" in the nest of civilization even in wilderness.

Andy's silver wake unrolled across the dark-blue, mountain-shadowed water. He rose away. Always that lift of the heart when the pontoons tilt up: "She's off!" He waved his wings as he circled and passed over us. Already Cris was loading his packboard, but I watched the silver sliver rise against the dark mountainside, grow small and disappear down the Alatna canyon. Then I turned to our work.

Cris had my packboard loaded with the most interesting object I had ever carried, the cage of wolves. A piece of torn cardboard tied to it, lettered by the Eskimos at Anaktuvuk Pass, stated: "Gray one name Trigger black name Lady."

Trigger and Lady scrambled unbalancingly in the cage as I followed Cris up the mountainside to the tent a mile away. Cris, whom I had not seen for several days, brought me up to date on our situation.

First, why only two wolves instead of the four expected? Two Eskimo youths had found the den, killed the parents and taken the entire litter—five pups. One "wouldn't eat" and they killed it. One strangled on the cord it was tied with. The third got loose and went to the chained Eskimo dogs, which killed it. The two survivors, backpacked a hundred miles to Anaktuvuk Pass, would probably have died of starvation before we reached them if Dr. Krog had not happened to be there. He bought them canned milk from the white trader in the Pass, at the rate of three cans for two dollars.

Next, why had Cris chosen this place? He wanted a spot

remote from humans, where he could rear the wolves in soli-
tude. He had it. We were three hundred miles northwest of
Fairbanks, a two-hour flight over wilderness mountains from
Bettles Field, and over a hundred miles of tundra walking
from the nearest other humans, the Eskimos at Anaktuvuk
Pass.

Cris had chosen by map only, as usual, and had a good wilderness reason for picking this particular spot, one I should
never have thought of. I had learned a lot about wilderness
from Cris but he was still my teacher. Four rivers headed
in or near this pass and he surmised wild animals might use
the pass as a crossover between them. His judgment was soon
to be somewhat hair-raisingly confirmed.

Already he had gratifying confirmation. During the long
day while I had waited restlessly at Bettles Field, four thousand caribou had poured through here, entering from the west
and going out toward the north. Cris judged from trails already beaten that this multitude was only the close of some
huge migration. He had got some footage that pleased him—
caribou descending the mountain and passing a blue lake in a
giant S, moving simultaneously on all its traverses.

Two people set down in the wilderness with their possessions are confronted not by dreamy leisure but by hard work.
My job was to backpack the dunnage from the lake. It took
several days.

Cris had a real photographer's job. He worked with desperate haste building a pen in which to release and photograph
the wolves. He wanted to record their baby look and it was
vanishing by the hour. Already they must be nearly two
months old; wolves are born about the middle of May. Until
the pen was ready, the pups had to stay in their plywood pen,
hidden from view and the beginnings of friendship, or else
tied unhappily to a yard wire.

For once Cris had sun to match his zeal for work. No sundown checked him, only the limits of his almost bottomless strength. He trenched the rocky mountainside to set the fencing deep, so the wolves could not dig under. When the fencing came he backpacked it to camp; the rolls were a bit heavy for me.

For the first day or two I was blind with fatigue, sleepiness and the general strangeness. There was something about this place I did not like. For the first time in my life I distrusted a piece of terrain. It was beautiful. The mountains across the pass from us rolled in sunlight and shadow. The gently rising floor of the pass below us, strung with lakes and ponds, was still a warm tan, often irised by rainbows.

Yet I distrusted the place. Over it, even now in July, hung the shadow of the Big Dark coming. And here Cris planned to winter! Not in a tent, in a "crackerbox" of plywood; he was not going to spend freezeup as we had spent breakup, in a tent. He leveled the spot and laid the floor joists when Andy flew them in. But I distrusted even the spot he had chosen.

It was between the tent and a naked gulch gashed clear from the top of the ridge above us. It looked to me as if we would be in a crossfire of winds—wind down that gulch and winds tearing through the pass. The crackerbox—it would be unanchored—might be shoved, rendered useless, in a storm. Already gales and sudden gusts ransacked camp. The tent bulged, pans sailed, the pups battened down their ears. What would winter gales be like?

Yet I felt guilty lest my fears hinder Cris's work. It was for a photographic reason—ostensibly—that he wanted to winter here. That huge caribou migration that had barely preceded our arrival might return through here, and if they came in October he could get the mating fights of the caribou bulls. It would be worth a winter alone here.

I never doubted we could survive. But I had a clear vision of the starlight, the intense cold, the darkness. Above all, the immeasurable loneliness. But to Cris it was a challenge. Was that the real reason why he wanted to stay? To myself I thought meeting a challenge was one thing, seeking it another.

On my first weary evening here, after a day of backpacking and camp chores and cooking on the tundra in a gale, a sudden demand arose for more strength. Cris spotted a grizzly ambling along the mountainside toward us on a course that would bring him by above camp. The wind was blowing up the gulch. He would smell two vulnerable attractions, the pups and their meat, brought from Fairbanks in my plane load and stored in a natural cave in the side of the gulch. Cris grabbed Andy's gun and climbed away, not to kill but to scare off the grizzly.

I sat on a rock watching till he was out of sight. The last thing I craved was to climb a mountain. For the moment I could not see the grizzly either; it had dropped into some ravine. Suddenly I rose and ran up the mountainside after Cris. I had just realized he could come over the edge of a ravine and fail to spot the grizzly in time; the evening shadows would favor the bear.

I was unarmed but I had a "secret weapon" in which I had justifiable confidence. Already on a couple of grim occasions in Alaska I had inadvertently saved Cris's life with it. It was the element of surprise.

I overtook Cris, but we failed to find the grizzly. Either it smelled or heard us, or had intended anyway to turn aside hereabouts.

Cris felt dissatisfied. "I'm not afraid of him as long as I see him," he said. "What would be bad would be for him to slip into camp after we're asleep."

Now, instead of sacking in as we sorely longed to do, we did an absurd but humanly inevitable thing. The plane was to make several trips, flying in fencing and posts for the pen.

We knew it would come toward midnight, when the turbulence would be less, but we did not know on which nights. So we lay down dressed, on top of the sleeping robes, ready to run for the lake at the first far-off roar coming up the Alatna canyon. Otherwise Andy could unload and be gone before we got there. It never crossed our minds to miss the chance of seeing another human being.

At midnight we gave up our vigil and sacked in. Not, however, to languidly prolonged slumbers. At three o'clock we were awakened by a fumbling crash at the tent door. Cris grabbed Andy's gun and, stark naked, crept out cautiously. He came back grinning. The tarp over the stove had blown down.

The next night the plane did come, and with it another precaution by Andy for our safety. He had rocked up and down the river at Bettles for miles, trying to take off with unscheduled additional weight, a second pilot, Dick Morehead. Andy had preferred not to be the only person in the world who knew where we were—just in case.

This precaution reminded me of what had struck me as a curious incident the previous year, when Bob Byers, our pilot on the Yukon, had nearly failed to keep a rendezvous with a couple in the bush. He flew a white trapper and his Indian wife into remote bush to trap for a year. (Incidentally the wife was very fat; when Bob saw her he warmed a bigger plane for the flight.) He promised to pick them up a year from the day he set them down. No one but Bob could ever have found them. Two weeks later he was struck on the head in an outboard-motor accident and lay unconscious for two weeks. During that time not only his life but those of the two in the bush hung by a hair.

An odd, hapless little chain of events was started by Dick Morehead. He went fishing up the creek flowing into the lake from our gulch and tramped on a duck's nestful of eggs, heedless of the bird's distress. (Early summer on the tundra is a time for great courtesy toward the wild things.) Cris was sorry because he had hoped to photograph the duck's young. But there were other consequences too.

The next morning, a still, gray day, I was starting breakfast and Cris was studying the vast tundra pass below for "subjects." He sat on a rock to steady the field glasses, big ones—the midgets we liked for backpacking in the mountains of the States would have been nearly useless in this vast tan monotone. It was expressly to look afar that he had chosen this high, inconvenient campsite. Through the slowly rising pass he could look north for nearly four miles.

Below us lay three lakes. We called them Landing Lake, Middle Lake and North Lake. From a little higher, one could see twenty-two lakes and ponds, the farthest of which had the distinction of sending a creek into each of three drainages—the Nigu and the Killik, flowing to the Arctic Ocean, and the Alatna, flowing to the Bering Sea.

I had just poured the melted butter into the pancake batter when Cris said, "Three white animals are down by the lake at our dunnage pile. They look like Dall sheep."

A minute later he said, "They're grizzlies, a mother and cubs. The old lady has spotted us. They're coming up here."

My first thought was the wolves. They were on the yard wire. I went gently to put them into their plywood pen. They shrank as if fearing me. I left them for the moment, to help Cris. He was hunting the four cartridges, mislaid in the dunnage on the tent floor. We found them. Cris took the gun and a grim object whose significance I noted but had no time for feelings about—the hunting knife for close quarters —and started down to meet the grizzlies. They were walking rapidly up the mountain toward us, in single file. I turned out the gasoline stove in case camp was shortly a shambles.

This time I put the wolves into the pen. As I tied the panels shut, I murmured, "You may starve in there."

Cris was crouching behind a gray rock outcropping. The grizzlies, still in single file, were nearing him. In an instant I threw together the most horrendous bear rattle I had ever made, dumping the powdered milk from a two-and-a-half-pound can and putting into it an empty evaporated milk can; also, for good measure, a couple of pebbles. Holding the rattle noiseless, I started down to join Cris. Instead I abruptly sank to the tundra. Not from cravenness. I had remembered my secret weapon.

Fifty feet from Cris, the mother grizzly paused and gazed at him, studying him, then turned her head and glanced at her cubs. There was no other movement. The cubs waited, Cris waited, I waited. The decision lay with the grizzly. A minute passed. There was not a sound on the gray mountainside. The two pawns in their dark pen must have listened with silent intensity.

The grizzly made up her mind. She turned and started back the way she had come, not hurrying, walking, followed as before by the cubs. We had no doubt it was on their account she had turned back. She felt the uncertainty of the situation and would not recklessly expose her cubs.

Now Dick Morehead's heedlessness led to a curious incident. The last cub stumbled onto the wrecked nest. At first he did not eat. He lifted his head and stared steadily ahead at the two grizzlies walking obliviously away. Then he bent his head and ate. We found hardly a shell there later.

At our dunnage pile the grizzlies paused to knock things helter-skelter, then headed away west and up a draw on the far mountainside.

I stirred the pancakes at last. Cris looked at me and said, "Let's say grace"—a rite often omitted these tumultuous days. We were glad. For the grizzly and for ourselves. She was the most beautiful grizzly we had ever seen—pure creamy white, more like a polar bear. Her cubs were big white puffballs.

It was not until a few weeks later that the last touch was added to Dick's heedlessness. We were by the lake and Cris looked at the duck, which all summer had stayed here alone. "Pole duck!" he said softly.

"Pole duck?" I inquired alertly, wondering at this new variety.

"Po' ole duck," repeated Cris, who is from Georgia. "Came way up here hopin' to raise a family. Has to fly all the way back alone."

Our troubles with grizzlies were by no means over. Every one that came through the pass—for some reason all came from the north at this time—sooner or later spotted camp; you could tell the instant it happened: the grizzly swung around methodically and started up.

Cris established a "dare line" in front of the rock where he had awaited the white grizzly. "Ole bear cross that, I'll shoot."

We always swept the pass with field glasses before starting down. Seeing no grizzly, we went down unarmed one day to net a few grayling. As we passed a tawny hummock it rose from the tawny tundra and stood, the grizzly darkness of its belly toward us.

There were only two things we could do: keep our eyes off the bear so it would feel safer, and plod steadily on. After we were past, the grizzly dropped to all fours and took off at a gallop, for once going northward, perhaps backtracking.

━━━━━━━━━━━━━━━━━━━━━━━━━━━━

Cris finished the pen in a week. Joyfully we introduced the little wolves to this space so laboriously achieved. As we had hoped, they went wild with delight. Cris recorded some footage of them, then at last turned his attention to improving camp, rather miserable until now. He repitched the tarp, not shedwise this time but in a V against the two prevailing winds. He brought up rocks from the creek bed in the gulch and made a table. It cheered me to stand up to cook, sheltered somewhat from the everlasting fierce winds.

His next improvement led to an entertaining result. He started a wood pile of willow brush. Now we could have a warming and drying fire in our new Yukon stove. But Cris soon abandoned this brush pile and started another. Two shrikes had adopted the first as their hangout. They caught mice back of the wolf pen and hung them limp on the brush. Other mice, with charmed lives, lived under the brush.

What entertained us was the varied and expressive muttering of the shrikes over a really fiendish problem they had, namely the presence of two wolves in a spot where so much nice potential food lay around on bones. The shrikes sat on the top wire of the fence and gazed down at the bones and the wolves until their feelings overcame them and they talked about their problem in sweet or strangulated or rasping cries and kissing noises. The difference between humans and birds is perhaps slightly less vast than we suppose, reacting as we properly do against identifying with them. The shrikes' feelings were clear.

And then neither their brush pile nor ours mattered any more. Cris stockpiled no more willows; he had given up his plan of wintering here. My argument about the winds in the pass had prevailed.

But now we were pitched into such a torment of indecision as I hope never to experience again. Cris had not given up wintering somewhere in the Range. And he still hoped to get the mating fights of the caribou next October. But where would those nomads be two months from now? We had to gamble on the answer and it was the anomaly of the Arctic that we had to gamble now, in July. Summer is pinched between breakup and freezeup. According to Andy the latter could start any time after the first of September. Before then, the material for the crackerbox must be flown in, several plane loads of it, and if possible the building erected.

We lived a double life these days. By day all was eventful and hustling. By night we lay in the shadowy tent, keeping vigil often for the plane, and threshing over our problem.

Cris said once, with a slight smile, "Getting an Alaska picture is like the gold rush. The stuff is there. You become ruthless and gambling." That is, we took chances one would not ordinarily take and we had to make decisive choices in the dark. "You spend your spirits, your life and your fortune. Maybe you get it and maybe you don't. It's there all right."

And once he asked a rare question for him: "What do *you* want to do, Lois?"

Helplessly I blurted out the truth. "Go home," I mumbled.

"Let's get the picture first," Cris said gently. "Maybe we won't do the wrong thing."

The humble words comforted me and I stopped jerking at the end of my chain. But what broke our deadlock was a daring, creative little act of Cris's. He is not a man to endure a deadlock. What he did was perfectly irrelevant; it had no bearing on our gamble. But it did take away the feeling of desperation and give instead the good feeling of being on our way and in command again.

Daily he took the wolves for a walk on leashes, wearing little harnesses, which betrayed his pride in his wolves. Surprisingly, they were the first pets we had ever had. Living in wilderness as we had done ever since our marriage, we could neither take a pet along when backpacking in the mountains, nor have a neighbor feed it while we were gone. There was no neighbor; we had always lived miles from other humans. Moreover, any pet would have either killed, or been killed by, wild animals. Yet Cris, I knew, still felt wistful over Tim, a cougar dog he had once had.

One afternoon when the wolves were leading as usual, like rocks or rebels, Cris suddenly said, "I'm going to turn them loose and let them follow us home."

"Oh, no! They can outrun us and we'll never see them again."

Cris knelt and stripped off the pretty harnesses. "It's a calculated risk." It was the first of a long series of bold gestures of friendship to the wolves.

As I feared, the wolves sped away. Then came a revelation —our first real nugget of wolf knowledge. Lady whirled and ran back toward Cris and as she came she demonstrated what is surely one of the prettiest, most endearing gestures in the world, the wolf "smile." We had not known it existed.

She smiled with her whole body. She humped her back like an inverted smile. She sleeked her ears into her fur and tossed her big forepaws gaily to either side as well as back and forth, as if they were on universal joints. Nearing Cris, she produced the most bewitching part of the smile: she tilted her head aside and lifted her opposite forepaw high, as if entreating friendliness. She looked up at Cris with an expression of pure joy, such as we had never seen on her keen little black face before. Cris's eyes too were wreathed in happiness.

For the first time we realized the beauty of a wolf's eyes. The whole wolf face is considered by Dr. Rudolph Schenkel to be one of the most expressive of animal faces, and much of the expression resides in the quick-changing eyes. You can never do justice to them until you are close to the wolf; from even a little distance black lines of fur and socket prolong them into slant slits. But when you see them a few feet away they are level and large and as clear as pure water, gray or gold or green according to mood and individual wolf. The changeable black pupils, enlarging readily with emotion, may be radiant or lighted by the fierce spark of anxiety or anger.

The rest of the wolf's face changes with feeling too. Eyelids knot or smooth, ears point alertly or snug flat in friendliness. Also—and this, says the animal artist William Berry, makes a wolf's face very hard to draw—there are changes in the slight but very complex musculature of the muzzle.

The smile goes on naturally into the "full wolf greeting." When the wolf tilts head aside, bowing his neck, he may proceed to lay his neck clear down on the ground and unroll his eel-supple spine to follow—a dancer's maneuver no dog could perform. A wolf can perform it without falling over only because he takes a remarkably wide base with hind paws. And he does it all in one fluent gesture, accompanied with the dazzling sweetness of the eyes.

Much has been made of the first part of the full wolf greeting, that is, "presenting the neck to the enemy." But the wolf is presenting his neck to the ground, preparatory to laying himself at your feet and it doesn't matter to him which way he turns his neck to do it. If he tilts his head away from you, "offering" his vulnerable neck, it is because he has an impulse to raise his paw toward you—lay it over your own neck if that has a low enough elevation at the moment, or lay himself at your feet.

From this day on, the smile was a constant feature of our lives. And always it warmed our hearts, made us smile too. We soon found that out on the tundra the most reassuring gesture we could make to the little wolves, doubtfully watching as we approached, was to do a wolf smile ourselves. We crouched, elbows to sides, and flipped forearms sidewise. A wolf reads the lowering of your elevation as friendliness. Whether they figured out that our idea was that we were smiling I don't know. But they took the crouch and paw flip as our regular recognition sign. They smiled and tossed their own paws sidewise and ran to us.

We thought nothing about it, but in the first instance of many we had imitated the wolf in order to control him.

And did the wolves follow us home on this day when Cris gave them liberty and received the smile? By no means. But they did glance back occasionally to see if we were coming! We did not have the ghost of an understanding of it yet, but we were part of their pack. The social wolves wanted us along, though personally they were so elusive they frustrated all attempts at cuddling them.

At last that day they were in the pen and fed, and you never saw such relaxed, contented little animals. Cris, passing as I got supper, whispered in my ear, half for fun, half shyly, "I like my little wolves."

From now on they ran free on our daily walks.

We had the brave indispensable "starting ignorance" that afterward one marvels at. We could not dream the turbulence ahead as we would try to live in a degree of freedom with animals not human-oriented.

We were motivated superficially by the desire to photograph the wolves. For us this was premised, of course, on friendship. And we wanted to photograph them in their

natural habitat because of the outlook dominating our thinking and even our way of life: we believed that the last frail
wonderful webs of wilderness now vanishing from Earth are
of some infinite value, a value only sensed and very deep—
and liable to perish and be lost in this day. Wilderness without
its animals is dead—dead scenery. Animals without wilderness
are a closed book.

So the harnesses were put away forever and I was horrified to see that harness marks remained on the wolves' fur,
dimly pale even on Lady's luscious black coat. Incredulously
I wondered if harness had touched fur at some critical point
in fur maturation. I did not know that "harness marks" are
the wolf pattern!

Now the wolves introduced us to the tundra as never before.
First they showed us each wee anonymous clot of bone and
feathers—birds that had died here this past spring. Sick, old,
tired, or perhaps caught in a late storm, they had made the
long flight to the great tundra where they first saw light and
heard song, and here had died.

Lady made her first kill, a mouse, and bore it to Cris when
he praised her. She danced clear around him, brilliant and
smiling with pride.

Next the wolves introduced us to that authentic mark of
wild nature, the Grimm's fairytale effect!

We were taking them by a new route one day and I glanced
back to see why Lady wasn't coming. The black wolf stood
by her first patch of newly opened dark-pink daisies, acquainting herself with them. She brushed her nose across them,
raised her paw and touched them. Long afterward we were to
glimpse other young wolves acquaint themselves in this way
with newly opened flower patches.

A wolf's curiosity is impersonal. It goes beyond food and
fear.

Lady patted her first puffball, sprang back and sneezed,

then patted it again. She ran curiously to where I sat picking and eating the first sour blueberries. I mashed a few, she licked them, watched attentively while I picked and gave her more. Then she picked and ate a few berries for herself. Wolves have to learn.

But those incidents had connection with food. Pure impersonal fascination with the unknown showed on the morning she first met ice. She stood examining the ice in her water pan, touching it with her paw. Even after I poured water over it, she reached her paw through the water and stroked that novel satin underneath.

There was a dark, puzzling side to the wolves' nature. Cris thought he would please them one day by taking them to a caribou carcass he had found. Instead of being pleased, the wolves acted dark and troubled. Then little Lady undertook a huge task her parents no doubt would normally have performed: she began to cache the meat.

She tore off a chunk, took it away and holding it in her jaws busily dug a hole. She laid the meat in the hole, covered it, not with her paws but with her slender nose, brushing duff over it, then hurried back for more. The wolf did not put all her eggs in one basket. Each piece was cached in a different spot.

And Trigger? He ate!

Was this a sex difference or a personality difference between him and Lady? Long afterward we watched Lady work like a dog in hot sun for two hours, caching a kill piecemeal, while Master Trigger relaxed nearby in the shade of willow bushes. But also we were to see him work even harder than Lady, carrying very heavy pieces a long distance to cache them; and when he did, it was invariably under stimulus of competition from strangers liable to get his meat. Lady's feeling seemed to be more generalized: you cached meat; that was what you did.

The two wolves were very different. Lady was wild; she was totally independent. She was fearless and gay and she always led, never at a loss for where to go or what to do. Trigger had a combination of traits that baffled me: he was lordly yet shy, perhaps a natural combination at that. He was mixed; Lady was single. Always she seemed to be "going someplace," as if to meet destiny. Trifles along the way were a matter of indifference to her.

Not to Trigger. He was luxury-loving. As a matter of course on hot days he took the one cool spot in the pen, a denlike hollow. Lady indifferently slept where she could, in the sun. When Cris dug a shady hollow for her too, she was distrustful of it for two days. Wildness.

Yet Trigger depended on Lady emotionally. There was no gate to the pen. We laid back the top band of wire at one point and stepped over the lower. Trigger lost his head one evening. We had lifted Lady into the pen unobserved. In fact Cris had carried her part way home. Trigger thought she was gone. He ran back to look for her and when he did come to the pen and she bowed and smiled, inviting play, along the inside of the fence, he was so distraught he would not let us catch him to put him in.

But once inside, the poor wolfie for once cared nothing for comfort. He wanted only to be close to Lady. Even the next day he deserted his shady hollow to lie beside her in the hot sun, one big bony leg across her tuffy baby fur.

Cris told me long afterward, "I aways thought that some-day Trigger might be dangerous, but never fierce."

The wolves had a strong property sense. They did not contend for food: whoever got a piece of meat first owned it. But if both happened to grab it simultaneously, there was a tug of war. The wolves didn't fight, they hung on. Neither one was going to let go of that nice meat. They flopped up, growled-and-tugged, sank, as rhythmically as to drumbeat.

Cris prepared one day to stage and film this tug of war. He set up the camera, then presented one big piece of meat only.

But Lady got it. Trigger merely glanced at her, then sat looking expectantly up at Cris, now and then glancing hastily over his shoulder in case he had overlooked "it." Cris laughed and yielded, gave him a big piece of meat too.

When meat ran low, the wolves never knew they could break our hearts by begging. They never begged us for food. When they did cry it was because we walked off and left them behind.

They were as gay and frustrating as dog pups. I stood in the rain by the Yukon stove one evening, patiently drying their gunnysacks, then spread them in the sleeping box in the pen. In frisked the pups, dragged the sacks into the rain, spread them with their paws and lay down.

Now and then that dark side showed, wildness. Cris spotted a grizzly coming south through the pass one morning. At first it looked as if he would turn aside into the Nigu drainage. But by the time I was rinsing the dishes he was passing North Lake, coming steadily, not feeding but traveling. We prepared. Stove out, rattle cans, Cris to the dare rock. I hoped for once a bear would pass without noticing us.

He was walking directly below camp. He was a monstrous big fellow and a beauty. His legs, paws and head were darkness. He carried his beautiful pale-tan coat as if it were a loose-fitting cloak. He had the most pronounced roach I had ever seen. It wobbled black, then tan, at each jolt of his front legs. When black-shadowed, it looked like a primeval spine slanting up from his low-carried head to the grizzly jut over his shoulders.

He looked up. At once he started up, as a provident bear should. As he reached the dare line we both stood up and rattled our bear rattles. He galloped southward, his original direction, risking only one half-turn of the head.

"Look at the wolves," said Cris in a low voice. "He's crossing the wind now."

They could not see the grizzly but Lady stood on the highest rock in the pen, Trigger below her, absorbed in garnering impressions. Her head was reared, her eyes were somber and shaded. "She looks all wolf now," murmured Cris. In the gray light she was almost fearsome-looking.

Wildness is a quality gone from human environment. Tameness is the air one breathes in civilization. People suppose wildness is ferocity. It is something far more serious than that. It is independence—a life commitment to shouldering up one's own self. For his safety and survival a wolf depends on himself only. It saddened us when we discovered that. The discovery occurred when the wolves saw their first caribou.

It was an event we had awaited with curiosity. The normal prey of arctic wolves is caribou; how would Trigger and Lady react?

On the walk one day we met a young caribou bull. The wolves were romping and did not notice him. He went through the caribou ritual, first a run, then a pause to look back. When he did that he froze, lost in contemplation of the extraordinary little group proceeding toward him over the tundra—two humans, the long-nosed black camera and two playing wolves.

The wolves saw him. They fled! Cris managed to stop Trigger but no entreaties prevailed on Lady. She kept going, up the mountainside until we thought she was gone for good. At last she considered it safe to turn and sit looking at the bull, now saving his own life.

You can tell a wolf you are friendly. But you can never tell a wolf a situation is safe; he will judge that for himself.

In part, Lady's action had been the terrible self-dependence of young wildings, almost exactly like that of a bighorn lamb, leaving mother and group to flee to a high rock for refuge. But there was something else. Cris sensed it.

"They didn't think we could help them." That was easy to see. "And they weren't going to help us either! If we were in trouble, that was just too bad for us."

It was a glimpse into unknown depths, into "wolfness" as well as wildness. And it was enormously puzzling because of something in ourselves, namely a prefabricated pattern for wolves. It was going to take Trigger and Lady a long time to break up and dissipate that pattern.

Everybody has it. Everybody "knows all about" wolves. There is no pattern for aardvarks but there is one for wolves, and people who have never seen a wolf will defend their myth-wolf pattern with betraying fury.

A wizard from Mars who knew the myth-wolf pattern would not know much about wolves but he would know a lot about humans. He would know we are a naked, nervous, angry species. We gluttonize on self-righteous fury.

Real wolves just are not a feisty, fighting animal. Dogs are and we can understand them. But how can our cherished, seething, hating species fathom a wolf?

I was more possessive with the pups than Cris was. Naturally he got along with them, at least at first, better than I did. Every morning as I prepared breakfast I glanced enviously at him sitting on a low rock in the pen, waiting for the wolves to play with him. We had soon learned we could not choose when to play; they chose!

Trigger was already that rare beast, more often claimed than found, a one-man animal, namely Cris's. He came to Cris and gave himself up to being gently wooled. Lady was nobody's wolf. She was elusive.

I noticed her standing behind Cris one morning, looking up thoughtfully at his Stetson; perhaps it was not detachable.

Then she burrowed her slender nose into his hip pocket and made a discovery. His red bandanna was detachable. She dragged it forth and ran flaunting it as a trophy for Trigger to chase.

From now on, that was Lady's game. Cris's bandannas were soon in rags.

Lady would try to get Trigger away from Cris, spreading her paws and smiling before him, if that failed nipping his hind legs. Then one morning as Trigger still leaned sunnily against Cris's knee, I saw Lady go off to the side of the pen and lie gnawing an old bone as if perfectly indifferent. But with a shock of surprise I noticed that her green eyes, empty of happiness, rolled often toward the pair by the rock. Lady was jealous! And we still thought Trigger was not!

As the personalities of the two wolves, so different, unfolded, an unanswerable question teased me. What would their dead siblings have been like? I could not construct in imagination any wolf personalities beyond the two I knew.

And another question. Could any of the siblings have been more wonderful than Lady? Sometimes I thought she must be a kind of wolf genius.

10   Wolves Hunting Caribou

An abrupt change in weather brought Cris two photographic opportunities, the second that of his dreams. On July 24 it turned hot for the first time since June.

At breakfast under the tarp shade that morning, Cris, glancing up at the skyline, remarked, "I don't remember any rocks like that up there." He left his breakfast, seized camera and pack and climbed swiftly away. The rocks had moved. They were the antlers of caribou bulls, moving like a river along the skyline, antler palms like plumes above them, attached by threads.

When Cris returned he brought footage and also the answer, or part of it, to an old question asked on the Wolf Walk in June: when do caribou walk the high ridges? When wind blows heat and flies away.

Warble flies now tormented the caribou. The main herds stayed high but stragglers were going through the pass. Often we noticed some caribou down there suddenly dash and reverse like crazy, trying, no doubt, to throw off a warble fly.

The tundra turned crisp almost in a day. Its color changed at last from tan to the gray-green of summer, as green as it would ever become. Our altitude of thirty-five hundred feet here was about like twelve thousand feet in the Colorado Rockies.

There was no shelter from the heat. I moved the can of butter around the outside of the tent as the sun circled us twenty-four hours a day. But one merciful respite there was.

Every day about noon great bluish thunderheads came over. The pass cooled and dimmed instantly, with a palpable, speaking dimness, like an act, or a word spoken. Personal-impersonal.

I was dressing in the tent on the morning of July 30 when Cris called me. "Wolves! I see two wolves, Lois!" I ran out barefoot.

Two long cream-colored animals tossed along over the tundra below, heading north between Landing and Middle lakes. All the animals we were to see on this remarkable day were going north, except for a cow and calf that had already passed, going south, and the wolves, which wove back and forth between the lakes.

There was to be no breakfast for us this morning. No sooner had I finished dressing than Cris called again. "They're after a caribou!" For the next four hours we were to observe wolves hunting caribou, a spectacle of which there have been few witnesses and almost no eye-witness accounts.

The dark-gray caribou was running north toward Middle Lake, the wolves after it. Suddenly all three seemed to increase their speed. Then the caribou drew away from the wolves. The lead wolf stopped, glanced sociably back at the other wolf and—sat down! The caribou was far off now, heading away toward the low arctic divide at the north end of the pass.

We hoped the wolves would now come to our side of the pass. But they trotted to the far side where, in a green patch, the bigger wolf, a male we supposed, jumped at something, dug a bit, then pounced again. Hunting mice probably.

All at once the smaller, more alert wolf, a female perhaps, started back toward Landing Lake. "Another caribou!" said Cris. On this chase we were to see a thrilling thing, wolves using tactics.

The female was apparently heading straight toward the oblivious caribou approaching. But no. She passed above him unseen. Not until behind him did she reveal herself, turn and chase him.

The bull ran—straight toward the big cream-colored wolf, waiting on a low ridge near the foot of Middle Lake. The bull sped along the side of the ridge. He saw the waiting wolf and sprang forward as if lashed.

"He's going to leap off into the lake!" said Cris.

At the same instant the bull swerved and dashed down the side of the ridge toward a green marsh by the lake, and the big wolf swept into the chase at a right angle to its previous course.

"The wolf will get him now," said Cris.

But the bull came swiftly through the marsh. The wolf struck it, sank from our view, lifted himself, plunging along, then dismissed the caribou and gave himself up to a good wallow, from which he emerged practically indistinguishable from the grayish tundra and dark rocks. Luckily for the camera, the other wolf was still clean and bright.

The wolves now headed at a desultory trot back toward Landing Lake. All at once the industrious little female broke into a run again. We did not spot her game at first.

Landing Lake was perfectly still. The reflection of the purplish and green mountainsides slanted down into its misty stillness like a mirage. At a glance, a stranger would have said no lake was there. Suddenly I spotted her game, a big caribou bull.

For the moment he had eluded the wolves. He was already in the center of the lake, a spot of darkness trailing a long silvery V. He was swimming toward our side.

The two handsome wolves trotted down the far side of the lake, starting calmly around it to meet the bull when he landed. At the south end of this lake, too, there was a green marsh. It gave them some trouble. They jumped along through it, the water slashing silver into the air. When they emerged, both wolves were clean. They seemed in no hurry. They started in a leisurely way up along our edge of the lake toward where the caribou was nearing land.

He had gained footing underwater and stood now, his white chest showing under his black muzzle, looking at the bank before him, then looking north as if intending to come out and go that way.

With anxiety I watched the two wolves coming closer, following the margin of the lake, its ins and outs. The caribou was wasting precious time. Finally he turned his antlers toward his right. Instantly he plunged back and swam, heading across the lake—not straight across but angling away from the wolves and toward the northwest corner.

The wolves turned and started back around the lake. Now it was a race, performed with deliberation. The caribou was striding, afloat in the water. He was nearly broadside to us, angling a little away. The black mass of his head and the jut of the guard palms over his nose were doubled by reflection, as were his antler palms tethered overhead. His back was a level brown streak. He did not go unerringly. He swerved a little now and then, but he was striding fast underwater, pulling the long V of his wake across the stillness again.

The wolves were coming steadily but not hurrying. It looked like an even break: they and the bull would make it to his landing point simultaneously. They rounded the marsh and started north along the far side of the lake.

All at once the lead wolf broke into a gallop. A new factor had entered the situation. The caribou cow and calf which had gone southward early in the morning were returning along the far side of the lake. They were ahead of the wolves and did not see them yet.

The wolves ran tandem along the lakeside, their reflections running under them. The bull was nearly to the bank. At the same moment he and the other two caribou saw each other. Each read the other as danger! Deer run from deer if surprised, a hair-trigger, life-saving response made before placing the animal they see. The bull turned without touching footing and swam back for the third time toward the middle of the lake. The cow, without seeing the real danger, the wolves, sped faster toward the north.

But the fawn did what looked like a foolish and dangerous thing. It turned at a right angle and ran up the mountainside, disappearing among the mottled rocks.

This act of the fawn put a pressure on the mother; her concern for the fawn handicapped her. She halted and glanced back. For the first time she saw the wolves. They were close and in plain view now. She turned and sped on. But she did not run with the single-minded purposiveness of the first two caribou the wolves had coursed. She slowed down, risked giving up her advantage, in order to stand looking back toward her fawn. She even circled. But at last she hesitated no more. She turned, fleeing away in a straight course over the great tundra toward the arctic divide.

Now I was at a loss. I could not locate the dark little fawn. I could not ask Cris, for he had moved the camera to a better vantage point. I could not even find the wolves for a while. Then one raised itself from a green hollow. Had they caught the fawn while I watched the mother? When she decisively left her contact with her fawn and set out running without pause, had she seen the fawn's death?

The bull irritated me. He was in the middle of the lake and I wished he would come on, get to our shore, rest himself. The wolves had dismissed him from their activities. But the bull apparently felt himself still sore beset, fleeing from wolves on one side of the lake, running into two animals read as danger on the other side.

What he was doing now was to zigzag in about the same spot in the clear, still, dark water. Now his head pointed toward us—"He's coming to land," I would think with relief. Then he swerved and his side was toward us. He never turned clear around. He faced north and kept making a half circle to northwest, then northeast.

But at last he swung toward our shore and began drawing the long V riffle after him, not so swiftly as at first. When finally he got his feet on a standing place underwater, he stood a long time, turning his dark antlered head this way and that. At last he stepped up onto the bank, his coat dark with wet. After a while he ventured a bite now and then, but hardly moved from his position, lifting his head, turning it, looking this way and that.

Meanwhile Cris had gone to the tent to reload. He had recorded that sweeping tactical run of the wolves, and also the wolves running, reflected in the lake. Now he wanted to get closer to them. We went down into the pass, intent on the picture, without a thought of the gun. On a rise with a swale between us and the wolves, Cris set up the camera. Here he could shoot over the heat waves; the tundra was vibrating. Neither of us knew whether the wolves had got the calf, but it looked as if they had eaten and were resting.

"They may lie here until four o'clock and the heat breaks," I murmured.

"I can stay here until four o'clock," rejoined Cris. The heat and our thirst were intense. Luckily Cris had thought to pick up an orange apiece in the tent when he reloaded. We sat by the tripod eating them and watching the wolves. The male lay stretched out, never raising his head. The female lifted her head to watch us but laid it down from time to time. At last, tiring of this half-and-half business, she rose, turned, and lay so she could watch us without raising her head.

Suddenly she rose and started back south. Cris whispered, "She smells something." I said, "She's nervous and leaving us." Cris was right. Another caribou was approaching from the south.

As before, she did not meet it head on. She by-passed it. Not until she got beyond it did she turn. Then she and the caribou came flying back toward the male wolf. Again she was using strategy, driving the caribou toward him. Meanwhile he had sat up, looked at us, then walked sluggishly after her, glancing over at us now and then.

Now an incredible thing happened. The caribou stopped and turned for the inevitable caribou look back. This was the wolf's chance. But no! The wolf stopped too. She sat down! The caribou stood and gazed at the wolf, the wolf sat and gazed at the caribou.

After a minute or two the caribou turned and started on, using the beautiful flying upward launch which caribou employ when no camera is running. The wolf rose and sped after her. "Do wolves hunt by Marquis of Queensberry rules?" thought I!

The caribou was running straight toward death. The big cream-colored wolf awaited her. "We'll see something now," Cris muttered.

We did. But not what we expected. At this moment what should burst into the situation but the calf! It had lain hidden all this time. As the cow passed, it jumped up and sped after her. Was she its mother, who had circled around the lake to pick it up? We soon had the answer.

By this time the cow, without seeing the male wolf, was passing near him. As before, he cut in at a right angle. But by now we knew the relative speeds of wolf and caribou; we knew she was safe. The female wolf had stopped; the chase was the male's. He ran after the cow but gave up easily. She ran on toward the north.

We were still sure the wolves would have their breakfast, the fawn was doomed. It was running well behind the cow. The foolish thing acted hesitant. It paused often, looking back at the wolves, both running after it now. They gained as it gawked. It sped on. But would it never stop its doubtful pauses to look back? At last it did actually overtake the cow. I felt relief. Surely now it was safe; she would lead it out of the country. But no! Wrong cow! Again the fawn turned and ran up the mountainside. The cow fled on away obliviously, a stranger.

It was our turn now. The wolves, having given up the caribou, trotted hesitantly toward us, the last things left to investigate. A head came up over the side of our mound, the body appeared. The female wolf paused to look at us, then came toward us.

It was a thrilling feeling, undeniably. I supposed they were timid, like Trigger and Lady, and would run like wildfire if we moved. Still it was thrilling—a smiling, delicious thrill—to have the wild wolf coming toward us, watching us. She turned and partly circled us.

The male came onto the rise and circled farther away. Then the "Grimm's fairytale effect." He yawned! A big calm luxurious indifferent yawn. The wolves trotted away toward the arctic divide.

"Decided we're not caribou," said Cris. "Not much afraid of us, but curious."

Breakfast at last, for us and the pups. "I thought for a while there I'd have fresh meat for them," said Cris, smiling. He was purring over the fabulous morning's work.

"Everybody robs the hard-working wolf!"

The talk-it-over was bubbling up. We had witnessed a spectacle we could hardly have hoped to view. "This makes me doubt the old-timers' stories," said Cris. "About wolves killing and killing for fun. Those wolves worked hard all morning and didn't get a thing. Unless maybe some mice over there."

"They should have got the fawn," said I. "If the male wolf had done his part."

"She was doing all the running, giving him all the chances," Cris admitted. "He didn't cash in on them."

A lot of surprises had come our way this morning. For one thing, how quickly the wolves had judged when a chase was useless. And then that built-in speed differential between wolf and caribou. A buck deer down in the States was clocked, according to the naturalist E. A. Kitchin, at forty-two miles an hour. Whatever these arctic deer, the caribou, could do, it was obvious that wolves could not quite rival it. Later, Eskimos from Anaktuvuk Pass told us that "a very strong wolf" could sometimes run "almost" as fast as a caribou. They considered even that very exceptional.

The crowning surprise had been the speed of that calf. He would be only about six weeks to two months old. Yet he had given the wolves every advantage and then outrun them with ease, simply floated away from them when he got good and ready.

As for that Grimm's fairytale affair, the wolf that seated herself and waited while her prey took time out! Should we ever understand that?

Meanwhile the answer to our old troubling question, where to winter, had ripened in Cris's mind. But Andy had ceased to come. I even pondered walking alone to Anaktuvuk Pass, where Andy touched down on a weekly mail flight. If we both went, taking the wolves, we risked losing them. The tundra made me feel imprisoned. A walk of a hundred miles was not serious, but on tundra it would be like two hundred. Besides, my pack would be heavy—warm sleeping bag for arctic nights, all my food, and fuel.

One evening as the shadow rose from the pass below and we were about to sit down to our hot supper, there came a far-off roar. The plane! We seized packboards and ran for the lake.

The plane floated on the dark clear water by the bank. Andy, chilly in south-of-the-Range clothes, stepped down onto a pontoon. He had waited in the cabin.

"Did you think I had forgotten you? Just thought I'd check up and see how you were getting along."

He flew Cris north to Tulialek Lake, where I had camped alone in April. When they returned the decision was final. They had found freshly rutted caribou trails. Incidentally my Blazo was still there; also they had seen several grizzlies. We would winter at Tulialek Lake. Andy was to return as soon as he could spare time, and fly us over. It would take several trips to move our camp.

Now we were beset by a puzzle in logistics. If we moved camp down to the lake, where we could depart whenever Andy came, we should have to make the wolves miserable by keeping them on a yard wire. If we stayed up by the pen, we could not possibly move everything to the lake after Andy came; it would require several round trips, and each took an hour.

Cris's solution was to pitch the mountain tent by the lake. We began moving all but a skeleton camp down to it. At that, it would need two round trips after Andy came. But meanwhile he could be ferrying our previous loads to Tulialek.

The wolves went wild with delight the first time we took them along to the lake. Lady sailed ahead into the lake until almost buoyant. Trigger hung timidly on the bank, at last gathered all his courage and made a great arching leap into the water. He never feared water again, even when he should have feared it. It was Lady who wisely feared the creek the morning after it rose white and roaring overnight.

The wolves ran off and disappeared in the tall grass. "They'll come back," said Cris easily.

They came on a run, Lady ahead, bearing the choicest trophy she had ever found, a piece of caribou hide in short brown summer fur. Trigger got it away from her and lay growling and wooling it. She pretended he was illimitably dangerous. Her eyes brilliant with excitement, she made rapier-quick darts at it. Then, when she got good and ready, she took it quite easily from surprised Trigger and bore it fully a yard before ditching it. She trotted to Cris positively grinning, as if she had played a great big wolf joke on Trigger and come to Cris to share it. It was the first time Lady had given us her heart in complete trust. Two days later we betrayed the wolves and she never fully trusted us again. Trigger got over it but not Lady.

It was on the day Andy flew in. On our last trip down from camp I came ahead. Cris was proudly bringing his wolves running free, joyous at coming to the lake.

I had Andy crouch in the mountain tent in order not to scare them away.

As Lady neared she halted and looked darkly at the tent. Then she fled. We had to trick her to catch her. Both wolves had diarrhea from terror. We had crammed Lady into the box both had come to us in. Her tail and fur billowed from it. Trigger would have to ride in front with Cris and the terrifying stranger. I learned later that he hid his face in Cris's arms.

There now occurred a faintly grim trifle, throwing light on arctic bush flying. I was to wait here alone for Andy's return from Tulialek; he would fly me out to stock up on supplies.

Cris was about to strike the empty mountain tent when Andy said quietly, "Better leave that for Lois."

Cris looked at him. "Oh! Sure."

This gave me a thought. I stepped onto the pontoon and pulled from the dunnage in the plane a brick of Tillamook cheese.

Nothing happened in my sunny hour alone by the lake. No grizzly came. Andy returned. The even, confident flow of life resumed.

Four days later, with the first load of two-by-twos for the crackerbox, Andy set me down by Cris's camp at Tulialek Lake.

Had the wolves made up with Cris? On arrival, he said, they would have nothing to do with him. Betrayed and terrified, they would not eat nor let him touch them. They strained away from him at the ends of their chains like two little draft horses.

"They're no good to themselves or anybody else this way," he thought. The next morning he turned them loose! It was his second calculated risk.

All day he followed the wolves as they slunk over the strange terrain, lying down when they lay down, going on when they went on. Toward evening he turned toward camp, not knowing whether they would follow or not. They followed.

After that he chained them only at night. By day they went with him to where he was starting work on the crackerbox site. They lay in the brush, he never knew where, but when he whistled and started for home, they crawled out from wherever they had been sleeping, and followed. He was proud of his new relationship with them.

"Don't turn them loose today," I begged, the morning after my arrival. I was a stranger to them in new shirt, shoes and dry-cleaned pants. Worse yet, three plane loads of lumber were due today. The wolves would never dare come to camp.

But Cris turned them loose and went off proudly to his work. At noon he returned alone. "I asked Lady," he said, his eyes shy and shining, "and she said she would come back."

The first plane load came about two o'clock. We thought the wolves took off then. Cris looked bleak and drained. He searched for miles. I stayed at camp in case they came home.

And Trigger came! He was walking along the bank above the tent. He was alone. He looked long-bodied; he carried his head not jaunty and high but level with his back. Tired, I thought. I flew for a pan of milk and held it out, coaxing beguilingly, "Here, Trigger."

The wolf stared at me. He was not Trigger.

This bemused wolf also met Cris. He too thought the wolf was Trigger. He ran toward it, the wolf ran toward him. Both realized their errors at the same moment: the wolf was not Trigger, Cris was not a caribou!

After supper Cris set out to search again, this time on the far side of the river. Young wolves are not self-supporting; they would starve if not found. Or be killed. Cris had seen a grizzly going upriver in the willows that afternoon.

He was wading the river when there was a big splashing behind. He whirled. Two strange wolves were lunging toward him. For a second it unnerved him. Then he recognized them! Trigger and Lady had found him and were beside themselves with joy.

All three splashed ashore and Cris lay down flat on the sand and let the wet wolves jump all over him and lick his face.

Now we put all our strength to building the crackerbox. It was no mean feat. Cris had only limited tools and no help but that of a woman. He was building in the wilderness and far from the landing lake. Every stick and nail had to be back-packed across Easter Creek (which was really a river), over a marsh and up a steep mesa a mile away. As in the pass, Cris had chosen a lookout site.

This mesa was an unusual formation here. It stood right at the foot of the mountains on the north side of the valley, near the confluence of Easter Creek and the Killik, flowing north to the Colville River. From the mesa we could look for miles up the mountain-lined valley of each river. Up the Killik, to the south, we thought we saw the pass where we had summered.

At first I backpacked alone. Cris dug a niche in the brink of the mesa for the crackerbox. More and more plane loads of lumber were set ashore by the tent. Could I ever move them to the crackerbox? But when Cris set his strength to the backpacking the pile sank fast.

We forded Easter Creek in wool socks and boots. The bottom was stony and the current bitterly cold. I changed to dry footgear only at evening.

The wind was fierce. Climbing the mesa with a load like a sail on my shoulder, I was often blown aside and backward. Anxiously I thought, "What will it be in winter?" This wind did not seem stronger than winds in the States; it seemed different in kind to start with. There is a quality of fearsomeness in arctic wind, no matter how slight its velocity. I resisted this wind too hard, because I was resisting with my spirit the unknown winds of winter ahead of me.

Bitterly I warned Cris, "It could blow the crackerbox off the mesa."

"I'll take care of that!" he said sharply.

The weather changed. Gray rolling clouds suffused the country. I felt a bit wistful, coming into camp at evening, my feet cold and soaked, to no warmth, no snugness, only cold and the chore of getting supper after the day's backpacking. (We had no time or energy to backpack willows for a warming fire in the Yukon stove; we cooked on the gasoline stove.) For four months we had lived in a tent. I wanted a house. "One's coming," I reminded myself.

In just two days after this cold weather, the tundra colored. The ankle-high birches, the wee "forests" of the Arctic, turned crimson. The willows turned pure gold. There were red carpets of arctos. Up on the mountains, the dark rock outcroppings, Concord-grape-colored, were wreathed with birch brush blued to plum color by distance. Distant mountains were dark blue. Clouds and mists crept over the land.

Overnight the river rose, racing gray in new channels. But Cris as usual forded with a load roped on his packboard, this time the first sheets of plywood. At noon he failed to return. All day I did not see his small figure working around the crackerbox. At evening I started downriver to hunt for a man lying face down under a stack of plywood. And I saw him coming! He said the high water had kept him from coming home for lunch.

After supper I went up the bank onto the tundra and just stood. So still. So full of color, movement, things. Drifting clouds, evening sunlight on the flank of a mountain headed in purple shadow, bright brush on the tundra, ducks floating on the dark-bright lake. "Nature never did betray the heart that loved her." What thundering poppycock!

The next morning not even Cris could ford. But the morning after that the water was down a bit, and he drove his powerful thighs through the gray surge. On the far side he set off his load and returned to string ropes for me to hold to in crossing.

All of a sudden, on August 27, the crackerbox was done. It took me by surprise. I had not realized how fast plywood goes up when you're ready for it. We brought our old "camp load"—the sleeping bags, stoves and cooking utensils—and put them in our house! One side where the windows were to be was still wide open, the Flex-o-glass had not come yet, but we had a fire in the Yukon stove. And that night I slept by an upright wall that did not slap or punch me.

In the morning I lay on the high bunk in the sleeping robes watching while Cris "raised" a fire. "Luxury puss!" he said proudly. I smiled co-operatively—he was fond of the myth of the sheltered woman—but I was speechless; a thought had just struck me: if Cris got hurt, could I cut and backpack willows to keep us going up here? I am not handy with ax or saw and the biggest willows were half a mile away, upriver.

This very day Andy flew in with the Flex-o-glass, Cris packed it over from the lake and we stapled it up. We really had luxury now.

I came to love the little crackerbox. It was planned strictly to be practical but it had much unplanned beauty. It was an eight-by-ten box, six feet high. The roof, like the walls, was of plywood, but was covered with a tarp against leaks. The door was in the center of the north wall.

On your right as you entered was the high bunk—high so things could be stored underneath. It ran from the north wall to the south. So did the high counter on your left. Before you on the floor sat the space-eating Yukon stove. The only movable furniture was a stand made of two Blazo boxes, one on top of the other, between the stove and the head of the bunk. You found yourself standing in the only free floor space, about a square yard. In the mornings I stayed in bed while Cris dressed. Only one could dress at a time.

The extraordinary charm of the crackerbox lay in the belt of windows clear around the east side and turning the corners to door and bunk. Also in the wall material, rough-textured, oyster-white Celotex. The windows flooded the tiny room not only with sunlight but with warmth. Often we had to open the door to cool the room even at eighteen below zero. A couple of willow sticks heated it.

The walls were like a thermos bottle. There were three

layers—the plywood outdoors, the Celotex for warmth indoors, and aluminum foil between the two.

Cris added a detail later that my eyes never tired of tracing. The Flex-o-glass "exploded" in shattering noise during gales, though we had tightened it with all our might when stretching and stapling it up. Cris tightened it now with undulating double lines of peeled white willow withes around the windows.

His next "improvement" alarmed me. Over my dead body, he breached our north wall of defense against winter storms. He cut a hole high in the corner at the foot of the bunk and inserted a joint and elbow of stovepipe, pointing downward outdoors. It was for ventilation, and after my alarm subsided I had to admit it worked very well. (The windows of course did not open, and in storms it would be impractical to leave the door ajar.)

He added one more provision for storms, an entryway. It, too, had a pleasing feature, though put in like everything else, strictly for use. It was a Dutch door, opening inward. We had no idea how deep the snow would get, but if it was deep we could always dig out at least the top half of the door and slide down inside on returning from trips.

He dug a path from the drop-off around the front of the crackerbox under the windows. He made it wide enough for an important feature, the "watch box," where every morning he sat with field glasses to examine the vast land for subjects.

As to my chief worry, the wind, I had to admit he had taken care of it. The crackerbox could not possibly blow off the mesa. Winds would only pin it tighter into its niche. The roof was almost flush with the mesa top. Also, Cris built a rock wall around two sides, stuffing brush into the space between it and the cabin for warmth. The crackerbox shuddered in gales but it could not budge from its foundation.

Cris pours his strength without check or withholding

into a project. When it is done, he enjoys it as frankly as a child. "I like our comfort here," he said. "So long we've been uncomfortable. In fact sometimes on the verge of being miserable."

On September 3 Andy made his last flight to us before freezeup, and paid me a courtesy I deeply appreciated, for I was lonely. I did not go over to the lake for this last precious human contact. Cris had waders now. But for bare legs the river had become almost frighteningly cold; it turned one's legs dark red.

I stood watching at the door of the crackerbox as Andy rose away from the lake. He flew to the mesa, passed me low and waved his wings.

12   *Arctic Fall*

"On the deck," in the company only of arctic wolves, we faced the most dramatic event of our lives so far, the approach of arctic winter. The land sometimes wore a look we called the "mystic-arctic look." The first storm of fall had that look, and the inner and haunting menace that gave it the mystic quality.

You could hardly call it a storm; it was simply an inimical condition. There was grayness in the air and the whuff of wind forever around the crackerbox. The most strange, unnerving fact was that the blurred sun was present but un-friending. It seemed—and not merely as a figure of speech—to have gone under a spell. It looked down upon a dead, nonmortal land, vacant and enormous, from which all small forms of life had gone in or away.

The mystic-arctic look took many forms. It appeared one still, gray afternoon when we camera-hunted a high ridge, filming at f 2 in the dark light. Twice the hidden sun spotlighted a cradle of land far off in the tundra below, gild-ing it. We stood looking down at the many waters—ponds, lakes, rivers, all gray—at the dim arctic mountains and that cradle of light. Merely as a statement of fact, Cris said, "Out of this world, isn't it!"

A haunting thing happened as we neared home this day. From a draw came a caribou bull, trotting purposefully. He was the first caribou we had seen since moving into the crackerbox, though while we backpacked the lumber caribou bands had passed going north, fording with tantalizing pic-turesqueness; we had no time then for cameras.

The bull's face was proud and sullen. A last tag of velvet hung from the tip of one guard horn. His antlers were dry but still blood-tinged and grooved as for veins. He was stately in his fall coat. A bull's fall coat is magnificent—sleek brown back, deep underhang of white fur on the chest. To us he was only himself. He connected with nothing. But some-where the big tide of migration was turning; this bull was a fleck of foam tossed ahead.

The oncoming of fall was slow. The climate north of the Range is arid, light snows came and went. But up on the mountains the grizzled whiteness moved evenly and inexor-ably toward our level.

The tundra froze leathery, thawed, then froze hard, and our feet hit like iron one afternoon as we went, with five-gallon cans tied to our packboards, to bring water from the river.

The spring near the mesa foot had frozen. The sun in the southwest, nearing the mountaintops, was a marginless radiance. The brown tundra was covered with amber light, through which snow sped horizontally on a north wind from down the Killik. When there was a gust the myriad traveling flakes, widely separated, accelerated to streaks.

It stopped us—the amber light over the brown earth, filled with those speeding specks of white, the winding ice-rimmed river, the white mountains standing off on every side. "Did you ever see anything like it?" Cris said softly.

A wind drift formed behind each shrub but over all the tundra still looked brown. But this snow would not melt until spring.

We had a new feeling. It was the "arctic euphoria," which comes when the mighty landslide toward winter is irrevocable. We interpreted it in old ways. Cris said, unemphasized, with a shy quick glance at me, "I kind of like the challenge of the—unusual."

I cast my own exultation in terms I knew better than arctic ones—in forest terms. People are free and of equality in a wild sunlit wood, I thought. There is no criticism or grading by any usual standard. Not by clothes, money, manners, knowledge, heredity, power.

No man is slave, no man is master, facing the sunlight on wild wood and wild fur and eyes. Liberty seeps like health into your heart. The weight on your heart of being an object, being manipulated and having to strive cunningly—all that is lifted away. A wild shy honest delight steals into you. You breathe in a part of your being that had unconsciously been constricted.

All my life I had taken for granted I was free. Actually, these past months, I had for the first time been exposed to genuine freedom and it was just now beginning to take. There are feelings not specified. The accepted, labeled range of feelings is so small. Far, far around, the mountains and tundra were inviolate now and they said something to the heart.

Our wolves were growing up. They would reach about adult size by Christmas. Cris was as proud of their size and beauty as if he had achieved both by his own efforts.

"Isn't Trigger getting a fine big head!" he purred. "He looks like an executive. Their fur is so deep they don't touch the ground when they lie on it—like lying on a pincushion."

Their fur was not harsh. It was luxurious to bury your hands in, wealthy-deep with thick new undercoats of wool. Blond Trigger had darkened surprisingly with new black guard hairs.

Hardly anyone realizes what wolves look like. I know of only two artists, Olaus Murie and Bill Berry, who draw real wolves; the rest draw myth wolves, stocky and brutal-muzzled.

Real wolves are slender, invincibly aristocratic-looking. They have disarmingly sweet faces!

They are slender all over and as sinuous and graceful as cats. Bodies are long, and carried high on long legs. Paws and legs are unlike those of dogs. Legs are twined "nervously" with veins and sinews. (By nervous I mean innervated, alive and sensitive all over.) Paws are nervous too—not mere clumps like most dog paws, but long-fingered and spreading. Trigger's forepaw made a track as long and almost as spreading as that of my own long hand.

Beside a wolf, the most graceful dog looks wooden. Wolves seem to have a fineness and delicacy of articulation lost to dogs through centuries of breeding. In motion they ripple, they flow. Even in walking, the spine has a slight sidewise ripple.

And how wolves leap! Lifting leaps—straight up, all bushy

and flowing, to the tip of the tail. Straight down. That is their way of participating in gaiety. They leap upward as if pulled at the shoulders by a skyhook. Or they leap perpendicular, standing straight up in air; that is the "observation leap." They leap sidewise. They leap backward. They twirl into a doughnut in midair and wind up the incredible act with a flourish—chest to ground, paws spread, and an inimitable, flashing wolf-toss of the head. Heads too are slender, long.

A wolf's most undoglike feature is his tail. He runs with his tail, thinks with it, marks mood with it, even controls with it. "They run with their tails as much as with their spines," observed Cris. The tail floats. The one position it never assumes is up and curled like a sled dog's tail.

We watched Lady think with her tail one day. She stood looking at a caribou skull, not really scared but skittish. She swirled and twirled her tail as a dubious squirrel will do.

The higher the wolf's spirits, the higher his tail. You glance at his tail to learn his mood. A typical tail position for a cheerful wolf is out an inch, then down. You can talk a gloomy wolf's tail into that position. Wolves are wonderfully responsive to a truly cheerful voice.

Since wolves have complete "differential relaxation," they don't wag their tails quite as dogs do. They wag them on about the same occasions but take the trouble to start only the base of the tail. The rest of the tail follows through, drifting languidly in a Delsarte gesture, the stump starting east while the tip drifts west. When the tail is not in use the wolf withdraws every ounce of residual tension; the tail hangs like a great tassel, subject only to wind and gravity.

On the other hand, wolves use their tails strongly and controllingly, like fifth arms. A wolf will flap his tail strongly over the back of another wolf running alongside. Legs are used the same way; that is, out at right angles. A wolf will lay not only a front leg but even a hind leg over the back of another wolf strongly and easily, as you would lay an arm. Also he can push backward hard with a forepaw. Strolling through a door he has just opened, he shoves it farther open behind him as you would do with your hand.

Undoglike too is his deep, narrow chest—deep from the side, narrow from the front, like the chest of a bull elk. A big male wolf may have less distance between the tops of his forelegs than a bulldog pup has. Not with any of the eight wolves we eventually knew could I insert my fingers flat together into that chest arch. I had to overlap them slightly.

Cris and I had a little ceremony every morning. It was going out to reap the wolves' morning welcome. We prized it so much we actually took turns. Wolves don't make a fuss over you any old time as dogs do.

I enjoyed their greeting of Cris almost as much as of me. I liked to hear his gruff pleasant voice as he undid the gate. "How's my little puppies?" The wolves danced and bowed along the inside of the fence. "Aren't they the nicest little wolves!"

He entered and the wolves all but knocked him down. Trigger stood up face to face, paws on Cris's chest, rough, heavy, beautiful, uttering a "half-howl" while Cris gently shook him by the furry jowls. Cris sat down on the ground. The wolves assaulted him from both sides and in a minute had him hunching his shoulders, giggling, gripping his cap down over his ears.

This was because Lady had invented a new game. She had stood up back of him one morning, forepaws on his shoulders, looking him over. (A wolf feels safer to approach from the rear for mischief.) She didn't want his fur collar; she didn't want his bandanna. Ears sharply forward she neatly untied with her teeth the strings holding up the ear flaps of his cap. From then on she untied them every time he sat down.

But still she was elusive; she would not let him hold her. She was quicksilver. She was a minx, a Cleopatra of changing moods. Trigger wanted to romp with Cris one morning. Obligingly Cris went for his gloves. But when he returned, Lady would not let Trigger touch him. She caught Trigger's tail, she bit his neck. He had to give his full attention to protecting himself.

"She's just made up her mind she won't let him play with me," said Cris.

He started from the pen, but this did not suit Lady either. She enticed him. She bowed, her eyes bright with mischief. But she still would not let him touch her. He turned back to Trigger.

At this Lady surrendered. She threw herself into Cris's arms, her pink tongue going in and out, trying to kiss his face, which he held back from her, laughing.

"You can't help f'm feeling flattered when a wolf plays with you," admitted Cris sheepishly.

He wanted to camera-hunt alone one morning but knew the wolves would want to go along. He waited in the little entry-way adjacent to the pen gate while I entered the pen to distract the wolves' attention. But they stood bright-eyed at the gate, relentlessly watching to spy that hidden figure.

"All right, all right," conceded Cris. "Let them go!"

Lady raced out radiant, rippling around the outside of the pen. Poor dignified Trigger stood bewildered. It wasn't walk time. Lady enticed him at the far end of the pen. She had taken a day's exercise already, racing around the willow bushes. Now she flowed back into the pen in one swift black invitation and smile. He followed her out.

And then the quality of happiness became visible, personified in Lady. She raced round and round the wood rick, leaping each time over the willow bushes at the end of it. Beyond the black wolf rose the smiling white morning mountains.

Big wolves are more exciting companions on the tundra than little wolves. The other wildings here were about the same as up in the pass during the summer: moose, grizzly, fox, caribou, wolves. But now Trigger and Lady could do something about them.

Lady gave Cris a scare the first time she saw as well as smelled a grizzly. She set out to chase it. If the grizzly took a notion to chase her, Cris knew she would head straight for him with the grizzly on her heels.

"Lady!" he yelled imperiously. The astounded grizzly reared to his hind legs. And back came Lady, but not purely from obedience.

She chased her first fox. She did her best but the fox toyed, not taking her seriously. When it saw she was gaining on it, the fox floated away. Foxes run faster than wolves. Another of those built-in governors on what wolves can do—like the speed differential between wolf and caribou.

Defeat made Lady morose. For a depressing companion commend me to a morose wolf.

Down on the sand bar one day she observed just the back of a moose moving along the high bank. She crouched and stalked as for sik-sik—parka squirrel. When she topped the bank and for the first time beheld the dimensions of a moose, she stood up, stopped trying to make herself small. She took a few faltering steps toward it. Then she turned and fled. She passed up Cris and me, hit the river at a bad deep place, plunged in regardless. On the far side, followed by Trigger, she disappeared into the willows.

Anxiously Cris headed homeward for his waders to cross and search for the wolves. Glancing back he saw them perched on the distant bank, their attention glued on the departing moose. "Not going to let that thing sneak up on them!" said Cris.

He blew his whistle and they came. But for hours afterward Lady felt glum. She snatched my whole hand in her mouth when I domineeringly continued to pet her after she warned me with a growl.

The wolves played one game so much we called it simply The Game. One wolf elected something—anything—as a trophy and ran with it, pursued by the other wolf.

Their other main game was pure histrionics. Down on the sand bars, where the matériel was easy, they played it. Never think wild animals don't enjoy ease. Lady would dig, look to see if Trigger was watching, then dig furiously, stopping to sniff the hole as if she had a mouse, until Trigger came over to see what she had. If he started a dig, each wolf tried to make the other come to his own dig. Usually Lady persisted till Trigger came to hers.

"She makes it look so-o-o attractive," said Cris.

In life-and-death affairs, as with the moose, the wolves asked no help from us. But they had one problem with which they felt our powers sufficed to deal. It was a social problem, and the last you would expect a wolf to have trouble with.

Lady came up to Cris on the walk one day, with an expression of distress and anxiety. She cried up to his face. It dawned on Cris what her trouble was: she had lost Trigger. He blew the whistle and Trigger came. The next time this happened Cris failed to catch on. This time it was Trigger who had lost Lady and come crying to Cris. After appealing vainly to Cris, the wolf hurried back along the narrow slough between willows, down which we had just come.

Then here came Lady, crying too. Cris caught on. He pointed up the slough. "Trigger went that way," he stated briskly.

Lady looked up at his hand, up the slough, then away she went. "She understood perfectly," affirmed Cris with pride.

One day the wolves lost us. We were on the lake, shoveling a landing strip for Andy. Bored, the wolves ran off up the far mountainside. When ready to start for home, Cris blew the whistle. The wolves ran down the mountainside all right, but picked up their own trail and followed it back up the mountain.

My stomach felt sick and hit. What did they mean to do? Leave us? They were so far away up there that only Lady showed up; Trigger's silvery fur blended with the snow so that he all but vanished.

"Maybe they don't see us," Cris said. He led back from the willow tundra onto the white lake and whistled again. The wolves raced down the mountain as before. This time they streamed on toward us, getting bigger, tongues flapping, ears flattened, perfectly delighted to locate us.

When I had not gone along on the walks for a couple of days it was worth it to see Lady's joy when I did go. Over and over she ran back, dazzling-eyed, to spiral to the snow in the full wolf greeting, until the serious business of the tundra absorbed her—rabbits, voles, parka squirrels, ptarmigan, fox.

"I like to see Lady the way she was today," said Cris. "Squatting down in front, ears pinned back, eyes shining. She's so tickled you're going."

She gave me a great welcoming run one day that warms my heart yet. I had joined the walk late and Cris and the wolves were up on the mountainside. The wolves froze, watching, until I gave our "recognition sign," the crouch and arm-flip.

Back went Lady's ears. She came tearing down the mountainside, sailed right over the willow bushes, and threw herself at my feet in a cloud of powder snow, in the full wolf greeting. Trigger followed as usual.

You can't help sharing a wolf's joy. And a wolf, it seems, shares your troubles. I had stayed at home to bake bread one day, when, far too early, I heard from the foot of the mesa the whistle that meant, "Wolves are home, pen them." I ran outdoors.

Cris was coming slowly, not by the roundabout trail, but straight up the mesa side.

"He fell," I thought. Trigger followed him. Lady, already on top, watching, acted nervous. Both wolves seemed upset. Cris had fallen on the imperceptible slant of the river ice, struck his forehead and, I guessed, had lain still quite a while.

We had lost our gamble for caribou, in coming to the Killik. There could be little doubt of that. Cris was cheerful as always but there was no élan about him.

The weather turned warm one night. In the morning we awoke to see the Flex-o-glass unfrosted and white mountains and blue sky showing through. Cris got up to start the fire. In a low, negligent, disparaging voice he mentioned, "Down on the gravel bar there's a band of—" I restrained myself from supplying "ptarmigan." "Of caribou," he finished calmly.

Calmly he dressed, refused to let me prepare hot milk, and plugged away, tripod over shoulder. I dressed and went outdoors. Cris was out of sight. On the marsh below the mesa grazed sixty caribou.

One big bull lay facing the sun. His antlers were the most arty, unnatural color imaginable—a pinky orange-red, due to the dried blood where the velvet had shed.

The caribou moved toward the river to ford. Was Cris getting it? This was photogenic! I balanced equally between two thoughts—that it would be a miracle if he had reached a vantage point in time, and that Cris was a miracle-doer sometimes.

He came home after a while. He had got it! "And them shaking themselves on the other side. The water flew up backlighted. And going in, the cows felt for each step as long as they could touch bottom. Long slender legs. Didn't move'm till they felt around and placed that front foot. A minute later and I couldn't have set up in time," he said. "Run like a son-of-a-gun when I saw they were going to cross."

We never said "set up the camera." To set up on a rough hillside meant loosening up to three knobs on the tripod so it could be set level, loosening horizontal and vertical control knobs on the camera so it could be swung to find and frame the animals, then tightening all the knobs, focusing and stopping down.

I felt pleased and amazed but Cris dismissed this triumph idly. He had another. "I got an old bull so close he filled the frame. Took nearly two hundred feet of him. His guard horns were red—like an arty artist's idea of Santy's reindeer. The velvet tattled. Hung in tattles."

"Tatters."

"Tatters. When he turned his head quick, the tatters swung like ear pendants."

The lightheartedness! The mirthful surprise! I sat on a box, my plate on my knees. Cris sat on the high bunk, eating pancakes. I grinned and glanced up at him. He permitted his pleasure to gleam back at me for a merry instant, undisguised. There was a boyish bright look in his blue eyes.

"Maybe he *is* God's little boy," I thought. Maybe in spite of Andy, the studio and me, he had been right to come to the Killik. I felt young, mutable, potential.

From now on, we saw caribou daily, though even a thousand looked no more than lice on the vast land. But how a land is furnished and comforted when its animals show up in it. Looking at land you know is dead gives you a different feeling from looking at land you know is alive.

Mostly the caribou came from the north, which seemed natural for fall. Sometimes they drifted west. But on September 17, with field glasses, Cris observed a counter-movement across the Killik. They were going north!

"I'd like to know what they're doing over there," he said. Were the mating duels starting? The next morning, carrying hip boots and camera, he set out to cross the Killik.

The day was mild and still, but seldom sunny. I took the

wolves for their walk, herding them anxiously because I alone was responsible for getting them home. They scuffled on the verge of a steep river bank and fell in. Of all things, they started to swim to the far side. They were bewildered! I called, but down in the roar of the current they did not hear me. I really yelled and this time they heard. They turned at once and swam to me.

After six o'clock I began watching for Cris. I watched across the Killik, but involuntarily every few minutes I swept a long look around. Up Easter Creek, south across the lake and mountains, up the Killik for twenty miles or more, then west to where Cris must appear. A vast and barren land, all tan, except as the mountains blued with distance, and savage white combs rose above the brown rumps of lower mountains. I could see for fifty miles and in all that land the most precious thing was one small object not over two feet wide and six long.

The color browned. I gave up the field glasses. I did the chores, then went to the west side of the mesa and sat silently on the dry moss, waiting. He was not lost. He could drown or get clawed by a grizzly or break a leg, but he could not get lost—not with the Killik and Easter Creek to guide by.

A lake of yellowish, rose-suffused mist filled the crotch of the mountains up the Killik. In southern lands that color would soon have been gone. But it mounted higher. An inverted cone of rose haze spread into the sky above the dark mountains. There was a crotch of gold under it. The ponds on the dark tundra below me were dark rose color.

The color left and it grew darker. I sat silent and swept the mountain-rimmed land automatically from side to side, but expected Cris at two points only. I was warm enough in his worn-out leather jacket. If he had to lie out tonight, I would take the first capsule from a bottle of Seconal sent by a friend last summer, and hunt tomorrow. A piece of plywood with four holes bored in one end for rope could make a sled. Could

I slope it up with canvas in front so I could drag it over hummocks and brush? It would not be very practical.

At the point where Easter Creek went behind the hill toward the Killik, there was an upright black splinter. I was motionless, sure yet waiting to be utterly sure. It moved. Still I sat, waiting to see how he would come. Then I plunged straight down the steep shale slide and went to meet him.

He smiled. In the half-dark I was sure of it. He let me take his pack. His wool shirt was black with sweat stripes where pack and straps had crossed it. We jaunted homeward, Cris in the lead, telling easily with frank pleasure what he had got. I made only two remarks. In a soft happy voice I reiterated, "Oh!" and "Well, I declare."

There was no fighting yet, he said, but bands of bulls were passing over there. He had got one wild strange shot of them filing along the edge of an abyss; immediately beyond rose the mountainside, and you felt the unseen depth.

And on the way home he had had an odd little adventure with a bull moose that cost a fox its hard-earned supper. This bull had fixed its gaze on Cris and kept coming straight toward him. Cris got a little worried. He blew his whistle. At this the bull turned away and for the first time Cris noticed the fox. The whistle had startled it too. It dropped a bloody ptarmigan from its jaws, scattering feathers, and ran away.

After supper as Cris lay on the bunk, his face smooth and ruddy as it always is when he is very tired and completely relaxed, I saw that he looked intent though his eyes were closed.

"What are you thinking about?" I said.

"Those big white bulls," he said promptly. "They fascinate me. The big ones kind of keep together in the herd. The young ones scatter through."

I envied him. I wished that I too might see the big bulls close up in their fall coats.

The next day about noon a dense band of twenty bulls

passed the foot of the mesa, traveling fast. They looked all white in the sun—chests shining white, a white stripe along each side below their "saddle blankets" of glistening brown, their rumps white. One bull had the most tremendous antlers I had ever seen—a quarter bigger than those of the other bulls. All the bulls looked magnificent, swinging along. Perhaps they were looking for a herd of cows and fawns to join.

A curious fact dawned on us as the caribou continued to pass daily: the same bands were repassing. They would go east, then south, then reappear a day or two later coming north. What caused us to recognize them was the "rocking-horse caribou," the ones that limped deeply, bobbing their heads to their knees. Some limped on one leg, some on another; there were crippled bulls and cows and fawns.

What did not dawn on us was that once before we had seen caribou circling like this, when the big bulls milled in the De Long Mountains in June, before the main bull migration. It was the slow swirling movement that presages the coming of a great migration.

13   A Drop

The event we looked forward to was a drop of mail and frozen food that Andy had promised to give us "about the last of September." The lake was not frozen yet and we hoped he would touch down. We prepared for a contact. Cris had twenty-nine rolls of film to go. I packed them in a knapsack along with towels and dry socks and laid out Cris's hip boots and my knee-high Eskimo water boots. The river had shrunk so much I had hopes of crossing without going in over knee-deep. The boot soles, of ugruk, were hard and slick, so Cris cut me a willow pole to aid in fording.

Chance noises these days made my heart stand still. A noise like wind or rushing water! The plane? No, a flight of ptarmigan passing swiftly.

Cris had a thought. "If I'm not here, look to see if he's on floats before you start over. If he's on wheels it's no use going."

The night before September 28 was cold. We awoke in the morning to see the lake still, smooth and dark. This was the freezeup. We had a slight feeling of awe and excitement. Of relief, too. Now we should not have the ticklish job of crossing. The river had been freezing out from its banks, over the riffles and around rocks. The current was doing unpredictable things—backing up, getting deep, running on top of the ice. Sometimes a shell of ice hid current running over bottom ice.

It was gray and there was a steady east wind. Cris started to the river for a load of willow. I was wiping the dishes when I sensed the far-off disturbance in the air. The wolves began to howl. Andy came over high, circled far to the west and came back low over the mesa. Two circlets hung below the plane; he was on wheels. I saw Cris, down on the marsh, hold up his red bandanna to give Andy the wind direction. Andy waved his wings.

Again he made the big circle that took minutes—out over the Killik, where the slight silver plane was camouflaged and lost against the black-and-white mountainsides and even its noise was muffled out.

Abruptly he was coming in level with the mesa top, his motor cut almost to soundlessness. I stood on the highest mound back of the cabin. A flat bundle fell close—the mail, no doubt—and he was gone, out over the deep air, to circle again. I ran all over the tundra hunting the bundle, like a foolish kitten that smells but cannot find a bit of food. Hurrying back to my mound to keep out of the way of the drop as Andy returned, I almost fell over the bundle. It was closer than I had realized.

This time a carton fell and the east wind carried it beyond the west end of the mesa. I noted the direction and waited. Cris joined me.

The third drop landed ten feet from Trigger and Lady in the pen. This wouldn't do. We hurried west, halfway across the mesa. The plane was coming in again from the west. A black-looking object dangled from the doorstep on our side. The plane was opposite us. With the same impulse we raised our right arms and swung them down, Cut! The package fell, a smiling brown young Eskimo face looked dimly down at us for an instant; Andy had a helper for the drops. I raised both arms in triumphant, joyful salutation.

After the final drop, to our surprise the plane came around again, with no package dangling at the door. A message! "There's a message in the mail to answer!" Cris exclaimed.

I flew to that first bundle, slashed it open with a knife. Nothing but magazines. I ran to tell Cris and he ran and slid down the steep slaty mesa side, to the broken carton that had missed the top. None of the others, we knew from our instant examinations when they fell, held the mail. I waited on the mesa brink. At this moment the plane crossed low again, and a scrap of cardboard fell, lighting on the mesa side. Cris climbed, hunting it. He read it. The plane was coming around again.

"Wave!" Cris yelled.

"What?" I bawled above the wind.

"WAVE!"

The message had read, "Hope we didn't forget anything. Expect to see you October 15. Wave if everything O.K." Nothing smartly military about it. It was the easy, friendly, responsible greeting and checkup of a bush pilot.

I stood lost in watching as the plane went movelessly east, smalling away against the white mountains. Then I took my packboard and went down to Cris, who was hunting in the wind for white letters on snow patches.

He gave me a dissatisfied look. "You nearly killed me," he said. "You started a rock as big as my head. I was reading the message and didn't see it. I couldn't jump. I ducked and it went over me."

A drop in the wilderness means luxuries and the wonderful human contact of letters from friends. But it does not mean all this at once. First we had many things to do. I spooned from the clean lichens the priceless food out of cartons broken in the drop—frozen raspberries, strawberries, corn, pineapple. Each bite wasted was a loss that hurt. We stowed away all our new riches. The fire was out and the crackerbox cold. But we could not restrain ourselves from riffling through the letters to read the return addresses, taking stock of our coming joys. Then the day's regular chores occupied us. Cris, with wolves and camera, went for the daily walk. I backpacked water from the river.

At last, in a warm cabin, after a voluptuous supper, we nestled in the sleeping robes on the bunk, leaning against the summer sleeping bags, which served us as pillows. With incomparable delight we began the reading of the mail.

Yet the delight was alloyed by pangs of a kind which only people reading mail alone in the wilderness can experience. Each impression and bit of news hits one hard. The impact is not spread by the many incidents of daily life among other people. Now we understood better the solitary old trapper on the Yukon, John Larson, who used to snowshoe to our tent door about six A.M. every few days and start talking as soon as he was in earshot, not about the situation we shared, but with anxiety about national affairs heard of the evening before over his battery radio.

Also we sensed vividly the whole situation of each friend. Loved new friends, once rich, now poor, had lavishly sent us a box of varied tidbits, packed flawlessly against the drop. Our wealthiest friends had sent a newspaper clipping. Both gifts gave us an aching feeling.

In the drop a gunnysack had squashed safely down, crammed with our long-awaited winter clothing, furs ordered from an Eskimo woman in Kotzebue in July—parka and pants for each of us. Cris's were of muskrat, mine of sik-sik or parka squirrel, a very lightweight fur, favored by Eskimo women because "you can wear it all day indoors and not be too warm and go out and not be too cold." This I found true even at fifty below zero.

We were saddened by a letter telling of yet another attempt by lumbermen to break the Olympic National Park, a wilderness we loved.

"Cris, don't you get discouraged sometimes?"

He glanced at me—an honest, uninflated look. "No," he said. Merrily he added, "Why should I feel discouraged? I've got a fine life, a fine wife and—fur pants! Think of all the hundreds of millions of people in the world, and very few have got fur pants."

October 1 was a new kind of day. It was radiant, cold and still. The mountains were white, the deep shadows on them sky-colored. The vast tan lands below were vacant.

When Cris came back for lunch at noon, bringing a pack-load of wood, I said, "Did you see any trace or track of animals?"

He replied as I expected. "None. Not a track nor a trace."

We were at lunch when there came a noise from the tundra below that caused us to spring without a word for the door, almost falling over each other. Cris swung the Dutch door wide. Below on the tundra was passing the exact spearhead of the fall migration, a dense column of caribou driving south-eastward to cross the Range for winter. Ahead of them was empty land. Behind them, unseen thousands would be gathering and following. The only sound was the *chuh, chuh, chuh* of hoofs on frozen grass, the brief *Mah!* of a calf. Otherwise they were passing like a shadow.

Cris took the camera and went up Easter Creek to a rock vantage point above where the column was crossing to swing away southward, up toward a pass.

I stayed on the mesa, going silently from the west brink, where I saw the caribou coming out of the Killik, white toward the sun, to the east brink, where I saw them going away shadowed into the vastness of the mountains. They were not wandering but going steadily, following contours as they went up Easter Creek, then crossing and bearing steadily southward up the great slope to the pass. Beyond it lay not their goal, the taiga south of the Range, where they would winter, but first other passes, other valleys to cross.

It was a spectacle like none other left on Earth now. It had power over the spirit. The power lay not only in what you saw—this slender column driving onward into wilderness. It lay also in what you knew. Arctic night and hunger coming. In-gathering far away somewhere of individuals into this traveling column, driven by the great seasons. Knowledge of danger and darkness and fear, built into their tissues by the centuries. Life and the cold Arctic before you for a moment in one silent sweep of land and moving animals.

Strangely enough what comes nearest giving the feeling of the fall migration of caribou is the "ice migration" on the Yukon the day the river breaks in spring. That too has the simplicity and endless oncoming of individuals—the floes—traveling purposefully it seems toward a goal.

It was not only in the lead caribou that there lay the sense, "This is the way." One file turned aside to ford half a mile ahead of the main fording place. They hit a bad icy spot and clustered, hesitating, for a while before returning to the main column. But some at least must have sensed that the river hereabouts must be crossed, the direction of travel changed.

Also a file left the main column and proceeded back of the mesa, going "right" but by a different route. Many followed them. Perhaps in all the caribou was a mystery, the sense, "We go; the way is thus."

Each caribou had its individual problems. None could help another. Each must solve its own problem or perish. A cow favored a leg. A big bull, almost white, held his mouth open panting; he closed it and went on. A big heavy bull walked at one side of the column. A cow drew to the side; her calf nursed. The bulls, the cows, the calves passed her. She pulled herself away from her calf and at once was trotting. The calf paused an instant shaking its head, then was trotting too. A big bull trotted past the trotting calf—two speeds. He was a mole-colored bull with silvery belly stripe and snowy under-hang or dewlap of fur; his antlers were high. He was limber power itself. His body flowed along. One sensed the reserve and depth of strength, the lightness and pleasure in control and in working far inside his strength.

The arctic sun was not high above the white mountains ahead of the column. The shadows on the snow were deep blue. The noise went on. Chuh-chuh-chuh—multitudes of hoofs hitting frozen grass. Clop, clop, clop across frozen ponds. Each knee joint lifted horizontal, foreleg trailing grace-ful and relaxed. Who was there but us to watch, to appreciate? But this was not to watch. Not for beauty. This was living-ness. This was the way for life—graceful, without excess, with-out awkwardness, perfect.

There was the small raven-croak of a calf. The great light gleamed off the ice of the river, off the mountains, off the antlers in very big silence except for the attentive small chuh-chuh-chuh. The line swung past. Mile—mile—mile eaten up by the migration swing, and they were past. Coming on out of the Killik; going very small in the sunlight, very many, away up Easter Creek.

Toward evening a hundred lay down on the tundra below the mesa. Two bulls engaged in antler play and Cris filmed it. It was not yet a real mating fight. "Like a ballet," Cris said. "They don't put any muscle into it. Just graceful." They en-gaged antler tips lightly, bowed their heads and jumped their hinds ends around.

That night Cris wakened me to come outdoors. We crouched at the edge of the mesa, almost stilling our breath-ing. Below in the darkness caribou were passing—clop-clop over ice, shuh-wih, shuh-wih over frozen grass, a noise no more than that of pouring granulated snow from one pile onto another. "Mah!" a calf spoke; a cow answered.

I had a wide, still feeling—wonder. Cris said, "Stars, Lois!" Till now we had hardly noticed their return after the long "day" of summer.

In the morning the lake "harped"; the ice made noises like wind across the mouth of an open pipe. Caribou still passed, in column formation but at longer intervals between bands. Poorer-conditioned animals were passing. Ribby cows but with chubby, well-furred calves. "Tired" calves but with nimble mothers. Something ailed those calves. A limping calf. His mother stood still, looking keenly ahead. She turned her head, looking back at the calf. She gave a small reedy grunt to him, turned and trotted swiftly, fluently ahead. The calf walked, bobbing his head up and down.

Cris took the wolves and went down, hoping to film them chasing caribou. Returning, he said they had chased a solitary caribou nearly a mile. "But a small bunch, no sir! They saw them, the little buggers. But they acted like they didn't. Wouldn't look at them. They knew durn well I wanted them to run them. But Trigger got very busy hunting a mouse."

Toward evening the main flow of the migration had stopped. Stragglers would pass for a few days yet. Cris estimated that eighteen thousand caribou had passed.

We had gone short on water and wood, hating to scare the column by crossing it to the river. Our spring near the mesa had frozen and dried up. I was about to start with a five-gallon can in a sack on my packboard to bring water, when we saw a calf coming back from the migration direction, but on the far side of the river and out of the main path. Trotting, pausing, veering, it was coming back in the brown evening light into hundreds of miles of emptiness. It crossed the river ice, hit the caribou trails and stopped veering. It hurried along them. But in the wrong direction.

"You're looking at a dead calf, Cris," I said.

I was halfway down the mesa side when Cris whistled and pointed. Around the foot of the mesa came the calf, very important, trotting swiftly behind a cow. They had found each other!

The next morning there were no caribou except a cow with sharp little antlers and a white cape, toiling along the migration route. She could hardly walk. Her right front leg was like a stump. Her head went away down, then up, on each step. A healthy calf trailed slowly behind her. Such a pretty little calf, with clear-cut, brief white cape and young spike antlers. The cow stopped, raised her head, ears forward, and looked off ahead trying to see the herd.

"A wolf would be a mercy now," I thought. Better the quick, exciting, terrible death than the unending toil and striving, to eat, to keep up with the nimble, flexible great travelers. When the snow came and the caribou had to paw through it for food, how could a cripple do that?

On the night of October 7, four inches of snow fell—the merest, puffiest snow I ever saw. It gave a feeling as of white smoke going up all around. From now on, the tundra like the mountains was white. There were no caribou tracks.

On October 9 we were coming up onto the tundra from the river bar when Cris pointed. A motionless small animal stood looking at us. A fox, I thought at first glance. It was a caribou fawn, and when it started to run from us, we saw that one hind leg was as if broken. The fawn got itself somehow down the steep bank and onto the lake. It crossed the flat whiteness, now hurrying, now seeming very tired and standing still. But it drove itself on. I thought it would lose the migration direction. But on the far side of the lake it turned southeastward again. A dot of life struggling onward in the white vastness, toiling alone up toward the pass, trying to catch up.

Six days later there were the tracks of ten caribou going past on the migration route. There was blood on the tracks as from bleeding feet. From now on, the land was empty of caribou.

Trigger and Lady had not yet seen another wolf, though three or four passed through now and then. Cris was a bit worried one day when three wolves passed below while he and our wolves were up on the mountainside. Trigger and Lady did not see them, but when they came to the fresh scent would they follow it away?

What shy Lady did was something she had never done before. She rushed to Cris and shrank against his leg, crying with intense excitement. It must have been a strange inner conflict for her, feeling the allure of her own kind, yet knowing only a human as guardian.

One thing we had awaited was our wolves' first howl. For a reason we did not understand yet they had never howled, though Trigger greeted Cris with what we called the "half-howl." In fact, we had not heard even wild wolves howl since we came to the Arctic.

I was stuck rebelliously in the crackerbox one afternoon, baking bread, while Cris and the wolves walked in the sunny outdoors. Suddenly wild wolves howled from the ridge back of the mesa. They must have stayed there, perhaps watching Cris and our wolves down on the tundra, for fifteen minutes later they howled again.

The sun was down, the light gray by the time I took the bread from the oven. But stubbornly I started for a walk. I saw Cris already coming home. He stood on the far bank of the river. I went down the back of the mesa, following his outgoing trail; it was too hard to break my own.

When I came around the foot of the mesa, Cris was still standing on the river bank. That seemed odd. I heard his far-off halloo. Suddenly his voice was surrounded by other voices. The cold still air was faintly thronged with the wild heart-thrilling uproar of wolves howling.

Were the wild wolves in the willow brush below him?

"Go to the tent, Cris," I thought. We had never struck the umbrella tent by the lake. "They won't go in there for a long time. *Go to the tent.*"

It was no use hurrying. In a few minutes I would only be out of breath, my heart pounding. There was just so much to be done before I could be of help. Climb the mesa and get Andy's gun, cross the marsh to the river. If Cris was in real trouble I could not possibly get there in time. Horror came over me. Then, as if my mind had gone through a door into another room, I was aware that anything was possible and that I would do what had to be done.

Rounding the mesa, I came into sight of the river again. Black and erect on its white surface came Cris. I ran to meet him, floundering through the unbroken snow. He told me it was Trigger and Lady, uttering their first howl.

Why had they howled? Their first thrilling hearing of the voices of their own kind since we had had them. And Cris trying different pitches to make me hear, to warn me that wild wolves were around.

There was a question in our minds that we never mentioned. Would our wolves turn on us sometime without warning? While they were pups and we were the stronger ones, all was well. But now that they were nearly full grown, I felt uneasy sometimes. Trigger, especially, mystified me. There was always something sidelong about him. And as always there was not one day when he did not growl at me.

One sunny afternoon in a blue-and-white world I was following Cris along the rut of a caribou trail when I became aware that Trigger was trailing me closely. When I glanced back he drifted aside as if he had not a purpose in the world. But the instant I turned my head he was at my heels again. Suddenly sharp fangs sank into my wool mitten. Trigger snatched it off and ran. He had a trophy for a romp! I felt relief. We had a free-for-all chase over the sunny snow. Trigger had made up his first game and, of all things, with me. Daily after this he played "mitten" with me. He gauged his bite to a nicety and never broke my skin.

The game led to a new insight. One morning in the pen he stole my mitten but, when I chased him, Lady set herself to hold my attention. For once she let me wool and maul her to my heart's content. Trigger paced around the fence, the unwanted mitten dangling from his jaws. When I finally went to him, he growled. So! Trigger was jealous!

I was horrified one morning to find a bloody incisor on the wolves' frozen water pan. I did not know a wolf's first incisors are deciduous. I blamed myself because in the night I had heard the wolves gnawing thirstily at the ice and I had not taken them water.

When they banged their pan the next night, I jumped up. The tiny white room was filled with the "moonlight" of the aurora. I pulled on pants, boots and parka, broke the ice on the water pail and went outdoors with a pan of water. The impact was always new. Not from one night to the next could one remember the awe of it.

All around rose the silent white mountains. Overhead the aurora moved in rectangles, parallel bright ropes and gliding curtains. My diaphragm had an eerie feeling of flinching. All that moving, those presences, noiselessly creeping above me, each more beautiful than the last but giving the impression of something purposeful yet not—ineffably not—animal.

The wolves were dark figures prancing shoulder to shoulder. Lady was full of black mischief. She nabbed my bootlace. She nabbed my braid, yanked and prepared to travel off with it. But when I set down the pan she stole to my elbow and drank. I could feel Trigger gliding close behind me. I withdrew to the gate. He snatched the pan, dumping the water, but he drank from the puddle on the snow. "Poor puppy," I assured myself, "he's thirsty but shy." I brought more water and again he dumped it. Long afterward I realized the wolf had been trying to start a new game with me.

The caribou came with the ice; the ptarmigan came with the snow. Bands of up to two hundred flew in from the north to winter in the willows. They came with a noise like rushing water. There was a whistling in the rush as they winged right over.

A wretched, misguided sparrow had chosen to stay by the cabin instead of migrating south. As the snow came he kept only a bird-sized hollow brown. Then it whitened. He moved only if we passed. He liked to sit on the bush in the pen above the sleeping wolves, possibly for some trace of warmth but more, we thought, for company. He ventured a few notes some mornings. Feed him or not? We fed him.

"The ptarmigan has more protection on one foot," Cris said, "than the little sparrow has all over."

"You don't want to shoot the little bird?"

"No. Let him try the enterprise he has undertaken. He just might make it. There could be an unusual winter—mild."

I was climbing straight up the mesa side one day and stopped to breathe. Up from the unbroken snow in front of my face rose a small brown head and shoulders. The loose snow fell away and a vole stood there in a black column of air, like that around an avalanche lily in snow. One moment of appalled scrutiny, then it vanished down into the snow, leaving no trace or sign but the hole.

The wolves shoveled their noses in the snow, snuffling for voles. They chased the ptarmigan and gave the little sparrow a routine chase when they returned home.

"I think he likes it," said Cris. "To have someone notice him." (He disappeared the day Andy came. A hawk?)

There was a mystic-arctic look one day such as we could never have imagined. We were on the lake shoveling a landing strip for Andy, who was due on October 15 for the first time since before freezeup.

We were working in vast empty stillness. The earth was passive.

"The air is blue!" Cris exclaimed. I looked up. Blue—blue-nesses—were in the air. It was still with a soft stillness you could feel. The faded little tent on the lake bank was a strangely vivid green, and my scarf that Lady had stolen and dropped on the ice was a vivid red.

Blue veils were over the mountains. Only one thin veil on the mountain in front of us. The other mountains were as clear in outline but veiled in shadows of blue as if night had looked at them.

Then the light began to play. We stood with our shovels, watching. Now this mountain was white against the strange-blue sky, now it was blue against a white sky. "The light is poetic," said Cris. "I never saw mountains like these."

Andy did not come on the fifteenth. When he did come, on the seventeenth, he brought a message from the studio that changed Cris's plan to winter in the Range. They felt it was too hazardous for us to winter here alone, so far from any other humans. Andy would return the first of November to fly us out.

From now on, I grudged every minute spent indoors. I felt as never before the strangeness and power and beauty of this great land. It was not only because we were leaving—forever, we supposed. There was an unexpected change in the Arctic. As the Big Dark neared, great beauty spread over the land that was going under the shadow. The temperature went down steadily but without much change between day and night. The winds that had troubled us since May, instead of increasing, were now laid.

We were in a world not of grim black and white but of color—blue, amber, white. Where snow met sky, the shadows were like gulfs of sky. The willows were amber. The sun, barely clearing the mountains to the south, cast our shadows **forty feet at noon.** Daily they lengthened. Pink sunlight crossed in front of blue-shadowed canyons.

The remembered beauty of the temperate zone seemed rich and tepid compared with this beauty, plain and pure.

On clear mornings in the west there was a color I had not seen in sky before. Not blue-pink as in white mountains anywhere, but a true orchid. The lightless mountains were carved in front of it before the sun rose.

I left the pancakes on the griddle to burn or not burn one morning and went outdoors just as the daily heart-stirring radiance of the sun glided from back of the mountain. All the way up Easter Creek each mountain was a light gray nothingness of shadow and would be for quiet hours yet. But far up the Killik those high lawns of the pass where we had summered were white, underscored with a blue slanting spear of shadow. Above the far side of them, the low blue mountains were cropped with sunlight. The air was so pure it seemed as if in four hours' walk one could be treading up there.

When I went back into the cabin, Cris, sitting on the head of the bunk, eating pancakes from his plate on the Blazo boxes, said briefly, "Lot of times we'll miss this country."

The wolves turned on us the day Andy came to take us out. He landed on the frozen lake, a mile or more away. We shouldered our final backpacks, closed the door of the crackerbox—forever, we thought—and each with a wolf on a leash went toward the lake. To our surprise the wolves led easily.

The high bank concealed the plane. I waited with Lady, out of sight of the alien activity. Taking Trigger, Cris went down to help load our dunnage.

Lady strained against the leash to escape. If I had fallen she would have dragged me. Then she sat down, gazing with clear eyes over the tundra and bright mountain world that had been her home. Here she had leaped with Trigger in play; they had dug for voles, raised white ptarmigan in clouds. Wild with delight, they had shoveled their noses in the first snow, found treasure to race with—the dropped eagle's feather, the shed caribou antler.

Again Lady dug her paws into the snow, striving with all her power to escape. Then she whirled and leaped despairingly at my face. I shouted for Cris. He put Trigger's leash in Andy's hand and came. He dragged Lady to the plane. Meanwhile, Trigger had bitten Andy twice. Our wolves had turned—how deeply and permanently we could not know.

On the flight out, Lady lay motionless, her face in a corner.

Trigger crouched by Cris's knee, looking down steadfastly. His eyes glared brilliant black and gold.

At Bettles Field, waiting a few days for a commercial plane to Point Barrow, where we were to winter, we chained Trigger and Lady near the roadhouse. They refused to eat, refused to let us touch them. Trigger was savage and brilliant-eyed, Lady dull-eyed and passive. Perhaps bright Lady realized more clearly than did Trigger the hopelessness of their situation.

At Barrow, Cris chained the wolves in front of our wanigan, one of a row of four or five empty wanigans beside the airstrip. They had made up a cat train. A wanigan is a narrow shack on runners; it can be drawn by tractor across snow or tundra. Ours had been the cook's galley. One end was nearly filled by a forced-draft range, the other by an improvised bed, consisting of a cot alongside a seat locker against the wall. A counter stood between bed and stove. Ducking an overhead shelf, one could pass the bed by a narrow aisle. Tight quarters these, for two people and all their gear.

Outdoors there was constant activity during the "day," which was dark, except for a few hours of twilight. Eskimos from Barrow village four miles away, working at the airstrip, snow weasels roaring, on some days a plane landing—all terrified the wolves. All decent privacy was denied them.

Cris said, "Lois, I'm going to bring them inside." He dragged the wolves, one at a time, toward the open door. They shot under the cot, seeing it in a flash as a den. Cris, talking quietly, ventured a hand and unsnapped their chains. The two hostile wolves were at liberty with us in the wanigan.

They lay quiet under the cot, except that each time we sidled past, Trigger nipped our ankles. The den had become his property and he resented encroachment. Cris hung a tarp over the side of the bed, giving the wolves and our ankles more seclusion.

The next night we were awakened by cold noses touching our faces. There was the smell of wolf fur, like the smell of clean hay. Shadowy forms prowled about our bed.

"Is that you, Lady?" we quavered. "Is that you, Trigger?"

Cris got the light on. The wolves, thoroughly recovered from the horrors of their transportation, were prepared to take the wanigan to pieces. They patted back and forth. Trigger stood on his hind legs and pulled clothes from overhead shelves, tipped over Cris's camera, reared almost to the ceiling, paws on the counter, and looked purposefully into the kitchen end of the wanigan. At the bedside, glancing at us mischievously without turning his head, he bit our new $130 sleeping bag. He burrowed his nose eagerly here and there in its softness. One leg, then all four legs, snuggled on top. The heavy wolf lay down and looked around happily. Always a luxury lover, Trigger had found new luxury.

At first we were amused. Cris got up and fed the wolves. For the first time in days they ate. Trigger with his bloody bone leaped onto the bed. He felt me move inside the sleeping bag. His eyes flared black, his mane rose. He lunged at my face snarling.

There was no time to think. I instantly began to talk "wolf." In Lady's brilliant, complaining voice, like that of a peevish woman, I said, "Do-on't, Trigger!"

The wolf's clear, intelligent eyes brushed mine. Cris took the cue. He began to coax. Trigger caught on. He got off the bed. Luxurious as it was, he understood that it was for us alone.

One thing I had not needed to worry about: wolves are just naturally housebroken. Each had one mishap only. Lady, starting outdoors after her first night in the wanigan, took one terrified look, saw something move, and fled back under the cot, where she urinated.

One morning before we were up, Trigger touched our heads, laid his chin on the sleeping bag and looked brightly and confidently at Cris. He made a terse statement: "Ow-wow."

That meant nothing to Cris but he soon learned. He replied civilly, rose and went back by the stove to dress. At this breakdown in communication, Trigger stepped up to what was now for him the most inaccessible spot in the room, the back of the bed. He urinated. Cris seized the broom. Trigger's eyes got black. He snatched the broom from Cris and flung it down. But he did get off the bed.

We were both by the stove when we heard a novel little sound. Trigger stood in the aisle, his back to us, uttering a small grieving howl all to himself. He had been scolded for the first time in his life, and unfairly at that.

We did not yet realize how strongly a wolf feels unfairness. Nor that the social beast always cries about it. When the sled dog Kipi was "jumped on" by his master once, Kipi jumped on Trigger and Trigger came to me in the dark, lighted by the open door, looked up and "told me all about it," how uncalled-for Kipi's action had been.

Two things impressed us about Trigger's mishap. First, the intelligent wolf had not dreamed of addressing a door; he had come straight to us when he wanted to go outdoors.

Second and more remarkable, he had uttered a brief, unemotional noise clearly meant to communicate something to us. He did not repeat, though we had failed to catch on to his intent.

Wolves have four main vocal communications. The famous howls, of which there are many kinds. Next, a whole range of expressive little "you-and-me" noises, protesting or cheerful. Third, the kind Trigger had just uttered, short, unemotional communications of fact that we called simply "speaking." And fourth, long, fervently passionate "talking."

These last two—speaking and talking—are all but unknown to humans. We never heard Trigger speak more than half a dozen times in his life. Each time he so plainly had something on his mind to communicate that if the situation did not explain it to us, we wondered forever after what he had meant. Incidentally, Lady never spoke.

The wolf talking is deeply impressive because the wolf is so emotionally stirred. His eyes are brilliant with feeling. He seeks your eyes and utters a long, fervent string of mingled crying and wowing, hovering around one pitch. It is like nothing else on earth. Later on, Trigger often talked. Lady talked only twice, both times under extreme emotional pressure.

One thing Cris never tried again was to punish a wolf. You cannot punish him. He takes your aggression as a fight. And Cris ruefully observed, "You can get along with a wolf all right as long as you do what's right in his eyes. Trouble is, you don't always know what he's going to think is wrong!"

A merry event took us by surprise one morning. Cris, as usual on waking, was yawning luxuriously. These sounds were very congenial to the wolves. They came yawning and stretching from under the cot, Lady only part way out into the dangerous lighted space between the head of the cot and the door. Man and wolves exchanged small comfortable sounds until the mood built up and all at once the wolves burst into a full-scale howl, the second of their lives.

Astonished and pleased, we glanced at each other and made a quartet of it. I leaned over the head of the cot looking down into the red cavern of Lady's mouth, fenced with white teeth, and she sang up into my face, her eyes blind and bright though focusing. It thrilled me to lay my hand on her fur and feel the deep vibration of her chest.

Trigger sang to Cris's face, stepped over and looked into my open mouth, brushed fur with Lady and brought his head near hers, but preferred to sing to Cris, in close harmony. Trigger had a natural talent for the barbershop style.

Lady's voice was deep and "dark." It had a strange, thrilling timbre, a mournful plangency. The howl seemed to be a catharsis for her, about the only emotional outlet she had these sad days. She took it with more intensity than did Trigger.

Also she sang with more virtuosity. Sometimes she ululated, drawing her tongue up and down in her mouth like a trombone slide. Sometimes on a long note she held the tip of her tongue curled against the roof of her mouth. She shaped her notes with her cheeks, retracting them for plangency, or holding the sound in with them for horn notes. She must have had pleasure and sensitiveness about her song for if I entered on her note she instantly shifted by a note or two: wolves avoid unison singing; they like chords.

Trigger's voice was higher pitched than Lady's. He sang up into a high treble, threw in short barks ending in the howl, "Yuh-yuh-yuh yoooooo."

From now on we always "had a howl" on waking up. Like a community sing, a howl is not mere noise, it is a happy social occasion. Wolves love a howl. When it is started, they instantly seek contact with one another, troop together, fur to fur. Some wolves, like Lady, love a sing more than others do and will run from any distance, panting and bright-eyed, to join in, uttering, as they near, fervent little wows, jaws wide, hardly able to wait to sing.

When, long afterward, a wolf or two would dig out of the pen at our home in Colorado, all we had to do to get them back was to start a howl with the other wolves. Down from the mountainside, out from the forest came the runaways, hurrying to get to the group and join in.

The wolves had one great unforeseen alleviation in their

captivity. In the small wooden station at the south end of the short row of wanigans lived Dean and Esther Phillips, the station manager and his wife, our only neighbors. They had dogs! Two ran loose and these gave the captive wolves something to look forward to. But the three wretched dogs that lay chained in the snow near the wolves were a help too: as long as those dogs lay there, the wolves seemed to consider their own fate not too *outré*.

The wolves were chained on a Y of short chains to one end of a long, steel-cored wire lying on the snow and fastened at the other end to a "dead man" under the snow. This gave the wolves a circle of a hundred and fifty feet across to run in. Trigger quickly adjusted and ran full tilt without jerking himself. Wild Lady ran in one direction only—away toward the level horizon—and the chain brought her up with a yank.

Kobuk and Brownie were the free dogs. Brownie was a six-month-old female. She tried to play but the wolves disdained her—at first. They courted huge white Kobuk. "They're discriminating!" said Cris. "They can't see what that no-'count pup could add to their lives. But that fine big dog! They'd like to belong to his pack!"

Kobuk ignored the wolves. At last they were glad enough to play with little Brownie. Trigger even stood gravely by and watched the cocky little dog eat his bowl of chunked meat.

He took a less favorable view of her stealing his bones outdoors; Trigger always liked property. Solemn and intent, he would catch Brownie by the tail as she absconded with a bone. The bone was at the other end but maybe if he hung on he might think of a way to get it!

We kept a box of bones at the foot of the cot for the wolves to amuse themselves with in the night. This luxury of the rich Hollywood wolves attracted Kobuk. Every morning as soon as our light was on, he stood on his hind legs on the doorstep and presented his broad white head silently at the high door window. We let him in and he stalked to the box and applied himself to choosing a bone to take outdoors.

Now Trigger and Lady were transfigured. They smiled, but more dazzlingly than we had ever seen them do. Lady dared poke only her head from under the tarp hanging over the side of the cot. Her eyes were black and brilliant with excitement. Whining urgently, she sniffed all over Kobuk's side with excited little sniffs.

Trigger bravely came clear out. Now we really saw what a wolf's courtship can be. (Wolves "court" for friendship.) More sinuous, quick and graceful by far than a dog could be, he bowed—not mere raw puppy squats of the front legs, but enchanting little bows and curves, accompanied with inimitable tilts and wolf-tosses of the head. He coquetted. He spread his forelegs in a V—"I am your slave!" He laid his arm entreatingly over Kobuk's neck. His eyes were dazzling.

Kobuk replied to all this brilliance and invention of movement with an insucked, outblown snarl, bit the nearest muzzle and turned back to his contemplation. The bitten wolf screamed, then courted him again. That beseeching shriek of a courting, rebuffed wolf!

Cris was putting the wolves out at night now. As he started one evening to drag Lady from under the cot, on which I lay, she talked for the first time in her life; and for the first time we heard that extraordinary kind of wolf communication. Looking up at me with black, anxious eyes, she talked, so passionate and troubled that we were touched. "She thinks maybe you won't make her go out," Cris said kindly, but he dragged her outdoors.

People who have never dealt with wild animals may suppose my language exaggerated. It is hard to imagine, if you have not experienced it, how fervent and intense wild animals may be in relation to a person.

The next morning we had brought the wolves in but had not yet removed their neck chains when Kobuk came. He chose a bone and went out. Lady, crouching low, shot out after him into the darkness, her short neck chain flying.

We were not much concerned, knowing she would not desert Trigger. What we did not know was that Kobuk occasionally ran off to the Arctic Research Laboratory a mile or so away.

Lady did not return. As gray seeped into the darkness Cris put on his parka and went to search for her. He found Kobuk at the ARL but not Lady. When he came back he looked drawn. "I think Lady's done for," he said. "Eskimo fox traps are lined up all along the airstrip and lab area. Dog teams going back and forth all the time."

He searched again, returning once in a while to see if Lady had come home. He looked tired and white. At noon he telephoned a fifty-dollar reward notice to Barrow village. At four o'clock, when darkness had come again, he raised it to seventy-five dollars.

I bathed my eyes and resolved not to cry any more. "If only she died quickly and cleanly," I thought.

Dean came over in the evening. He said, "A wolf is worth eighty-five dollars dead in the village."

Cris raised his offer to a hundred and Dean went home to telephone the new price to the native store at Barrow. Half an hour later he came back. "A native boy saw a 'big black fox' in a trap," he said. "The boy doesn't speak English. An Eskimo is bringing him here in a snow weasel."

The two Eskimos with Dean and Cris set out into the night, riding the weasel. I waited and prayed: "That Lady may do the right thing. That Cris may do the right thing." If it really was Lady in the trap, when the yellow headlights of the weasel rolled toward her in the darkness, or if Cris walked up to her too fast, she might tear herself from the trap and escape, injured, never to return.

After a while Dean's unsmiling rosy face appeared at the door window. "Do you want to come, Lois?"

"Is she badly hurt?"

"No."

Outside in the dark the snow weasel stood at Dean's door. Black figures of men were going into the station. I went to the weasel. Cris, in the back, pushed a big hunk of blackness toward me, through the window, the only exit. "Can you take Lady?"

I wrapped her chain around the wrist of my leather-and-wool mitten. For an instant I held and hauled the dear huge bushy form. Then Lady tore herself from my arms. She rushed me along the brief row of empty wanigans, lunged uncertainly toward the first, but at ours knew it. The power-ful wolf leaped at the small window, smashing it. I dragged her down, wrenched open the door and Lady shot in and un-der the cot.

Cris came in after paying the reward. His eyes were happy. Blood smeared his parka and the floor under Lady's paw but her injury was not crippling. Cris told me what had hap-pened.

In the beam of the weasel lights they had seen the black wolf standing, paw-held, in the trap. Her chain was wrapped around it. Cris went to her, talking gently. He lifted the trap and foot to his knee. The trap was too strongly set for him to open. He called an Eskimo to help. The man was afraid to approach, so Dean came up and tugged the trap open while Cris held Lady.

"She never offered to bite. She never whimpered or uttered a sound," he said with proud wonder. "Most dogs would have gone crazy."

Lady slept awhile, then Cris opened the door and Trigger came to it. In the rush of her entrance he had not come up. All day he had stayed outdoors, refusing to come in. Once he stood at the door and looked searchingly in, especially at the "den." He had gazed south all day, the direction she must have vanished in, and a few times he had uttered a sound new to me and to him—the wolf mourning call.

Now Lady came from under the cot and she and Trigger did something that surprised and moved us. Gently they touched noses and drew them across each other. "Wuzzling!" said Cris.

He never dreamed of making Lady stay outdoors this night. She slept on her reindeer robe under the cot. In the morning it took her half an hour of painful, agonized indecision and crying and rushes back from door to den before finally she was out. Then Brownie and Trigger crowded around. They couldn't get enough of smelling her.

All did not return to normal. Lady was traumatized. Day after day she lay motionless under the cot, except when we put her out for a while. I began to feel a touch of fear. The wolf could not go on this way, she had to "break." Would her withdrawal end in a berserk attack?

One day I tried to help her but made a mistake. I laid a carton by the cot, hoping she would amuse herself by tearing it up. Presently I heard her drag herself stealthily to it and tear it. "Good Lady!" I exclaimed. Instantly she froze again.

Yet a few days later I had a gentle little surprise. I had lain down on the floor at the head of the cot, hoping to be company for her, and my eyes had closed. Suddenly I felt fine pricks on my eyelids, like a row of needles. Lady was picking up the merest skin of my eyelid with her teeth, giving me grooming nibbles.

When Cris came home I told him about it. He, too, lay down to see what would happen. Sure enough, Lady nibbled him—not his eyelid but the rim of his ear. Such fine tooth-work made us surmise the wolf might like delicate attentions herself, instead of the robust slaps usually dealt to the dog kind.

Her trauma continued. Meanwhile I became acquainted with Trigger as never before.

When Brownie was not outdoors, he entertained himself by running up the eaves-high drift beside the wanigan and flowing down as fast as he could.

Sometimes I played with him. There was the yellow light from the windows of the wanigan, and my eyes soon utilized the dim light from the snow. He changed his old game of "mitten": he snatched off my mitten but dropped it. The best of the game, when Lady was not here to chase him, was the stealing.

Sometimes I played "pounce." He liked that. He watched intently and leaped away when I jumped. Or I chased him, then discovered to my pleasure that he would also chase me. But I was only the pretext for his run. When the great wolf streamed by me in the arctic night, mane flowing, head low, shoulders reared and forepaws flung ahead of muzzle, he was almost terrifying in his speed.

With wild animals the most important events are often not the big ones but the very little, almost imperceptible ones. Trigger now guided me to a leap forward in the "magic" of communicating with wildings.

I was alone with him in the wanigan; Lady was chained outdoors. He lay in his den. He growled warningly when I lay down facing his head, at the head of the cot, and burrowed my fingers in his deep warm ruff. As usual, I felt intimidated.

But this time, summoning all the love I really felt for this animal, I kept my hand on his fur. I felt a tuning of love with him as strong and definite as a harp chord strummed. I sensed him as a wild free being, neither doglike nor humanlike, but wolf and wild. His eyes glanced across mine. His defensive growling ceased. From this moment on he was less defensive with me.

But what on earth had happened? Just this: the wolf had

read my eyes! The thing happens so fleetingly, the animal's wild inexorable intelligence seizes the knowledge so instantaneously that the wonder is I ever blundered into awareness of this deepest range of communication. It is, I think, the inner citadel of communication: your true feeling looks out of your eyes, the wild animal reads it. The wolf has a characteristic way of looking at your eyes. He does not stare, his eyes merely graze yours in passing. I learned at last to have my eyes ready for that unregarded instant when the wolf's eyes brushed mine. (It was to be months yet before I proved all this with a stranger animal than a wolf.)

As for me, it was no small achievement to have realized that Trigger was "wolf." It is hard enough to realize the selfness even of another human being. When you are learning a new wild animal there comes an unexpected moment when all at once you realize his "selfness." It is a flash of creative awareness. It is the break-through out of anthropomorphism. An opaque fog of humanness surrounds our understanding as our human scent surrounds our bodies unaware. Each human whose human fog dissolves and who spies other-than-human beings about him is another stout Cortez and may have the authentic delight of spying new worlds.

I stumbled onto one more way of communicating with wolves. They had a problem and I strove to help them with it. They were often tense in the wanigan, heads too alert, eyes too bright. "Wildness" commanded them to fathom the least noise; in wilderness the crack of a twig could mean something deadly. What might not the rustle of a broom or rattle of a pan be leading to?

With my naïve trust in words, I exhorted the wolves. Then one day in desperation I stumbled onto the right thing to do. I yawned and stretched. I sighed luxuriously. And the overbrightness faded from the wolves' eyes. They eased their heads to the floor.

I told Cris and from now on you would have smiled to observe us grunting and sighing comfortably as we worked.

When I was alone with Trigger again one afternoon during Lady's trauma, another slight, significant communication occurred that impressed me more than any other so far.

The wolf lay silent by the door, head up, looking up with wolf attentiveness at everything—shelves, hanging light bulb, then me, sitting on the cot. On impulse I deliberately stretched and spread my fingers. Trigger, watching them, spread his own long "fingers" very slightly, the merest hint of a stretch. The wolf empathized!

Two weeks after Lady's trapping, Cris had chained her outdoors and paused by the door to watch her a minute, when he called me imperiously. I ran to look. Lady was playing! She was running and romping with Trigger and Brownie. Her long trauma had broken and in a good way.

But all was not well with her yet. Every morning, just before eight o'clock, there would be a crash at the door, a glimpse of powerful black shoulders at the high door window. The plastic glass bowed in, Cris sprang to open the door and Lady's bushy black form, crouching low, shot in and under the cot, still attached to the yard wire outdoors. Sometimes she plunged through the window before Cris could get there. We taped the broken pieces of Plexiglass together instead of putting in a new piece, so she would not hurt herself.

It was Cris who finally realized her difficulty. She was in terror of the snow weasel, arriving with the Eskimos from the village for their day's work. The "eyes" of the weasel searched the snow in the darkness for the chained wolf as they had searched when she stood trapped.

"Lady doesn't associate those 'eyes' with being rescued," said Cris. "The rescue occurred when she got in the door and under the cot and she performed that herself!"

As in a roaring tunnel of darkness and work our days sped. Chores take more time in a tiny, inconvenient dwelling. That seems obvious, but our friends always supposed, because we lived without conveniences—running water and a sink, for example—that time hung heavy on our hands.

Getting water took time. Cris sawed—quarried—snow blocks at a distance and bore them to the wanigan one at a time on his shoulder and slid them into a giant aluminum kettle on the range that held two blocks. That was our water supply.

The wanigan was essentially cold though the range roared day and night. Metal wall bolts below table level were always white with frost. The frosty window by the stove let in snow as well as cold. Bread dough set on the stove itself would hardly rise.

For me the horrors of the Arctic are represented by that stove. The day-and-night roar of its forced draft dulled my ears. Cris refused a respite of stillness for even half an hour. "No, Lois, everything would freeze—the potatoes, the eggs, your ink." Sometimes our airborne vegetables from Fairbanks did freeze, even while Cris dragged them on his homemade sled the short distance from plane to wanigan.

"What do you do with all your time?" wrote a friend. I replied, but the gaps in the narrated time puzzled me. There were none in the real day. That evening I paid attention to what we did. We were keeping the wolves in at night now.

Bring them in for the night at a quarter of nine, feed them, speed cannily to bed to get some sleep before they wake up in the night.

Sure enough, about two A.M., they waken us. They crowd around us. Lady rears at the door looking out. She launches through the window. Now one of us must leap up, put on fur slippers, mittens and parka and manage the chains. There is an in-and-out indecision of the wolves. At last chains are all unsnapped, no wolves lost, resnapped to the yard wire. We are thoroughly awake.

At eight A.M. in crashes Lady, terrified. But once in she wants Trigger with her. She cries. Brownie eels in around the door. Cris holds Lady's collar while I transfer chains. "Master Trigger, will you in or out?" In!

"Fix them some eggs, Lois," says Cris, hoping food will tranquilize them. I boom the stove, set on the iron skillet. Trigger starts out the window. I gather an armful of deep tawny fur, deep wolf chest. "Wait, Trigger!" Gently I try to move him back to drop into the room.

Trigger is silent. He is almost always silent. But he curls his strong paws and toenails and grips the open window ledge like a person, till his leg quivers. Then he turns his beautiful head and launches back into the room—himself. He is not going to be made to do anything. He will do it himself.

With entreaties to Trigger to stay in, I get the sluggish pan warm, scramble the eggs. They are cheerfully "wolfed." I use the word as an exaggeration. Actually, with his slender jaws, the wolf is a slow eater compared with even a little, shovel-mouthed dog pup. The wolf can snatch tissues from a bone; he's fitted for doing that. But he often strangles if he gulps prepared food fast. Then he rears his head and utters a low moan, the most spine-chilling sound I know, aside from the warning "bark" of cow elk in deep forest at twilight.

But the wolves are still determined to go outdoors. Parka on, mittens on, chains unsnapped, untangled, Cris holding Lady, Trigger out, Lady out. "There you are!" we tell the wolves. "Now you can go." Away they race, on the circuit of the yard wire.

And the time? A quarter of nine. Just one of those idle empty hours on my page written to our friend.

At our door was the presence of the Big Dark. It was illimitable. It went away over the polar ice and wide away over the limitless snow. It was not depressing—more so were the few hours of twilight. Rather, it kept one's spirit at a somber tension.

The cold differed from the cold in the States. Thirty below here was not like thirty below in Minnesota. No sun, no change would alleviate this cold. It wasn't a "cold spell." This cold was relentless and undeviating. It went down to permafrost, up to the aurora, north to the Pole.

Failing to understand its power, I often ran out without my parka. Extreme cold can take down one's strength like surgery. By spring I learned that. And was told then, too late, that one needs extra amounts of vitamin C when exposed to prolonged cold.

Cris often came in with his nose yellow-white in his dark-red face. It became a glass nose, freezing easily. I frosted my fingers to dark-red blisters by handling the wolf chains without mittens in emergencies. We were constantly in and out of doors, living "on the deck."

But we did have two luxuries. One was warm feet. We wore mukluks with a stack of two or three wool inner soles and two pairs of wool socks. Even walking on the snow for a couple of hours at fifty below zero, our feet felt as cozy and dry as if propped by a fire.

The other luxury was the cold air itself. At forty below it was delicious. When one first went outdoors there was a gasp to get it down past one's throat, then the invitation to breathe more and deeper. Each breath was delicious; you thirsted for more. It was a beauty known only to the buried lungs, in their own terms.

Like the darkness and the cold, the snow here differed from that in the States. Or even in Fairbanks, in central Alaska. It seemed never to snow and always to snow. Whenever I went outdoors, a steady fan of tiny snow was passing the red field light that burned high on a post back of the wanigan. Drifts changed and climbed. New snow cleaned old snow.

The drifts did not crust, they hardened. This was igloo-building snow. It sounded light and hollow underfoot, like plaster-of-paris. Mukluks were all one needed for walking on it—not skis or snowshoes. An Eskimo laughed at a picture Cris showed him of an igloo in the Colorado Rockies. "Snow soft!" he said.

It is *lèse-majesté* to say it, but the aurora was often only a smear. Yet one night when I went out to the wolves, beyond them, down the darkness to the snow, swirled thin greenish curtains, their texture moving.

And one memorable midnight when Cris and I were out walking suddenly all heaven broke loose. Always the "lights" move, but slowly. Now they moved with intense speed, in iridescent whorls. The whorls spun but not as wheels turn. They revolved by jumps. It was as exciting as tremendous noise. But in silence the terrific movement occurred. Matter showed its strange properties—it was here, then there, and there was nothing in between.

It was all over in a minute. If I had so much as stooped to tie a mukluk thong I should have missed it. In that respect it was like all wild nature; there is no announcement, no retrospect—the eagle stoops to tease the white rams on the crag, they flee; if you see it, you see it.

The Big Dark was so strange and dominant, and we worked so busily and hard, keeping warm, fed and clean and keeping the wolves from being too unhappy in their captivity, that the thought of Christmas seemed remote—like the glitter in department stores a thousand miles away.

An incident purely arctic turned our thoughts to Christmas. We stood silent in the black shadow of the wanigan one night, watching two arctic foxes play. In the starlight and snow-light their immense eyes looked black. Except for their deep white fur they seemed no larger than kitties.

One fox lay down and moved himself ahead merely by rolling zestfully from shoulder to shoulder; this scooted him along. He evidently liked the drag and feel of the snow on his furry belly. The other fox smelled some frozen morsel; his little paws flew faster than a hand could scratch, digging for it.

Then the foxes became very stern. Brownie had barked off somewhere and they answered—menacingly, from their point of view. One barked, but the sound was only like a very small dog barking softly at the bottom of a deep well. The other growled; it sounded like a tomcat purring.

They were the lightest things on their feet we ever saw. A cat is light but he makes preparations for his effort—crouches, then springs. The foxes made no preparation. They did not bounce, they did not spring. They "floated." Touch, touch, touch, like soap bubbles.

Suddenly the fairy foxes froze. From the level darkness came the sound of a man singing, "It Came upon the Midnight Clear." Somewhere out there an Eskimo was passing with his dog team, taking dead foxes from his traps. One of the doomed foxes near us bounded like a feather to the top of a drift and poised, its delicate head reared. The other fox rose to its hind legs and actually hopped a few feet toward the song of peace: "It Came upon the Midnight Clear."

The landing of a plane in a lonely arctic storm is a demonic event. It is not like a landing on even a storm-swept airstrip in the States. The storm rules the dim world. Black and roaring, yet hardly heard in the storm, the plane rushes down, half vanishing in steam and prop-raised snow and arctic twilight. How did it find and dare this markless spot in storm? The beam seems an irrelevant abstraction. The plane rushes into the reality, a demonic apparition.

In a storm landing like that, our Christmas mail arrived. Plywood Cris had ordered was whipped away as it was unloaded. It took two men two hours to find it in the darkness and storm. When they picked up a piece, Cris told me, "It blew straight out—like holding one end of a stretcher."

In the mail were gifts of perfume. Before retiring I rubbed some on my forehead. I was awakened in the night by a hard, hairy jaw stroking my forehead. Then a wolf's chest began rolling over my face. Cris got the light on. It was Trigger, in ecstasies over the perfume.

I felt startled and put upon, but Cris was interested. "Get some of that stuff for me," he said.

We perfumed our hands and let the wolves roll on them. Lady forgot herself and came clear out from the den. The wolves' eyes flashed, their white teeth showed. "I like to see 'm enjoying themselves," said Cris. "How much does that stuff cost? Let's get a pint for the wolves."

We tried other perfumes on them later. For the record the wolves preferred Chantilly.

Cris gave me my most treasured Christmas present, a barrel of fuel oil. He hooked it to a fanless, noiseless stove in an unused barn of a building. After a day or two the room was warm enough so I could sit in my parka against the stove jacket and read or write letters with icy fingers. My ears had a holiday from the roar of our own stove.

We were safe. Nothing was required of us that we could not meet with springing vigor. We might come home to find Lady had got scared and leaped in through the window, leaving it open, and the front end of the wanigan was two feet deep in snow, the bed half drifted over. Only inconvenience was involved.

But around us was the inexorable fact of one of the mightiest forces on the planet, the darkness and cold of arctic night. From time to time like the somber stroke of a great bell the reverberation of danger sounded.

At the native hospital in the village a nurse and I paused by the bed of an old Eskimo who had lost his way home one night from a village toilet in the middle of the street. He looked up at the nurse with the wide, merry smile that seems *de rigueur* in Eskimo culture. "Cut!" he said. He held up the frozen hand and sliced the other across it. The hand was not repulsive. The blackened bones stuck neatly beyond the flesh.

The nurse smiled and shook her head. As we walked on she said, "We don't dare operate. All the doctors in the Territory would be on our necks." There had been no resident doctor at Barrow for months. The nurses *de facto* diagnosed and treated syphilis, measles, etc., but dared not admit they had any notion of what the maladies were.

"Fly him to Fairbanks?"

"You have to go too high to get over the Brooks Range. He has heart trouble."

One noon twilight a peculiar-looking plane touched down in front of the wanigan. It was a squat gray triphibian—motors high, tail fins jutting aloft, a ski dangling from each wing-tip float. One word was painted black on the nose and by the pilot's window: RESCUE. The plane was from the 74th Air Rescue Squadron, on search for a pilot who had disappeared in his small plane on a flight from Bettles Field to Barrow. After his plane was found abandoned on the ice of the Beau-

fort Sea, the interstices between busyness were shadowed for
me by the knowledge that a man was walking alone in the
darkness on the polar ice. The temperature ran fifty below.
Soon my thoughts turned to him as to a dead man. But on the
afternoon of the day the search was to be ended, the flight
engineer, looking down through the haze of ice crystals in the
twilight, thought he glimpsed a dark figure. Jeul Thibedeau
was found. He, too, was in the hospital awhile. There were
offsets on his fingers where the flesh sloughed, but amputation
was not necessary.

The storms were worse than ever but the wolves stayed out
in them. It broke my heart. Curled each alone, thus not icing
the other's fur, mounds of mere survival in darkness and
storm, they lay with no lee from winds across the snow. It
was not that they were indifferent to comfort, but that they
valued safety more. As their fear of things outdoors grew less,
it seemed safer to them—at least more tranquil, demanding
less watchfulness—than the wanigan. I did not know it took
nearer three years than three months for a wolf to learn to
sleep peacefully on the bunk while I washed dishes.

Sometimes we dragged them in and tried to tranquilize them
so they would stay. We pressed the cold out of their fur so
the slight warmth of the wanigan could enter quickly—in case
they did go right out again. We offered them reindeer meat
from Nunivak Island.

But the wolves did a new thing: they tossed one's hand away
with the muzzle—a controlling gesture. "They don't doubt
they can control you," said Cris. "It's not enough for them
to know they don't want it; they have to let you know."

Trigger would have stayed in; he loved luxury. He stepped
up and down the aisle, congratulating himself in small pleased
sounds. But when Lady left, he left too.

One day Cris started outdoors while they were in. Lady
actually cocked her head with the sharpness of her attention,

watching to see how he operated the door bolt. As soon as he left she took the bolt in her teeth and tried to open it. But it was set on a slant to prevent accidental opening when the wanigan was in motion in a cat train; the slant defeated her. Next she turned her attention to the high door window, stripping off with her teeth the adhesive holding the broken Plexiglass.

Trigger stood waiting to follow her. I stood between him and the door, coaxing him to stay. He tossed my hand away with a brief "curse" and looked at me with so clear an awareness that only I stood between him and the door that I preferred to stand aside. It was only a matter of moments anyway till Lady would get herself out. I opened the door.

Change was afoot. Color was coming back to the Arctic. In the noon twilights the snow was blue-dappled. To the north, the thin air had a tinge of true lavender. To the south, color glowed for hours along the flat white horizon—sunrise-and-set color. The last of January the sun rose. Not dramatically. It rolled low in horizon mists, sending pale gold light over the snow.

A grim arctic thing happened, common enough but new to us. A lead opened offshore. (A lead is an opening in the ice.) Black "smokes" went up from it against the rosy sky like smokes from a row of bonfires. Eskimo seal hunters were trapped on the far side of the lead, in danger of being carried to sea.

Sternly the Eskimo, Ned Nusinginya, told me, "A man can do *some*thing. You don't have to stand still. And you don't have to run. You can walk along the edge of the lead. There are floating ice cakes and sometimes they have points, or they jam. You can jump onto them, work your way across." The seal hunters saved themselves in this way.

Change was ahead for the wolves and us. One thing we longed for—that wild Lady might taste freedom once more before she died. (Freedom meant more to her than to Trigger; she took captivity harder.) It seemed impossible. Then the impossible happened: we were to return to our old cracker-box in the Killik.

But there was a difficulty I dreaded. How would we load the wolves onto our chartered plane? They weren't pups now, in spirit or size either. Trigger weighed a hundred and ten pounds, Lady ninety. And we knew they would fight.

Cris thought the problem was solved when we obtained knockout pills. But the instructions gave us pause. "The wolves should go under in about an hour. The plane should start at once." Our flight would be long; the wolves must not wake up before we unloaded them. Could we control the promptness of departure?

"The sleeping wolves must be kept warm." How could we manage that with our slight matériel when we laid them onto the snow in the Killik? Could we drag those heavy bodies up the steep rough mesa to the pen? "They may be slightly crazed when they come to." Would they be permanently harmed in some way?

Cris decided not to use the pills. Instead he ordered muzzles and built a box to crate the wolves. As for getting muzzles onto the fighting wolves, that troubled him not at all. The wolves were more submissive with me. I was the mouse that must bell these cats.

The Hermann Nelson roared into its white canvas hood, warming the engine of our chartered Norseman—it was thirty-five below zero—when Cris called me outdoors to muzzle Trigger. With all his strength Cris held the fighting, terrified wolf, while between slashes of Trigger's fangs I tried to catch the muzzle over both jaws at once. I got it on and Trigger was dragged to the box.

I trembled as I waited to muzzle Lady. Trigger had fought with his strength; Lady would fight with her spirit. Cris held her. She reared on her hind legs, snatching at me. Never shall I forget her eyes. Greenish-opaque, they bulged with total black fierceness. I muzzled her and she too was dragged up to the box, snapped to a chain leading out through a hole in the back and dragged inside.

We flew across the white monotony of the deadly arctic slope, our part-Eskimo pilot to my admiration discerning the imperceptible courses of frozen, snow-covered rivers and keeping his way in unknown country at a hundred thirty miles an hour by sight and the map on my knees.

We were troubled when the Brooks Range appeared to the south to see that it was fogged in. We found and entered the Killik valley and flew "on the deck" between fog-hidden mountainsides. The pilot, used to the level arctic coast, got worried. Andy had flown a barrel of gas to our old camp and our pilot was to refuel there. But he might miss the turn-off up Easter Creek.

"We'd better turn back while we've still got gas to get somewhere," he said.

Anxiously I traded places with Cris, and he helped watch for landmarks and emerging mountainsides. (It was unthinkable to rehandle the wolves.)

The fog thinned. We flew up Easter Creek in sunshine, and over the little old crackerbox, still fresh and new-looking, on the mesa. With all my heart I wished we could parachute the wolves into their old pen beside it. I feared getting them out of their box and somehow dragging them fighting up the mesa.

The pilot gave us a tundra landing right at the foot of the mesa, to shorten backpacking distance for us. He gassed up, bobbed plane-shakingly off over the hummocks and rose away. We were alone in stillness among the sunny white mountains with our dunnage pile and box of wolves. It was only twenty below zero here.

The first thing Cris did was break trail to the crackerbox and start a fire. We ate lunch, then started down to get the wolves. I was trembling again. I knew I had only a minute or so to banish this fear; the wolves would know it if I was afraid. By good luck I thought of my real joy that they were soon to be free. Shakily I hung on to it.

Cris picked up one of the two chains lying out on the snow from the box. There was a growl from inside. I stood unprotected by the door and raised it. The wolf that came out, crouching and peering, was Trigger. I picked up the other chain and raised the door again. Lady came out, took one wild look around and—knew where she was! She dragged me up the trail so fast I was panting. "Wait, Lady," I begged.

It was hard to get the wolves' winter-rusted collars off. They managed half-bites through their humanely loose muzzles. The worst was that Lady's buckle had rusted shut and Cris had to haggle her leather strap off with his pocket knife while we both held her down with all our strength. When she felt herself free at last of the collar she had worn for four and a half months, she sat leaning against the fence half fainting.

We backpacked the meat and soft food from the dunnage pile up to the crackerbox, so the wolves would not be self-sufficient when released.

The next morning, in the gruff pleasant voice the wolves had always seemed to like, Cris sang out the old happy question, unused since November: "Want to go for a walk?" Free and collarless the wolves ran out onto the great tundra.

It was a beautiful arctic spring day. Wind rose in the afternoon but now it was still. The shadow off each hummock and mountain was the purest, softest blue; it mached the sky exactly. Fresh rabbit roads, patted eight inches wide, ran through the willows by the river. A "glacier" hump on the river was robin's-egg blue. There were ptarmigan nestle holes in the snow and the lace of ptarmigan trails. Ptarmigan themselves ran on fur-thick, pure-white legs.

Two hundred of them sunned like white statues on a white hillside and Lady with calm joy went up to raise them. The first strip of birds toddled ahead of the black wolf, then rose, and she trotted, not ran, back and raised the next strip. The last strip of ptarmigan just sat there.

As the four of us proceeded, each full of purpose and busyness, electric thrills of happiness went through me.

But would the wolves come home with us? This day they did.

Then one day they did not. "They took part of my life with them," Cris said. "But they were lonesome and bored: they missed the dogs at Barrow." Had they started across the desolate arctic slope to find them?

Whenever we went outdoors, our eyes searched the wide whiteness under blue-carved mountains not for first-returning caribou, but for a black and a blond wolf.

At twilight on the second day Cris had gone out for one more long sad look over the tundra when I heard him say very gently, "Why, Lady! Where's Trigger, Lady?" I ran out.

We "loved" Lady; she greeted us happily. But where was Trigger? Then here he came, from the direction of the pen, where he must have looked for food. We gave him the welcome of Lazarus.

After we had penned and feasted the wolves, irresistibly we went out one more time in the twilight to "love" them, and this time two mystifying things occurred. First, Lady, all by herself at one side of the pen, suddenly went into a perfect fit of elation. She bowed and smiled and raised her paw to the side. We stared.

Then Cris said, "I think they thought they were lost and she found the way home." Lady always led. "And now she thinks she's a regular little heroine!"

Next Trigger did something almost unique: he jumped on Lady. Wolves, unlike dogs, practically never fight. The fighting wolves reared up and came down on top of Cris, who scrambled from under. "I didn't want to be bottom dog in *that* pile!" he panted.

Now why that little scrap? It was over in a minute. Again Cris guessed. Trigger might have been set up over our big, unusual welcome to him and become jealous when we petted Lady.

A couple of nights later there was an omen of things to come. We were awakened about midnight by the wolves' howling. It was a new howl, one we had never heard before, and very probably the most beautiful animal sound in the world, the "call howl" of wolves.

The two voices changed incessantly, rising and falling, always chording, never in unison. The chord changed in minor thirds and fifths. Sometimes there was a long note from one while the voice of the other interwove around it. The notes were hornlike and pure. The wolves would break off suddenly and there would be listening silence. We were sure they heard the voices of other wolves at the margin of sound.

We lay listening, only the thin wall between, and I almost feared. Not real fear; I would have gone out to them without hesitation. But uncanny fear because of the wildness of the sounds. "It's wild and beautiful and eerie," whispered Cris.

There are many howls—the happy social howl, the mourning howl, the wild deep hunting howl, the call howl. All are beautiful. The wolf's voice is pure except when the wolf is crushed by despair. The only set pattern is that of the mourning howl. The others vary but the meaning is clear. Mountain men in the old West gathered valuable clues about movements of Indians and wild animals from the changeful voices of the wolves. Few humans now have ever heard the howl of a wolf and at that only the captive howl, like the howling of the slave dogs of the North.

On Tuesday morning, a week after their return, Trigger and Lady idled down to Cris. He was working at the dunnage pile and had no time to take them for a walk. They returned to the mesa top and played awhile but I too was busy, in the cabin. They left and did not return.

It was evil on top of the mesa. There were wind and eye-whipping fine snow. The next day there was a ground blizzard all over the country. Not on the mesa top, for that had been scoured bare. The mountain tops were visionary-looking from powder snow blowing off them. The tundra "traveled."

On Thursday I looked down at the misty wastes, still blowing, and wondered whether Trigger and Lady were down in that smother somewhere, trying to find their way home. Or striving northward on the deadly arctic slope. Or

The quints newly taken from their den.

The baby wolves are introduced to Trigger and Lady.

Lady was soon taking the pups for a walk. (She is bleaching and shedding—it's June.)

A baby wolf at the mouth of the den Cris dug for the pups.

Cris cuddles the baby wolves.

The pups liked to gnaw on his boots.

When Trigger returns from a night's hunt, the babies besiege his mouth for a handout.

The pups were affectionate with Trigger.

Caching food.

The first kill—a parka squirrel. Perfectly amicable but nobody dares to let go —or no meat.

The wolves returned over and over to old carcasses found on the tundra.

A favorite food, rich in calcium salts, was caribou antlers in velvet.

Wolves have a strong sense of property rights (someone encroached) but spats like this were rare and brief.

Lois and wolf pup.

Life with the wolf quints was less hectic after Cris made a feeding tray.

Lois calls "Meat!" and the wolves mob her for morsels.

The wolves liked to play in shallow water. "Water dogs."

Gnawing ice to quench thirst. There's an interval before the snow comes when ice provides the only liquid on the arid frozen tundra.

Mr. Arctic, and all the other wolves, liked to be "loved."

The only invitation the wolves needed to play piggyback was for Cris to kneel.

The expressive wolf face. Miss Tundra, gnawing a bone, catches sight of the being upon whom she has bestowed all her affection—the hostile dog Tootch.

Instantly her face and eyes are suffused with heart-melting affection.

The wolves idolized Tootch but were afraid to come close; the dog bit their muzzles. They were *moonstruck* over her.

Cris stands guard to keep Tootch from biting the affectionate wolves as they circle, courting the dog.

Wolves are "animals that look up." Miss Alatna directs the famous, impersonal wolf attentiveness on a bird in the air.

Wolf-raven fraternizing. A raven chose to play with the wolves, alighting beside them over and over, calling if their attention wandered. The two predators like each other's company.

The wolves liked to have a leader to take them "someplace"!

Mr. Barrow ahead, graceful Alatna, Miss Tundra—going places.

Chasing the leader, especially if he bore a trophy, was the favorite game.

Five-month-old wolves are interested in caribou but afraid of them.

Andy drops supplies, also a message in a roll of toilet paper.

But a wolf captures the message for a trophy.

Finis. The wolves, who have never had even a thread around their necks, must be chained and crated to be flown to the Crislers' home in Colorado.

trapped, for by now, traveling twenty miles in a night with ease, they could have reached the traplines of the Eskimos of Anaktuvuk Pass.

"If they have found Them," said Cris, meaning the wild wolves, "it's hard to see how They could resist them. They're so courteous and winning." It was true that there was a kind of wolf courtesy about them. We had stood watching them in the pen and Cris had commented, "They have their own little courtesies and darings and jokes." It had been another of his true insights. Wolves have that hint of ceremoniousness.

He tried to cheer me. "You still have one wolf! Teaching there at the university before we were married, you could never have imagined being way up here in the Arctic, crying over two lost wolves."

I did not smile. Seriously he went on. "We've been very free from grief, living the way we do. Big families have it you know. Dying all the time."

It did not seem irrelevant when he told the somber story of his Grandmother Bruce's brother, a Northern prisoner in the Civil War. They got a letter from him at the war's end, saying he had been wounded but was on his way home. They never heard from him again. But all her life Grandmother Bruce looked at every stranger whose buggy stopped at the farm to see if it was her brother.

Friday morning was clear and zero. There was the unearthly beauty of an "ice storm." In the shadow off the mesa, sunlit particles stormed and scintillated; they touched your cheek.

Toward evening I forced myself to start down to the dunnage pile to bring up a load. At the foot of the mesa there was a touch on my hand. I looked down. It was Trigger!

Whimpering with emotion, he spiraled to the snow, giving me the full wolf greeting. I knelt, laughing and crying, for the absence of Lady was ominous. "Where's Lady, Trigger?"

The wolf growled, rose and trotted up the familiar path I had thought no wolf would tread again. But instead of going to the pen, he halted on the mesa rim and gazed at the white ridge to the north, just across the draw.

"Cris!" I shouted, fearing the wolf would drift away in the direction he looked toward before I could get to him.

Cris came without parka or mittens. "Where's Lady, Trigger?" I heard him ask tenderly as I ran to the cabin for meat to bait the wolf into the pen. I brought it and Trigger took it from me gently, as always, but he moved away from us to eat it.

"He's a different Trigger," said Cris. His demeanor was grave, preoccupied. Never before had he kept his tail curled under his belly; it had always hung loose, unregarded. He jumped a little if we touched a paw.

"He's been running," Cris said. Frost was white around his muzzle. We looked at the wolf intently; he knew what had happened to Lady. Was she in a trap? Had he stayed with her a long time? It was too late now to take him and try to find her. Already, across the lake, only the tops of the mountains were sunlit; their bases stood in blue shadow. The gold light was dimming on the white ridge Trigger watched.

Cris said, "I'll go in the morning. Take food—and Andy's gun."

"You may have to kill her."

"Yes."

We got Trigger into the pen easily after he had eaten. Cris, wrapped up now, sat on the snow and Trigger went to him. I kept my hands off his fur, for he was looking into Cris's face and eyes, both heads on the same level. He made a small sound and his soft lip sides trembled. He offered Cris's face a quick lick and endeavored to sit down closer against him than he could get. I started into the cabin.

Cris called me. "Lady's coming! I can't see if she limps or not."

Like a black post on top of the ridge she stood surveying home. I called and she came to the brink but stopped there and lay down. Cris was already down in the draw on his way to her, perhaps to help her in if she was hurt. He told me later she sidled and skittered down the steep hard snow to him and was so pleased to see him that she wriggled and twisted and smiled.

Meanwhile I was having a bad time with Trigger. He was trying to get out. It had scared him when he saw Lady stop; maybe she wasn't coming home. He made a determined effort to get out such as he had never made before; it was knowing and self-helpful. He knew he couldn't make it around the gate. He left that side of the pen, though it looked toward the north ridge. He gave his attention to the back of the pen. It was weaker and the wolf knew it, had the knowledge stored up so that he never wasted a moment on the strong part. Cris had cut a new door there, straight into the entryway. Trigger looked up studyingly at Cris's toggles, then made a gesture I had not seen before—the wolf observation leap. He leaped up perpendicular, like a man, and descended with apparent slowness.

I hurried into the cabin for rope to tie him and to my surprise found him crowding in with me, with none of his usual hesitation at the door. He made straight for the windows. Standing on hind legs, forepaws on the counter, he edged clear along it, looking with fierce purposefulness at the windows. In some casual-seeming glance he had stored away the knowledge of possible exits here.

To get Lady into the pen without letting Trigger out took both of us. She did not greet me. She was wolfishly hungry and, after eating curled up in her usual hollow, working on her paws. As the moisture from licking froze instantly, she laid her tail around her nose and the old trap-hurt paw and went on working at it in this seclusion. She growled when I petted her—a very businesslike wolf, resting up to go out, she had no doubt, and join Them in the morning.

For by now a strange thing was clear to us. From every move our wolves made, we knew the wild wolves were on that ridge, just out of sight. Trigger and Lady must have come home as the wildings passed near, or more likely by their assured bearing had convinced Them they knew where to find a square meal and had led the wildings here.

Trigger still expected Them to follow him in. To our surprise, for the first time in his life he was not satisfied with Lady alone. He sat by the fence, still looking over at the ridge. The soft furred part under his black nose tip gathered in minute sensitiveness incessantly, inquiring of the air for Them.

"If those other wolves would follow into the pen," said Cris, "he'd be perfectly happy."

Cris's eyes were full of sunlight. We gave each other happy glances but busy with the wolves had no time for a kiss. Our eyes, though, laughed at ourselves for grieving while the wolves had been having the time of their lives.

"This is a funny experience," said Cris, "to have a pair of wolves that go and live with wild wolves and then come back and live with us."

We thought of it the first thing the next morning. We lay whispering, not to let the wolves know we were awake. It was five o'clock, the stillness benign, and out the shaded windows rose the sunny white mountains, the shadows on them so frail, so nothing.

"Trigger would be completely satisfied if you would go out and join the pack," I said.

Cris was proud and touched by Trigger's greeting the night

before. "Thinks I'm kind of a decrepit, immobile wolf but he's attached to me."

He went on slowly. "Our relation with the wolves is the most understanding, kind and desirable that's possible between humans and animals. We've never scolded or taken a stick or thrown a rock. Only confined them against their will sometimes. And yet they'd rather have their freedom and be hungry. It's true of humans too. When you have to pay freedom for security that's against human nature and it's against wild nature."

There could be only one sequel to Cris's thought. A few days later he propped open the gate of the pen for good. From now on we lived with free wolves.

For a while Trigger was tied to an old habit. He arose from wherever he lay—the wolves now sought lees from wind, or sunny spots, in general conforming to comfort—and stalked gravely to a certain corner of the pen to urinate.

He started a new custom. Every evening as Cris sat on the watch box, Trigger, waking from his nap before leaving for the night's hunt, came to Cris, raised his long head and cream-colored neck and, leaning against him, "talked." "M-m. L-l. R-r. Um-moom. Oooo."

It will be forever impossible to convey what it was like. Anyone else would assimilate it with his idea of a dog's talk. Neither in sound, way of delivering nor intent was it like a dog sound. The utterance was extraordinarily interesting and pleasing. It was long and varied, inflected expressively, a hoarse mellow wowing. The wolf's voice resembled Cris's. He looked up at Cris genially with bright friendly calm eyes.

Cris did not pet him much but what little attention he did give, Trigger seemed to feel as brotherly. The wolf was content if Cris's hand rested on his ruff. But if Cris paid a little attention to Lady, Trigger took his pants leg to get him back.

It was borne in on us that what the wolf wanted was for Cris to go hunting with him. As he went off, he would look back over his shoulder at Cris.

The wolves were often gone overnight, sometimes for a day or two, but never again for four days. We took it less hard though we knew their risks. At least we were sure now they would never get lost. Only one more time were we really upset.

We came home from a walk one day to find Trigger had returned alone from his hunt. Lady was gone—the little black wolf so passionate, determined and whole. Had she gone to find the wild wolves? Had Trigger been kicked out?

The corners of his mouth hung slack. He tramped recklessly in and out of the cabin for handouts, with none of his usual shrinking at the door, filling his belly to ease his heart. When he lay down, tired out, he still could not rest. Every minute or two his head came up with a jerk, for one more somber look eastward over the tundra.

When I went out once to his and Lady's old favorite lounging place, where he lay with a bone, the wolf brought his bone and dropped it at my elbow, to lie close to me gnawing, as he used to do with Lady.

We induced him to come for a walk. Over by the lake he picked up a piece of hide he and Lady had often played with, and stood holding it, looking far around with searching, sun-filled eyes. It was Lady who had made the game, the racing and the joy.

That afternoon I started out to offer him my company again. A sober little black wolf was walking along the path in the sun. Our spark-plug, Lady! So usual-looking I could hardly orient for an instant. She turned and simply stood looking at me till I gave our recognition sign; then she ran up gladly.

By this time Trigger's big tawny head reared over the willow bushes, looking to see if what he heard was true, the wind being from him to us. Lady went toward him. And what did he do? He ran away! Piqued because she had chosen this first separation of their lives? Or challenging?

She followed and courted him. "Can't she play in the most sweet and tantalizing way!" murmured Cris. Shoulders down, head tilted bewitchingly, she looked up at him, laid an arm across his neck. From a crouch she made a sweeping leap right over him, all one gracious fullness and softness even to the tip of her bushy tail.

And he stood taut and tail-wagging and challenging, like a male dog. The corners of his lips were firmly elevated. He did not growl once at me the rest of the day—his heart was "good." He even surprised me with one of his demure little games, coming up as I sat on the watch box—flattered, I thought he wanted me to pet him—and snatching the handkerchief from my shirt pocket.

And then of all things, when we went out at evening, he was gone. Lady came up and whimpered a little. "She's had her fling, she doesn't want to leave again so soon," said Cris. But leave she did.

"Think you've got'm pegged," said Cris, "and they do something different. Think Trigger has decided to stay—leaves Lady, comes home. And then when Lady comes and wants to stay, he leaves."

"While you're answering that," said I, "answer this one: why did he run from Lady? And why do they just stand and stare at us when they first come home?"

"What keeps coming to my mind is this," Cris said. "Do people know *anything* about wild animals except skull measurements! It's only since they've been completely free, here in their own country, that we're beginning to learn much about them—their real selves."

An evening later the prodigals came home. Cris saw them coming and had us sit down in a level spot to receive them.

Up the mesa side they came, toiling as fast as they could,

Lady's ears forward, then back—first a look, then a smile and redoubled climbing. Both made first for Cris. Tongues flapping to kiss his face, both wolves reaching for his face, both circling as close around his shoulders as they could get, jumping over each other. Trigger's tail wagging, Lady's rippling and spiraling. Next the ceremonious wolves came to me and greeted me.

Then Lady led out to the Dutch door; they were hungry. Cloud-gray and calm gold eyes watched Cris chop a bone.

"You never know what mood they'll be in," said Cris. Silvery gleams were in his eyes, compressed by laughing cheeks. "They're mystifying. Guess they always will be, as long as we know them."

Unanswered but out of mind was that old question of ours: will the wolves turn on us unpredictably sometime? They had turned on us a couple of times but both times had been predictable. That question in due time was to be answered fully and forever. But now it was superseded by others. Will they go off for good someday with Them, the wild wolves? Shall we ever see them meet the wildies? Might they even bring the wild wolves home?

18   First Kill

Spring began with a bang the day after we returned to the Killik. We had arrived here from Point Barrow at the exact turn of the season. All through the Big Dark the snow must

have lain as it fell, knee-deep only. Now the gales of spring
and summer started. Snow drifted. The roof blew off the
dugout toilet. The tarp threatened to leave the roof and we
weighted it, not with stones, which we could not get, but with
five-gallon cans of Blazo. The cabin thundered and jarred to
the period of my windpipe, which jarred too.

The previous year we had seen the close of spring. This
year we were to see each solitary first-arriving animal, flower
and storm, until the great tide of spring should pour beyond
all itemizing over the tundra. We seemed to have no inner
life these bright changing days, only the outer, which rushed
us along in labor and wonder and homely detail.

Spring came not evenly but in a series of waves or climaxes.
The first was the small, magical one of dehibernation. We
awoke the morning of April 9 to see, on a south-facing snow
bank at the foot of the mesa, a small animal sitting dark on the
snow, the first parka squirrel in the whole valley to dehiber-
nate.

He acted about like a marmot on its first morning out—
dopey, staying near the hole he had just made in emerging,
soon going in. Wisely had he chosen his dehibernation day.
Passing up a premature warm spell a couple of weeks before,
he had come out on this first good day after storms.

The next morning there he was again, this time a good six
feet from his hole, which he had now enlarged. A little black
pillar, he sat on his haunches, bending gracefully around to
look without moving his pedestal. Gazing about.

A curious situation—to sleep for six months, then waken
alone in an empty, pleasant, promising world. Look as he
would, no other of his kind was on top of the shining floor
of the valley—yet.

The great climax of spring was beyond our imagining. Indeed, we had no doubt we knew it perfectly. It was the spring
return of the caribou and that we had seen the year before.

At first the land was empty of the great wanderers. Then

on March 29 appeared two bands of eight each, trudging westward. A few days later Trigger and Lady brought forty caribou down from the mountains south of the lake. We first noticed them as they stood by the willows on this side of the river, looking back as if for their pursuers. A few started this way, then that.

Then out on the wide blank white of the lake came two small figures stretched horizontal, the wolves. The caribou turned with one accord and fled. It was a beautiful thing to see. In the low sun the fawn-colored bodies swerved lightly, as a unit, over the snow, running grouped. They sped up the mountainside, bent to their migration course and away.

Trigger stopped on a mound in the marsh and looked upward. Lady kept running but stopped and the wolves walked together. "I'm more convinced than ever," Cris said, "that unless the caribou is sick or disabled the wolf hasn't a chance."

From now on, bands of caribou passed through daily. We still expected nothing. And then, the last week of April, the unearthly spectacle began—the spring return of the caribou directly over the Brooks Range. All week they poured through, a thousand a day, coming not in the column formation of fall, but in the spring formation, in countless bands, on a wide front.

They unrolled fabulous tracks—down from the mountaintops, midway along savage steeps, around mountain bases, descending to cross the Killik, then up to the tops of the highest peaks west beyond the river.

Tracks plunged from the skyline down past the end of a crag. A track girded the side of a steep ravine in one wary slender line. Tracks sprayed wide on the great mountain paw we called the Hippopotamus, where the caribou ran carelessly down.

Any time I stepped outdoors I saw new bands coming. We were on the north side of the flow; they were passing on the mountains to the south, across the lake. I saw them coming for two miles back, each band like a string of pearl- and fawn-colored beads strung on the blue track line of their own shadows. Implacably each lead cow steered the course onward into the mountains.

It gave me a feeling of "break-off" with the planet. Those caribou over there in that stern azure-and-white world were as if on another planet. The long line of white mountains, deepened with blue shadows, the shelf of high tundra along their bases, my awareness from our island in the sky of the whole, mighty, majestic setting—all made the pretty living forms not "frame fillers" but rather the heightening and gratification of the whole. I thought, "Now the caribou have nothing more to show us."

During that week we went southward up the Killik one cold sunny day on a den hunt, a project I will explain presently, and as far as we went toward April Creek, bands were coming down from our left, crossing the river ice and going away up the mountains to our right.

That ice crossing worried them. One band after a bad crossing sprinkled the snow for a hundred yards with black pellets; every member of the band must have had a bowel movement, a sign of tension.

One band waited ten minutes while their lead cow studied the crossing. She teetered part way across, then stood still; it was a bad place. When she finally gave up and turned to go back, her hind leg skated aside like a fan opening. She walked down the bank, looking for a better place, perhaps where a sand bar would shorten the distance on ice.

But her band still stood there, governed not by docility but by the big slow pulse of danger, sun and cold. It swelled in them; slowly they turned and followed her.

Across the baby-blue, snow-swirled ice came a black-looking grizzly. Unarmed, we watched attentively. He disappeared up a canyon and a few minutes later out of it stormed three hundred caribou on a dead run. They took the ice crossing recklessly, where they came to it. None fell. It was when they went slowly that one might slip, tangle its legs and fall.

We broke through the crust unexpectedly, to hip or knee, and once five caribou did the same. We thought they would perish. Nearing a rock promontory above us, the lead cow and main file went up and over—the hard, safe way, where the wind-blown, sun-exposed snow would be shallow. The foolish five took the easy way, straight ahead, and in the inevitable drifts below the rock they floundered and sank to their bellies, but struggled and jumped and got out.

"The empty dead Arctic!" thought I, following Cris. There was the wheet of a redpoll, the sweet comment of the many-voiced camp robber waiting on a bare willow to watch us curiously as we passed. A parka squirrel watched too, standing like a black finger on the snow.

There were tracks of all kinds of animal, even of a solitary wolverine. Wolverines need a large range in order to make a living; most predators do. Unlike wolves, they have a solitary kind of temperament. Hence, wherever we went in the Arctic we found one wolverine only.

Never underestimate tracks. They give a pleasing and populous effect. After we came to the tracks of three wolves, I watched, hoping Trigger and Lady might join us, tickled to death as we would be too, to meet us away out here in the wilds. They were off on one of their hunts.

The sun was behind the mountains when we neared home, Cris ahead as usual. From the willows by the river came a negligible gray-tan animal, gaunt as a fishhook from famine. Trigger, bee-lining to Cris!

He curled to the snow at Cris's feet in the full wolf greeting, whimpering and whimpering with emotion. For the hundredth time I thought, "That animal loves Cris." It was we, not the wolf, who ended the love feast. Then Trigger, empty as so often after a vain hunt, went ahead and dug up a frozen, cached ptarmigan of his and lay gnawing.

The joy of his return gave me regardless wings. I had felt almost too tired to drag but now I sped up the white rope of the trail, embossed above the snow, and lightheartedly prepared hot milk for the three of us before starting supper. Then here came the little thick-wooled, rusty-black wolf too.

She had a surprising lot of dusty cream color on her now. Both wolves were bleaching in the always-sun. Trigger looked vanishing-pale on snow; the silvery light on his fur blended with that on the snow. Both wolves now had fire-red ears.

Cris as usual had a main photographic project in view for this season. He wanted to find a wolf den and photograph the pups. There was no time to lose. It was true that the pups would not even be born until the middle of May, and he would not attempt to photograph them until June. But arctic snow vanishes fast and before it did he must, if possible, find den signs—tracks leading toward a chosen den site.

We had no luck the day we went down the Killik; it was dead country indeed—not even a fox track. But two pleasant incidents happened, one of them downright flabbergasting. The first was Lady's joy at the first warm thawed clay bank of the year. She scampered silly. Chest to ground, paws wide, ears back, she darted and broke direction like foolish. She actually turned a somersault.

About one o'clock Cris decided to start home. He did a one-eighty without pausing but after a hundred yards stopped to take sandwiches from the knapsack on my back. It was too cold to sit down to eat.

At this, Trigger, who had run silently with Lady all morning, came directly to Cris, looked up into his face and made a brief decisive statement; he "spoke." Then he turned away.

We looked at each other completely baffled. Then Cris stammered the only explanation we have ever thought of. "He's so mysterious and sure of himself . . . Anyway it was something definite. . . . I think maybe he approved of our going home."

On the way home a raven picked us up and followed along in the blue. The wolves were jumping for bites of our crackers and peanut butter. In purest, madcap "cosmic gaiety" I called imperiously, "Here, raven!" and threw him a bite. I knew he would not take it.

We had luck beyond our dreams the day we den-hunted up Easter Creek. We found a wolf "road." It led north up the sheep hills and south far up the great tundra slopes to the pass toward April Creek. At that end of the road Cris believed there would be a den. We began preparations for the den hunt.

By June, when he would start, the river would be broken up and in flood. So Cris built a boat, using plywood scraps from the building of the crackerbox. He whittled a paddle for it, but that was for emergencies; he intended to pull the boat across the current hand over hand along an anchored rope. He anchored the rope on each side of the river to posts of the Arctic—bundles of willow withes held upright in monuments of rocks.

Meanwhile there occurred an event we dreaded but that was bound to happen—our wolves' first caribou kill. Would they be fiercer with us after that? Would they even return to us, once they knew themselves able and self-sufficient? The kill occurred near the east end of the lake. Cris took the camera and we went over.

The wolves were clearing spots on the biggest part of the carcass, the belly. They tore out clumps of fur and shook them from their teeth. Trigger applied himself to one spot. Lady wasted efforts here and there.

Cris went up to them and Trigger made a button of his nose among bared fangs.

Cris manned the camera and ordered, "Get him to do that again."

Distrustfully I approached the wolves and kill. Trigger seized my instep and held it. "He feels he's just being firm with you," stated Cris. "He's pretty gentle at that. I don't want to scold him. I don't like to scold an instinct too much. Let'm feel their full emotions, not have to suppress them."

Suddenly the wolf left the carcass, lay down on a bit of thawed turf and thrust his nose into it. Cris guessed his trouble. He pretended to play with the wolf, spotted a splinter of bone shoved down beside a tooth and, brushing his gloved hand across Trigger's mouth as if in play, pulled it out with a dexterity I admired and could never have matched.

When we returned to the crackerbox we were still anxious: would the wolves ever come home? It wasn't long before they came—not for food but just to be with us and at home.

The ordeal of the first kill was safely over for us. But a change there was in the wolves. Cris summed it up. "A wolf has more authority after he's made a kill. If there's a situation he doesn't like, he feels he can do something about it."

For two days Trigger and Lady lived the lives of young gods. They ate all they wanted on the kill. They raced on the snowfields above it. We laughed with joy—and envy—to see their snow play. They pitched recklessly down steep banks, tackled each other. Lady somersaulted, head, neck and back. She slid ten feet on her side, biting Trigger's leg. Their eyes were bright with happiness. They panted, snatched snow, watched passing caribou. They climbed far up the mountains, then sailed down and down over terraces and banks, to lie and eat again.

"This is the way Lady always thought things ought to be," said Cris. "She always thought if she could just get loose she could make it this way. I'm glad they had a whole kill to themselves this once." (He referred to our guess that they might have shared the wildies' kills.)

There was one thing that at first Trigger resented. A kill is public domain and wolves are public servants when they make one. This situation was new to Trigger; he was not used to contending with ravens and eagles for food. Once we saw him heading for home, bringing along a caribou leg and shoulder. It was quite a sight.

The wolf trotted along the white river, carrying his load crosswise in his jaws. Behind him frisked Lady. Every few minutes he laid down his burden to rest himself. Finally he abandoned it. A fox found it the next morning and dragged it into the willows, as much seclusion as a fox could hope for. Once we saw Lady, passing by, run over and toss it, big as it was, into the air a few times from sheer high spirits.

The ducal ravens disliked wolves interfering with them. They liked to sit unmolested at the kill. Sometimes they dived the wolves. But that was a transient stage.

I was getting breakfast one morning when I heard Cris laughing, out on the watch box. I ran out. For a minute I stared, incredulous, then laughed too. What I beheld was a Grimm's fairytale situation.

Trigger stood down on the river, his back toward the bank. He was wagging his tail and watching a raven hopping around him. Finally it hopped right across in front of his nose. Four more ravens joined it, alighting near the wolf. They were initiating the young wolf into the fraternity of the lonely tundra. He stood and turned and stepped gently among them, wagging his tail. When Lady ran down from the kill she was rougher and the ravens flew up.

Now at last we understood an incident that had puzzled us long ago. In the Olympic Mountains in Washington State we had watched a coyote stroll in among a flock of sitting ravens. The birds hopped carelessly about; they did not fly. The only guess we could make then was a conventional one, that the coyote slyly planned a kill. Now the Grimm's fairy-tale facts of the wilds had provided us with the real and wonderful explanation.

Many a time after this we saw wolves and ravens fraternize. Why had the ravens—which, according to Dr. Konrad Lorenz, have the highest mental development of all birds— chosen to teach friendliness to the wolves? Of course the wolves helped them. Both are predators or scavengers. Wolves make kills; ravens eat on them. And it is remotely possible that ravens help wolves. Circling over a dead caribou they could reveal its location.

But to us it looked as if the ravens and wolves just liked each other's company; it pleased them. Maybe it entertained them. "Maybe they get lonesome," said Cris. It is lonely on the big tundra. A fabulous incident is told by Mrs. Olaus Murie. A raven liked to nestle in the box with her Siberian wolfhound and puppies; it was smothered accidentally.

There was a hint of things to come at the kill one day. Cris went over to photograph two shy eagles working on it. They flew away. But while he was still there, Lady picked up a bone, brought it and laid it by his foot. Then she stood over it, wagging her tail. Cris bent to pick it up but she growled and cautiously he straightened up. Still the wolf stayed there, looking up at him. So he bent again and took the bone, and this time she did not growl. Uncertainly he said, "Did you bring me a bone, Lady?"

It was a statement of one of the most awesome themes of

the wilds, feral generosity. We did not recognize it yet. But we did recognize that Lady had followed to the dot a pattern Trigger had followed once. He had found a frozen ptarmigan in the willows. He lay gnawing it. Lady lay watching, now and then giving a quick lick of her saliva or sliding her paw irresistibly toward the bird. "As if she can't see the deadline, has to feel for it!" said Cris. "Touching it is like touching a live wire!" Trigger would snatch and growl, then gnaw again.

But presently, when he had eaten over half of the bird, he rose, carried the carcass and laid it a foot from Lady's nose. Then he waited beside it, in order to snap, once only, as she delicately took it.

"She knew she was supposed to have it," Cris said. "She waited very patiently. And she didn't grab when he gave it to her."

It was spring all right. The lantern was put away for the summer. Things left touching the window did not freeze to it. A terrific blow followed by a hailstorm brought the caribou down off the mountains. It was time anyway. Ridges and high slopes thaw or blow clear earlier than low places. But the valleys were thawing now. The Killik marshes were brown and caribou were drifting back from west or northwest to graze here a few days.

Things were easier for the caribou now. They had a little fat along their spines. Their tissues weren't famine-blue; we had noticed that on the kill. They even had a little play in them. Madcap young cows rushed down a bank into the herd, startling them. They stood on hind legs and playfully dashed their front feet at each other. A third "climax" of spring was at hand.

For over a week now the ptarmigan flocks had been broken up. Their sweet courtship voices, used once a year, filled the air. On the evening of May 1 we noticed a cock strut before a hen.

The next morning was beautiful and bright. The wolves' fur was warm as they lay, breathing fast, in the sun—the inescapable sun of the Arctic. The cabin was still except for the tick of the travel clock. For days there had been no silence day or night, but the huff of wind and flame in the stove, the shatter-chatter of Flex-o-glass, the wuff of wind incessantly around the cabin. Now one's astonished ears sat congratulating themselves. This was zero decibels.

Before we got up we heard the excited, cheerful chatter of the ptarmigans. As Cris sat on the watch box looking the world over while I got breakfast, I heard him chuckle. "Cock's out here with two hens," he called. "One ran in front of him to be chased. Other one ran and stopped and did the hula hula. He took out after her."

After breakfast as Cris stepped out the Dutch door in cap and down jacket to leave, I followed. Our eyes met, smiling. "It's a wonderful life," I said, meaning all the activity and pleasure around us—the busy ptarmigan, the wolves home from a trip, fresh caribou trails in the snow on the mountains.

After he was gone I myself sat on the watch box and observed another ptarmigan triangle. What gave depth and sparkle to my amusement was neither anthropomorphizing nor its salutary corrective, "fero-morphizing," but gay greeting to the life that flows through all alike.

The cock chased Hen One, leaving Hen Two behind. She began purring. He turned his head to listen, turned himself and ran after her. She circled, fluffed herself—so did he—and in running passed near Hen One, who had presented herself hopefully in the way. Hen Two rushed at her, pecking, then resumed her sweet little courtship running, the cock after her.

All over the tundra couples were courting. The wolves were so absorbed in sleep that their tongues fell aside in their mouths, just fell out if they yawned. The Killik marshes were empty of caribou for the first time in days.

That afternoon the bull migration started through. Cris took the camera and wolves and went down to await the first band—they had paused at a distance to graze. He hoped to get the wolves in frame with the caribou.

But before that could happen, there occurred an unforgettable incident, the clearest statement thus far of the theme of feral generosity.

The wolves had not noticed the distant caribou, and Cris gave each a parka squirrel to hold them with him. Lady, for almost the only time in her healthy life, got sick—perhaps she had overeaten on the kill. She lay with her head against her squirrel, then got up, went off and vomited.

Now the remarkable incident happened. Trigger looked sharply over at her, rose at once and carried his squirrel to her. He gave it to her, wagging his tail. (Tail wagging is not so common with wolves as with dogs.) Lady wagged her tail a little, bowed her chest and looked up at him brightly and gently. She received the squirrel gracefully.

The incident by no means closed on this lofty note. Lady returned presently to her own squirrel and cached it. Whereupon Trigger hunted up his gift squirrel, carried it far off and buried it. But not so privately as he had in mind doing. Lady followed silently at a distance, watching sharp-eyed to see where he put it.

By now the bulls were coming and Cris did indeed get some footage of the wolves in frame with them, starting the tactical maneuvering that is in their very bones and nerves. They chased the caribou in vain.

Returning to Cris they took him by surprise, nearly knocking him down, trying to include him in a big romp. Each wolf ran full tilt into him, not blindly but deliberately, half a dozen times, coming up from behind and hitting his legs at the height of a wolf. When a wolf says hello that way, it makes your knees buckle.

On the evening of this varied day I asked Cris, "What did you think was the most wonderful occurrence of the day?"

Without a moment's hesitation he answered, "Trigger picking up his squirrel and going over and giving it to Lady when she was sick. She looked up at him so appreciative and quiet."

The sunlight the next morning was softly pink on the mountains at three A.M. Ptarmigan were still courting, filling the quiet air with their activities.

This was the day Cris started his arctic garden. Never a spring since our marriage but he has had his garden. This was one of the more unusual of them. He planted the old reliables—radishes, lettuce, turnips. But how to water the bed?

His answer was an arctic one, in terms of the local situation. He blanketed the bed a foot deep in snow. When, soon afterward, he fenced the garden it was for a reason that struck me as romantic. He fenced it not from cows and chickens but from wolves and caribou. The wolves loved to romp in that soft earth.

Icy north wind the next day stopped the ptarmigan courting. It soon turned warm again, but those sweet, high, excited voices of the pursued, or asking-to-be-pursued, were put away for an arctic spring we should not see.

The next afternoon was warm and signalized by the last, wonderful climax of spring. A gold-colored grizzly, hard to spot on the tan tundra, had discovered the kill and was spending his ample time there. The skull was still intact and meat remained on ribs and backbone. Luckily the wolves were off on a trip. That afternoon the grizzly moseyed among the willows by the river, full fed, with not a thing on his mind to do but poke and smell into everything. He fell asleep in the sun across the draw from the cabin. What would happen if he returned to the kill and the wolves found him there? We went with rattles to move him up Easter Creek if we could—that was his usual beat; he came through about once a week, going upstream.

We stole up on the dozing mound of warm tan fur with the usual thrill of trepidation, sure he would run, yet never quite sure. We shook our rattle cans.

The grizzly galloped off in the sunshine, heading up Easter Creek. We stood watching to be sure whether he kept on going. Startled by the grizzly, a fox bounded into the air like a balloon and looked all around. He saw the bear and ran.

"Boy, look at him take off!" said Cris. "Can't run straight. Has to run sidewise, looking back to see if the bear's going to follow."

A pair of ptarmigan flew up ahead of the fox. A dozen bands of caribou bulls were in sight, near and far over the vast land. Some were bareheads, having shed their old antlers. Others had thick, velvety new antlers a foot long, like black bars over their heads. Four cream-colored Dall sheep browsed in the sunlight at the foot of the crags above us. It was not "scenery," whatever that queer, perverted abstraction may mean, but a great living whole, with its proper inhabitants going about their business.

I felt "inside." The land and its animals gave a feeling more pleasing than beauty could give. A feeling at the opposite pole from that of Virginia Woolf's disillusioned words: "The leaf hides nothing." Promise is the word for wilderness.

It was not just this moment. History was here too. Millenniums of plants finding their place under the arctic sky, of

animals spreading against each other until all were corrected
and moved in a living dynamism.

The great "surround" was marked by tranquillity. It was
poised changing. We were in it, part of it. Every creature
pursued its own destiny intently—caribou on the tundra, Dall
sheep under the crag, moose in the willows along the river,
birds choosing their nesting places under the Big Light. There
was a great health and a promise that said, "Come. Act. Behold."

We were not like landlocked trout in a mountain lake.
The swing and flow of great movement from great distance
gave horizon. Beyond this valley were other lands also free
and healthy, alive with spruce hens and lynx and the faraway
trees.

19   The Eskimos Come

Unbeknown to us, the last days of an era in our lives were
ticking to a close. Breakup was nearing fast. Puddles on the
ice one day; flowing water the next.

·Lady liked that flowing water, her first since September.
She lingered, waded back and forth, looking down as if it
were a live thing. She lifted a paw and touched it, acquainting
herself with it. That non-esurient wolf curiosity! I had to
call her to come along. She had observed the water for ten
minutes.

The next day there began the lone come-and-go roar of the river that would fill the air all summer. The riffles of snow on the lake subsided. A raven standing all alone out there on the blue ice bent his head and took a drink from a surface pool.

Andy brought our mail, his last charter trip to us until after breakup. Already, he said, a DC-3 and a Cessna had been damaged by landing on rotting ice south of the Range. Potholes are hard to spot from a taxiing plane.

Before leaving, he flew Cris over the far end of the wolf road, on April Creek. The area was enveloped in willow brush and alive with rabbit trails; Cris was more sure than ever that a den would be found there. Andy was flying from us straight to Anaktuvuk Pass on his mail run and he agreed to try to engage an Eskimo there that afternoon and fly him and his dogs to us at once. Cris wanted pack dogs for the den hunt to April Creek.

That evening was happy. Afterward we were glad to remember that. We read our mail, then discovered that Trigger and Lady were lying on the mesa, home from a trip. They wagged their tails and kissed us and lay down in the full wolf greeting and smile. Then they put on a memorable exhibition of play to our laughing, praising audience, which incited them to still more gaiety.

It was pure wolf play. There was much shouldering. They shoved, flapped tails controllingly over each other's backs, put an arm over the other's neck. But above all, they leaped! Lady leaped six feet sidewise. She leaped straight up, her back arched like a cat's. She whirled clear around in midair as if her forepaws pivoted on an invisible turntable. Then she lay looking up into Trigger's face, both arms around his neck. The whites of her eyes showed as she looked wickedly aside at him, nose tip buttoned between her lifted lips.

The wolves were not hungry but Lady came inquiringly to the Dutch door and Cris gave each a piece of dried salmon, more as a token than as food. As Lady turned away with it in her jaws, she looked up at Cris with serious clear eyes. It was a little thing but it impressed us.

"It's the little things," Cris said, as the wolves buried their salmon, "the run of little things, that makes the wolves so precious. They're sweet animals."

"They have a strong sense of—of—" I stammered, feeling for the name of some essentially undoglike, purely wolflike ingredient in their make-up.

"Of relation," said Cris.

He was disappointed in the morning, when, on rising at five to go with them when they left, he found they had already gone. He left at six with his camera.

About ten o'clock an ominous thing happened. Lady came home alone. She had never done that before. And she was terribly keyed up. For the second time in her life she talked, looking up into my face and ow-wowing interminably. She was so upset that I stayed outdoors with her to comfort her.

Toward noon Cris appeared. He looked around gravely. "Is Trigger here?" he said. He made no comment when I said no. Two Eskimos, he said, were here and would be up shortly for lunch; they were pitching their tent by the river.

At lunch I met them, Jonas and Jack Ahgook, the first humans besides our pilots ever to come to one of our camps. They had left Anaktuvuk Pass the day before, with ten dogs and a sled, an hour after Andy had touched down there. They had driven all night, arriving here just now. Their haste was due to the fast melt. They had followed frozen watercourses where possible but part of the way had driven on bare tundra.

They were Nunamiut, "Caribou People," who are taller than most Eskimos though still short by white man's standards. The Nunamiut, a band of half a dozen families and the only

Eskimos living on or north of the divide in the Range, were one of the last two groups of nomads left in North America. They were centered now by the tiny, new post office at the Pass.

They were changing swiftly from Stone Age to mail-order age. Until recently the Nunamiut had worn caribou skins, made shelters of them and lived chiefly on caribou meat. A purely artificial arrangement, the bounties on wolves, now gave them cash income and they preferred canvas tents and "store" parkas of fur cloth.

Jonas, the elder brother, was a slight, quiet, polite young man, subdued, I guessed, by his eight years of working on the railroad in Fairbanks. Eskimos are unskilled labor in civilization, however skilled in the wilds.

Jack was strong, quick, defiant and full of pride. He had a victorious young look. His brown face looked straight into the sun, his black hair tossed unkempt. It was clear from the dignity and eagerness of both men that they wished to do all things well, render a good account of themselves.

Not until they went down to their tent to sleep did Cris tell me what had happened.

He was on a mountainside up Easter Creek when he heard three shots down on the river. He hurried down and met the Eskimos. He asked if they had shot a wolf. They said they had shot at a caribou and missed. They had wolf traps on their sled, though Cris had stipulated through Andy that there was to be no killing whatever of animals in our walking range, except caribou for the dogs. The men had seemed astonished to learn our wolves might roam so far from our camp.

We had little doubt of what had happened. "I wish we could have taken Trigger and Lady home to the States," I said. "We have room, we could have built them a two-acre pen."

"It would have been no life for them compared with the

tundra," Cris said. "It isn't just the space. It's the whole thing —ptarmigan and caribou and parka squirrels. Those are the things that make it home for them."

He was going back to the place of the shots to look for Trigger's body or if he was wounded to put him out of pain.

"May I go along?"

"No. Don't, Lois." I was crying. "You go in. Read a story."

He was home by nine. He had found nothing.

The next day was bad. Lady moaned at intervals of a few minutes all day. It was the wolf mourning call, almost exactly like the long-drawn o-o-oh of a woman in tragic grief, starting in the middle range of woman's voice and dying in anguish. It went into my heart; I heard it when she was silent.

In the evening the Eskimos started—with guns "for target practice"!—to hunt a den nearby. I felt so clashing inwardly that it was almost unbearable. Cris said, "There's no one to talk to. No way of escape. We're just boxed in with our grief."

In the night I was about to get up for a Seconal when there was a slight howling in front of the cabin. Cris said in a light-hearted, quiet voice, "Lois! Trigger's here!"

I fell out of bed and out into the gray light. And the visionary, pale-buff, unbelievable thing was there, black-eyed and handsome and confident, his fur combed fine and flowing by wind and rivers and brush until it was like some intangible of nature—like wind or light on the tundra. Trembling with cold, I "loved" him.

He howled for Lady, who as we knew was down at the tent vainly courting the dogs, and was astounded when the dog crew answered. But he lay alertly, with composure, watching.

We went back to bed gay, into the first deep sleep since the Eskimos had come. Our guess was that Trigger and Lady had been with wild wolves, that the shot had put the latter to flight and Trigger had chanced to flee with them, Lady the other way.

Ten assorted doggies with curly tails, who ate a caribou every five days. (They were not matched like show teams in towns.) Jack and Jonas started stockpiling caribou. When we went down to their tent the next morning Jack was harnessing the dogs to bring in the first caribou they had shot. Trigger and Lady, who had followed us, kept a respectful distance. They accompanied Cris and Jack to the carcass. Cris said Jack never lost track of where they were.

The carcass was thrown down by the tent; the staked dogs could not get to it. But that night Trigger discovered it. It was now his meat. Once we saw him toiling up a distant ridge, carrying a ham of caribou in his mouth to cache far from the danger zone near all those dogs.

The next day when we went down with the camera, Jack was harnessing to bring in another dead caribou. As the dogs were led to the traces, they found themselves standing by the first carcass. They ate on it.

Trigger became insanely jealous. They were taking "his" meat. To him, each dog had become an enemy. As the team started to move, Trigger howled, yapped and crouched and started purposefully to close in on the dogs.

"Get sticks!" Cris said, fending the wolf off. I brought slender dead willow branches. "We can't do this," I said. "We can backpack the meat in for the Eskimos."

The scared driver held the dogs to a walk so we could keep up. Trigger uttered strange, furious half-howls. Again and again he circled to evade us and rush the dogs. We ran to intercept him. His eyes flashed across mine, measuring me and my willow stick.

When the dogs were tied at camp once more, Cris and I, standing guard, looked at each other in despair. It seemed the wolves would have to be killed. Cris said, "Ask the Eskimos if they have a rope." This meant he was going to make a try for the wolves' lives—try to lead Trigger home.

I brought the rope. I could not say anything. If I undermined his courage the wolf would know Cris feared him.

Now began a strange unequal struggle. On one side the man, armed only with his love for this animal. On the other, the crazed wolf, full-grown, a killer. His jaws could open to encompass half of a caribou's neck.

The wolf avoided; Cris followed. Finally he got his hand on Trigger. The wolf snarled and snatched for the hand as the rope went swift and easy around his neck. Cris gripped it at the nape of his neck to make it harder for him to bite his hand. Even if he had dared to relax his grip to tie a knot, he would not have dared to move away or Trigger could have leaped at him.

Holding the wolf this way, he patiently led him over the snow and bare tundra, spoke to him in a friendly plain voice as always, fended Lady off from playfully biting Trigger, waited when the wolf absolutely refused to come farther.

Cris brought the wolf up the mesa and waited while I ran to get meat. "Go in!" he said. "Go into the pen with the meat." The wolves followed along.

In the cabin at last, Cris stepped to me, his shoulders slumping, and clung to me for a minute. "Trigger is so jealous of those dogs!" he said. "His little heart nearly burned up when he saw them taking his meat. If only I had thought to throw him some, he might have quieted down."

Solemnly, with a bright inward look, he added, "Trigger didn't *want* to bite me. I didn't care if he did bite me. He tried to bluff me. I thought he was bluffing. But I didn't know."

It was true. Trigger had been half permissive. He had pulled his punches. I never mistrusted the wolves again. If Lady growled at me I hugged her. The margin of mystery was gone. We felt that we knew our wolves to the center of their hearts and that not one cell of them would ever be hostile to us except in perfectly understandable cases of pressure on them.

That night the wolves extricated themselves from the pen. But the upset was over; they were not only friendly toward the dogs but again courted them as they used to do the dogs at Barrow. Wolves like dogs. These dogs however were hostile, doubtless because their masters feared the wolves. They stoned them.

This led to a curious discovery: Trigger and Lady generalized about human beings. At first they supposed all were friendly, like us. But after they were stoned they became wary of us as well as of the Eskimos. Apparently now, all humans were animals that threw stones. It took us a few days to teach them "some." Some humans are friendly.

One thing about the Eskimos disturbed Cris. "They shoot in a funny way," he said. "Like throwing stones into the herd. They don't try to hit any particular one." Often they began shooting wildly when the caribou were still distant, even though the animals were coming toward them on a fixed route—their migration route passed between mesa and tent— and the wind was with them so that they could not smell the men.

The bulls came backlighted out of the east over the tundra in the morning. They looked at the tent of the sleeping Eskimos. They grazed. They passed each other within the group, in an inner atmosphere created by their being together, as if they spread a gauze of safety among themselves, moving alertly over the tundra, exposed to all—the helpless heat and cold and flies.

The dogs would howl, the caribou retreat. But after their fear dissipated they essayed their route again. And the Eskimos, roused by the dogs, started banging at them. One or two might fall but struggle to their feet and stagger on. The Eskimos did not bother to follow and kill the wounded.

The aimless shooting, the indifference to the wounded, went against Cris. He undertook himself to keep the dogs and men in meat. He had been an excellent hunter and had graduated from that stage, as men often do who live much in the wilds and really observe the animals.

It is well to understand that Jack and Jonas killed and felt pride in doing it not from malice but from historic background. Eskimos did not kill unduly, were not out of balance with their environment, when white men first came. They hunted skillfully but with native weapons. Now they are armed lavishly with white men's weapons but retain the imperative of men armed only with Stone Age weapons— kill regardless.

That of course is the attitude of most white men too. But the latter lay some dawning restraints on their use of weapons. And until recently there has been another big difference between them and the Eskimos, not in attitude toward wildlife but in the fact that the Eskimos are on the ground twelve months a year, "armed" with the really surprising mobility of dog teams. But with the military incursion of DEW line into the Arctic, white men too are on the ground twelve months a year. And their killing, like that of the Eskimos, is now governed by a mentality suddenly prehistoric, for it is facilitated by new weapons of mobility: helicopters and light planes.

Thanks to Andy we now made the acquaintance of the last animal I had ever expected to know personally, one so veiled by myth and distortion that the animal itself was a surprise.

I had been indoors all day baking bread. The caribou eaters liked bread and every other day I baked eight loaves, two at a time, in the oven Cris had made from a Blazo can, to sit on the two-burner gasoline stove. Cris and Jack were off den-hunting locally. Jonas was laid up in the tent with an ailment dangerous to Eskimos, who lack the immunities of white men—a common cold.

About eleven P.M., I set out westward along the mountainside, overlooking the tundra. I hoped to spot Cris and Jack below, on their way home, and join them. Pink clouds floated over the mountains to the south, across the valley. The mountains ahead of me were black on one side, tawny sunlit velvet on the other. A white-crowned sparrow sang its self-righteous little song. A male horned lark climbed like a longspur but instead of gliding and singing to earth, hovered warbling, then fell like a plummet.

It was a peculiarly poignant evening. I felt the youngness and eager desires and sense of importance in all creatures about me. Two mated seagulls sat in the sunlit draw where they would nest; an unmated gull stayed near. Trigger and Lady were off on a trip. I thought of the Eskimos—Jonas subdued but Jack still feeling that all was important and that, given a chance, he could do anything; burning to show his importance and ability. I thought of the two grizzlies we had watched with pleasure that morning, traveling high and far and fast together on the mountainside above camp, pausing to eat beside a snowbank, then impatiently traveling on. I thought of the little long-legged lambs waiting for death— all life awaits it—growing with the utter intensity of wild things, up on the black mountainside above me. Of the wild wolves, few in number, that would be in their dens now with the blind, passionately eager puppies.

I froze. The plane was coming! The roar silenced over the lake, presently resumed and the plane came into sight, low, obviously searching for us. Andy was not reckless. Why had he risked a landing so near breakup? Already the river had gone out; the lake was pocked with potholes.

I ran toward the nearest snow, where Andy might spot me and drop a note. The plane passed over before I reached it. It circled out of sight toward the lake and again became silent. Andy was waiting.

I saw the small figures of Cris and Jack, coming on the amber-lighted tundra below, casting pencil-long shadows ahead. I hurried down a staircase of crags and joined them.

Now I made a fearful anthropological blunder. Cris was not rushing, whether Andy left before he got there or not. He kept his steady pace, one I knew he could hold all night, even though he had worked all this day; and I knew he could work on, if necessary, after the walking and build a camp. Jack had slept all day. Impatiently I stepped ahead of Cris. Jack hesitated. He, too, stepped ahead of him. From now on he was to be arrogant with us.

Cris climbed the mesa for our one pair of hip boots and crossed the river to the lake. I waited on the river bank. The plane rose away. Only Jonas and Jack returned. Jonas told me why Andy had come. He had heard over the radio of two baby wolverines for sale. Cris had stepped into the plane as he was, and flown to Fairbanks to bring them back.

As I returned toward the mesa, Jonas pointed with silent pride to the foot of a snow slope. There lay the two young grizzlies, shot. A male and a female, Jonas said.

I slept that night. I was tired. But the next night I could not sleep. The needless killing of the grizzlies saddened me for its own sake. Also it impoverished our environment and violated the agreement to kill no animals but caribou in our camera-hunting range. Still another disturbing thing was Jack's new arrogance: he had refused to help backpack from the lake the supplies Andy had voluntarily brought on his unexpected flight.

About one A.M. I got up to take a Seconal. At the same moment I heard the roar of a plane. It was too loud for a Cessna. I looked out the Dutch door, the sleeping pill in my palm. Fog made a low ceiling over valley and lake, but right overhead there was a tear in the fog and through it sped a black Norseman. It was not Andy. I swallowed the capsule and the plane came back low, preparing to land on the lake. It was Andy! I dressed and ran for the river.

Downriver, Andy had found a place to get under the fog. From the air, as I learned, the river looked impassable, foaming white and brown. It had risen during the men's twenty-four-hour absence. Cris, it seemed, would have to spend the night shelterless by the lake. It was eighteen above zero. Andy performed a wilderness courtesy for him. He left him the wool liner of his emergency sleeping bag, not to be picked up until after breakup.

However, wise Jonas had found a new fording place, where the water was still only hip deep, and Cris came home.

Why the Norseman? The wolverines, it turned out, were

not babies but adult and fierce, confined in separate cages too large to get into a Cessna. Cris and Jack brought each cage over on poles the next morning, submerging the floors in the current, and set them at the foot of the mesa, where Cris would build a pen.

It was our fate in Alaska to deal most with the animals we had least expected even to see—grizzlies, wolves, now wolverines. We had had a few priceless glimpses of wolverines in the wilds—a wolverine with caribou, a wolverine braving Cris, even a set-to between a wolf and a wolverine, a strangely temperate affair, for the wolf had used not fangs and fury but fast footwork to head off the wolverine from her den.

I peered curiously into one of the dark wet cages. The occupant made a hissing lunge from which I shrank in spite of the bars. We named this wolverine Sickie because she had lost half of one of her huge front tool-paws in the trap that had caught her. The wound was healing. We called the other wolverine Scrappie.

Sickie rose to her hind feet easily, like a bear, as if the move were habitual, and half lifted her good tool-paw to the metal ceiling. She must have known by now, from desperate attempts, that there was no escape that way, yet still in her helplessness she had the impulse to try.

Jack left and now the wolves came up to view the strangers. Lady was wary, but Trigger stood by the bars. Like me, he jumped automatically when the wolverine lunged at him. She "seethed" continually and sometimes practically barked. Trigger took it just so long, then involuntarily made a delicate perfunctory sketch of a snarl and a sketch of a snap, his eyes very wide and clear and mild.

The wolverines had one amusing but troublesome little habit: they used their water pans as flush toilets. Each pan fitted so tightly at the bottom of the iron grill that I could hardly wrench it out. But the wolverine, after backing up to it neatly and excreting, rammed it easily from the cage. Water to clean and refill the pans had to be backpacked.

Cris liked the dauntless wolverines. He preached me a sermon on the text of their intractability.

"They're in a miserable situation. Iron bars, wet sacks, big superior animals coming up to them. And they don't lose their spirit. You'd feel awful discouraged in a predicament like that." I grunted and laughed. Cris followed it up. "Big superior animals come up to you and you'd go off in a corner and whimper and wail! Wolverine says, 'What the hell! Wough!'" Then Cris generously included himself in the sermon. "If we had half the spirit those little wolverines had, we'd probably be a lot better off."

Cris now set to work to perform the impossible, that is, build an escape-proof fence for wolverines in the wilds, with only a woman to help him. Jack sometimes sat and watched, but our deal with the Eskimos included only den-hunting.

Cris trenched the rocky soil knee-deep, to set the fencing he had brought along from Fairbanks. Then came harder work—trudging up the mesa side to hunt big rocks, heaving up each one and lugging it down to the trench. I helped as I could. By evening my back would feel broken and my legs pulsed. Cris would be so tired he could no longer lift a rock by muscle, only by straightening his back.

Meanwhile there came the heaviest snow we had ever seen in the Range. It was knee-deep. Marginal birds perished. I found the floppy-necked body of one of the two robins that had hung around the mesa. It was only bones and a size-shape of feathers.

It was apparent on the first sunny morning after the storm that a melt was due that would flood the river the highest ever. But the Eskimos, who had crossed the river with the boat the evening before, then walked upriver and waded back to this side, on arriving at their tent about seven A.M., sacked in tranquilly, leaving the boat on the far side. Cris was vexed but left them to solve the problem they had created.

"They don't think ahead," he said. "They don't see what the consequences are going to be. They gather willows only for this burning."

Perhaps the Arctic is an environment so overwhelming that the future is best not thought of; a spurt at a time is all an Eskimo can manage.

On the last day of May Cris had accomplished the impossible. The pen was finished, twenty feet square, with an overhang of wire and a hole cut for Scrappie's cage entrance. He would not release both wolverines at once for fear one might kill the other. He moved Scrappie's cage to the hole in the fence, knocked off the side rails, pried off the cleat over the top of the door and pulled the door up.

The wolverine ran out and raced around the fence in desperation. Our tall figures on the scaffolding overlooking the pen on one side were no comfort to him. (The scaffolding was for the camera.) He leaped up onto the wire so high I was sure he would go out by the overhang. He got behind the plywood panel at one side and it bulged. "He'll break that!" said Cris. "He's as strong as a man and more determined."

His appearance surprised us. Gaunt, arched spine, orange fur, coat in terrible shape from shedding, a hunk of fur dangling from his tail. An ungainly, *déshabillé* weasel.

He went into his box, growling. We moved it back from the fence in order to insert the water pan.

Cris cut a hole on the opposite side of the pen for Sickie's cage and we moved it up. She left it quickly and flew at the opposite side of the pen, launching herself here and there at the double or triple wire netting, hitting it with her face at each rush across the pen, so that I gasped. Her appearance, too, was a surprise. She was beautiful. Lustrous deep soft brown coat, compact body.

Then she shot out!

"Stop it!" I shouted, with a confused thought that the other wolverine would escape too. I did not realize what the opening was.

Cris groaned. It was so easy. The wolverine was galloping away, a bushy soft brown oval, low to the ground. She paused and turned to look back frequently. She went up the hillside back of the mesa. So normal-looking. So catastrophic. It hit Cris hard. He had simply not closed the opening in the fence when Scrappie's cage was pulled back.

I felt horrified and hilarious. And of course later there was the stunned ache. "All hard work and no fruition," I said bitterly.

Cris's eyes were joyless. "Everything has been against my intuition this summer. I didn't want to come back here, I wanted to work on polar bear and walrus. I try to get something anyway, by sheer weight of work."

At seven o'clock this golden evening, with irrelevantly somber hearts, we chanced to witness one of the stately, unheralded events of the wilds, the departure of the sea gulls. Yet not wholly unheralded: there had been a sign.

Spring had come in pulses, or days of climax. Such a day had been May 16, the first truly warm day; then had occurred the first marked influx of birds, including twenty-seven sea gulls. Of these only five would remain to nest here. The others were northward bound, detained only by the procession of caribou carcasses on the sand bar by the Eskimos' tent.

The sea gulls had cried and mewed here in these inland mountains. Yesterday and today the sign had occurred: very sweet cries mingled with their mewing. Northward to the nesting grounds they knew they must now be off; they could loiter no longer.

Wheeling, sunlit, shadowed, first white, then gray, they rose past the black mountainside, one sea gull ahead, a second behind, the others bunched, then lining out like geese. Wimmering white, beating along in the sunshine, they turned and crossed the crest two thousand feet above us and the beating, wimmering line, flashing white and gray, was lost in the blue over the Killik.

Cris let Scrappie into the pen the next morning and began photographing him. I stayed up in the cabin, baking bread. When Cris came up, he told me with the respectful admiration of one dedicated worker for another how the wolverine had conducted himself.

"He uses his whole body as prize and wedge. Makes you think of a bee when it's excited and stinging you: it just jumps on you and doubles all up. He tries to pull a rock and he strains on it like a man, till his body quivers. He works with his whole body—teeth, claws, chest, head. He uses his whole body as a lever or pry. Upside down, standing on his head and his hind paws in the air—any way it works. His whole upper end just pivots around on his neck, head and front paws. He's not intelligent like the wolves but he's so aggressive and determined."

"Brave and strong and busy," said the old Eskimo wolverine song. Every word was confirmed. The uncles of Andy's wife Hannah had seen a wolverine perform a nearly incredible feat: it dragged off a moose ham over its shoulder. We did not doubt it.

I recalled the coolness and energy of the small cousins of the wolverine, the weasels. At my open kitchen door in the Olympics once a weasel had reared his head and stared boldly from his hot little weasel world into my big alien one, instead of scampering away as any other tiny animal would have done. And as Cris and I rested our packs on a log by the trail one day, we heard a rustling and from the brush by our

feet emerged an object so strange it took us a minute to sort
it out. It was a weasel dragging a flying squirrel bigger than
himself, which he must have just slain in the tree back of us.
He toddled off down the trail, head high to avoid tripping over
his monstrous load.

I hurried down eagerly the next morning when Cris went
to photograph Scrappie again, to behold the wolverine work.
He did not work. He had tried that yesterday, there was no
percentage in it; today he took his ease. He dug himself a
hollow under the willow bushes and reclined, cuddled onto
his back, opened his pretty pink mouth, disclosing dental
arches of teeth functionally assorted as to size. He reached
for an overhead twig and toyed with it.

All the while, though, he growled continuously until it
was impossible not to think of the sound as a purr. The purr
sank diminuendo. He was silent. A ptarmigan clucked in
the sunshine, a golden plover called. The wolverine slept.

"His composure!" said Cris. "He's so relaxed. Curl up and
go to sleep with us right here."

21 The Den Hunt

The den hunt to April Creek started on June 2. When we
got up that morning we saw that the Eskimos, so often asleep
or away, were at their tent. Cris took his pack, ready with

tarp, sleeping bag, et cetera. "But how . . . ?" I began, wondering about the boat ditched across the river.

"They think white man manage," said Cris with a grin.

From up on the mesa I watched the struggle to get it back. The dominant actor was the wide race of muddy foaming water. The men were black ants posturing beside and across it.

Jonas followed Cris into the torrent and was whipped off his feet. Cris could not have known he fell. The uproar would drown a shout, the racing, hip-deep surge would shove Cris, the seethe unsteady and dizzy the eye. I thought Jonas would drown.

He shot or strove across the mouth of a creek and struggled and got to his feet. On the bar he stood on one leg, then the other, like a dancer trying a split, pouring water from his hip boots. He hesitated. I did not think he would try it again. But gamely he got a pole and entered the current. Of all things he had tried it the first time with no pole.

For two hours the men worked to get the boat across. One end of the anchored rope had torn loose and Cris strained to pull the rope across the currents, now so many, so wide. His body was a black slant against the dingy silver.

He was beat out when he came up for lunch. "You are a brave, capable man," I muttered rather formally. Then I sensed that really he was exhilarated.

With packs we both went down to the river. At this juncture Jonas sat on the ground in the door of the tent, mending the dog pack saddles, which we had had flown here by special charter the day after the Eskimos first arrived!

The chained dogs were shrieking with excitement. Trigger and Lady were not far from the performance, trust them! We knew the Eskimos had stoned them and that the wolves from their own point of view risked a stoning now, but better twenty years of Europe than a cycle of wilderness Cathay.

Trigger ventured tall observation leaps from behind the willow brush.

Cris ferried the packs across. Next he took Jack, who vowed he would not make that trip again.

Meanwhile I ran errands for all. I lugged the radio up to the mesa and brought back Cris's forgotten things. That radio gave me grim amusement. All the previous winter it had whispered or stayed silent at Point Barrow. Twice it had gone to Fairbanks for "repairs" that left it still speechless. Jack and Jonas laid hungry eyes on it the minute they first entered the crackerbox. They bore it to their tent, where half an hour later we found them reclining on caribou robes, the radio bawling at their elbows. The Stone Age men, so tenderly regarded by the anthropologists, had strung a horizontal aerial, for some arcane reason adding broken glass to it, had changed the setting by which only certain stations could be dialed, and now enjoyed a flood of general reception.

I went to the mesa again for tin to make a door for the gas-can stove which the Eskimos, on Cris's pattern, had made some days previously. This was the moment when they recalled there was no door.

Now at last the dogs were turned loose to swim the river. Instead they seized this opportunity to take out after the surprised wolves, who until now had apparently been persuaded the dogs if only free would play like Brownie at Barrow. A black dog chased Trigger three-quarters of a mile up a ridge, the wolf barely holding the lead, then heard the authoritative voice of duty—or futility—and ran back, Trigger hot on his heels. The red lead dog Tootch chased Lady downriver.

But how to induce those ten dogs to swim the brown-and-white torrent? Jack, on the far side, fired his gun and yelled faintly. The ambitious red lead dog plunged in but glancing over her shoulder saw she was not followed and turned back. Jonas fired. All was commotion. At last there was the low slant of ten heads and necks driving into the current, drifting fast downriver. I thought the dog Snyder, an old dog always given the heaviest packs because he was faithful, was going to drown. All made it.

Now general commotion on the far side. Why don't they chain the dogs, I wondered. Cris returned for Jonas. Jonas tried to help, paddling so hard the wrong way that Cris's straining hands were yanked from the rope. He pitched head first toward the torrent. I looked to see him drown. He recovered himself. The boat shot downriver. Paddling furiously the men beached it and dragged it back.

"Let me handle it till we hit the eddy," said Cris mildly, "then try to keep this end headed into the current." Jonas nodded.

They crossed. But now the dogs streamed down the far bank and started swimming to this side. I tried to pitch the black dog into the current as Jonas had done but he crowded against me, bracing himself and shivering. At last all were on the far side again.

But now back came Cris with Jonas. I splashed out to meet them. "What is it?" I yelled above the noise of water.

Cris's eyes met mine, he grinned. "Dog chains. They forgot the dog chains!"

Order over there at last. The dogs were loaded with their caribou rawhide pack-sacks. The little party straggled away through the willows. And on this side Trigger and Lady lay on the sand bar beside me, watching. This was a good surprise. We had feared the wolves would go along, creating innumerable problems. I talked them home, all heartiness, till my voice broke out harshly with fatigue. It was four P.M.

From the mesa I saw Jonas far ahead with a cluster of pack dogs. Next Jack with another cluster. Neither Eskimo carried anything but his rifle on his back and a staff to control the dogs. Last, Cris, trudging with camera pack and tripod and camera over his shoulder. At the far end of the lake the men got together. Half an hour later they were on top of the ridge, lying down, probably eating a loaf of bread. Then they were gone. I was alone.

The wolves had suffered a "lupine conversion." They were never to hang around the dogs again. It had happened fast. But at Barrow we had seen a lupine conversion in slow motion. An ugly dog, Weenok, used to come over from the Arctic Research Lab and harass Trigger. The first stage of the conversion was Trigger's tolerance, even courting of the dog, not for days but for weeks. The second stage came in the wink of an eye: withdrawal. Trigger's eyes changed. He did not attack but he did not run away either. "Weenok had better look out," said Cris. The third stage came a few mornings later: attack.

Cris, of course, did not know Trigger and Lady had undergone a conversion, and that fact was to lead to a big innovation in our lives.

I was grateful for the wolves' company, but after their supper they left for a trip. Now I was alone indeed. Even caribou no longer passed these days. Fumbling to fend off loneliness I idled down to the wolverine, the one living thing left in my world. A temptation came to me which reason assured me I should never yield to. I was ninety miles from the few Eskimos at Anaktuvuk Pass, hundreds of miles from doctor or nurse. Cris and the Eskimos were gone for a week or ten days. This first evening reason controlled me.

I sat down by the cage door and looked at the wolverine. I repented my bitter words when Sickie escaped. I thought, "Cris puts in train so many projects." The wolverine looked at me. Unlike a wolf he looked steadily. His eyes were different from the wolf's transparent orbs that reflect the slightest nuance of mood. They were beady flat black buttons, the pupil not distinguishable from the iris. They were small for the wolverine's size. He looked as big as an arctic fox but his eyes looked a quarter as big as a fox's eyes. Were they the weasel eye expanded to its utmost limit?

My temptation became very strong. Those small, matter-of-fact, observant eyes and the wolverine's round innocent forehead reminded me irresistibly of Erla Olson, a childhood playmate.

The wolverine gave me a sullen withdrawing glance. He sat up on his haunches like a little bear. He bowed up his neck, turned his head and picked up a hank of hay and looked back at me, holding it in his mouth and sucking in a growl on every breath. Seizing the hay was a substitute action, I supposed, for some aggression or repulsion against me. Could there be any rapport between a human and a weasel?

I summoned my honest feelings and spoke, not in a flattering but in a truly admiring tone. My eyes must have changed. The wolverine stared at me with hard watchful eyes. Then— suspicion relaxed from his eyes. He cuddled himself and yawned—pretty pink mouth, neat triangular wide tongue— and fell to doing his chores. He licked his wide tool-paw underneath and between the toes, cleaning it after his meal, which I had brought down to him. He lifted the paw so cat-like beside his cheek that I thought he was actually going to wash his face. Then he did. He wrinkled up his nose and face like a little old black man, gripped them between his paws, hiding his eyes, and dragged the paws down over his cheeks. One nonretractile, slender white claw caught lightly on his lower eyelid. He did this several times. Really I had the impression he was showing off in response to my fussing over him. Next he groomed his fur, pulling out clumps of the shedding underfur.

And then, to my wondering surprise, he sat up on hind

legs again and bent his head over as if he had in view inspecting his navel. He curled over onto his head, tipped over and prepared to sleep. He laid one broad paw like a bandage over his small dark eyes, calmly excluding my presence and the quiet gray light of the arctic summer night. He slept.

The next morning I fed him, brought water, cut dry grass and made a fresh sweet bed in his cage. Then Desire took the bit in its teeth; Reason chattered helplessly. Standing on the scaffolding I lowered Cris's homemade willow ladder into the pen. Reason screamed. I climbed down into the pen and pushed up the door of the wolverine's cage. I took one snapshot of his distrustful striped face at the opening to show Cris what had become of his wife in case wolverines are all they are cracked up to be. Then I sat down and awaited fate.

Scrappie came out. He circled the fence, watching me warily. I turned as he circled, holding out a morsel of meat to him. A cream-colored sash went around his low-slung orange-brown body, deepening into a bertha around his rump, narrowing to gray arches over his eyes. He bounced even when walking and deliberately, gracefully, laying down each huge front paw. (Was the size of the track the reason why people thought wolverines were big animals?) He arched his spine at the rump. From there it flowed downward to the tip of his nose. I thought the wolverine gallop, that everlasting hustling lope or gallop of a wolverine on the tundra, must come easy as a result of shooting that rump-hump out straight.

The wolverine fastened his inscrutable black eyes on mine. Did he have in mind giving me the bum's rush? I sat motionless, in trepidation and delight, holding out the morsel of meat. His harsh little furry muzzle brushed my fingers. Delicately he abstracted the morsel.

From now on I fed the wolverine by hand for fun, not starving him but feeding him first, then releasing him into the pen and letting him take extra morsels from my hand.

Once I held my hand out empty for him to smell, as I thought he might like to do. He smelled it, then very delicately took one finger with his short even front teeth between the canines. Gently he pressed. I distrusted him and withdrew the finger. This scared him so that he fled into his box.

And once he reached up from inside the box and took hold of my gloved finger through the slit by the door. Gingerly but firmly he held on. The glove slid off and tumbled on him, scaring him.

The big heat, the big sky, the big loneliness. I busied myself with work but there was an ache. Sometimes I even had a what's-the-use feeling. In spite of myself I looked often toward the empty ridge where the living dots of humans had last showed. I knew there would be nothing there. Indeed I hoped there would be nothing, for the river had continued to rise and was now appallingly high. I hoped the men would return in the small hours of the "night," when it would be a trifle lower.

On the hottest afternoon thus far, the sky was littered with blue-floored clouds. A single huge white one filled the whole head of Easter Creek valley, so that the sky dominated the mountains and I thought of the Great Powers. Then I was busy with work. About six o'clock a fierce wind came from east and north, an unusual direction. It shattered at the windows like a hailstorm. It was fearsome. The mountains were obliterated in storm-darkness moving rapidly down the valley toward me. Above it reposed dim white cumulus clouds. The upper heavens had no gale like that on earth.

I prayed for Cris, presently for myself, and got my boots on in case the tarp left the roof. Otherwise there was nothing to do. But the uproar was too intense and thundering for me to settle to any work. Yet I could not help feeling exhilaration, though it was blanketed by concern.

About eight o'clock the wind abated to merely rough and strong. It had come too early to break up the lake but a lead had opened on the far side.

The next day was intensely hot again and I "draped" the cabin, that is, hung a tarp around the outside of the windows. Inside it was stifling and shadowy. About noon I had a hunch. I dropped my mending and hastened outdoors. There was nothing to behold—nothing at all.

I sauntered to the west side of the mesa and there on the tundra below came four caribou bulls from the north. It was hard to believe after our long dearth of caribou. In another minute there was an explosion of excitement. I had forgotten the wolves. At home for once, they were sleeping out the heat in the wet marsh. The bulls almost walked into them. The bulls sprang to a run. The wolves laid chase but were outdistanced. They stopped and stood watching.

Now the caribou could have escaped easily. But no. The caribou vacillation came over them. They stopped and looked back. They came back! Right into the arms of the watching wolves. The wolves leaped into a run. The bulls split, two toward the mountainside, two toward the river. The wolves ran for the latter. The bulls fairly flew along the gravel bar against the brown shine of the water. They lashed into the current and swam, heads and antlers above the current. The wolves sped along the bar, wet their feet willingly but turned away from the current.

In the gray light about two o'clock one night I awoke suddenly. A burly bearded man filled the doorway. It was Cris.

He kissed me in a strangely perfunctory way, though electric with smiles. He stepped to the foot of the bunk and forth from his shirt brought one furry dark form after another and laid them on the sleeping bag. Involuntarily I shrank.

"Wolves," he stated. "I have them named." Totally disconcerted, I felt this to be one of the least important elements in the situation. He lifted each. "This is Miss Alatna," he said with éclat. "And this is Miss Killik. And this is Mr. Arctic. The Eskimos are bringing two more, Miss Tundra and Mr. Barrow."

This subject clarified, I sprang up and dressed. Cris mopped the sleeping bag with one of our two dish towels and set the pups on the floor. I was preparing warm powdered milk when a loud yell at my feet startled me. There sat Mr. Arctic, head thrown back, howling imperiously for food. (Trigger and Lady had not howled till five months old; this fearless howl from the new pup gave us our first glimpse of what our first two wolves must have suffered during their month with Eskimos before we got them.)

I cradled each little wolf in my arms while Cris spooned warm milk into its jaws and wiped its face and my shirt with the other dish towel. While the wolves slept he told me what had happened.

As he had expected there was a den on April Creek, where Pass Creek entered. But it was in willow brush and could not be photographed. He had expected to camp a few miles away and sneak up daily to photograph. On the spur of the moment he decided to bring the pups home. Jonas, the slenderest of the men, crawled into the den and brought them out one at a time.

Two wolves, the parents no doubt, bounded around crying. They were beautiful wolves, with deep black-bordered capes and fur so long it waved in the wind.

Now a crisis arose. The Eskimos prepared to shoot them for the bounty. Cris argued. Finally he said, "Okay! Shoot them. But if you do, the rest of the agreement is off too: no pay." (The agreement was to shoot no wolves.) The Eskimos put up their rifles: they never forgave Cris.

Cris slit his wool undershirt and inserted three pups. For once he permitted his camera outfit to be dog-packed, asking only that the dogs not be allowed to swim with it. With a doughnut—or heap—of little wolves around his bare waist he speeded straight homeward over the mountains. The Eskimos with the other pups came low, around the foot of the mountains, arriving in the morning.

At one point they had feared Cris was lost and had gone back to search for him. "What did you think when you thought Cris was lost?" I said.

Jonas looked quietly into my eyes. "I think he got no gun."

Miss Tundra, one of the two pups Cris had entrusted to the Eskimos to transport, had been traumatized by terror. She refused food. She sat in the corner of the bunk facing the wall, her head bowed, shuddering. "She has a will to die," Cris said. He stripped to the waist and lay down on the bunk. He took the little wolf in his arms and held her on his warm naked body. I drew the tarp curtain that shaded the bunk.

When I peeped into that twilight nook later, man and wolf were fast asleep, the wolf curled on Cris's breast.

When they awoke two hours later, a kind of miracle had happened. Miss Tundra had a will to live. She drank her milk thirstily. Then she toddled to Cris, crawled into his lap, bit his beard, licked his ear lobe and fell asleep again in his arms.

The wolves learned with stunning rapidity. They drank from a pan the second day, learned the door from both sides, left their enclosed box in the shed to urinate, climbed back in.

As for me, I could not have been busier if human quintuplets had been dumped on my hands. One of the worst troubles was the shortage of cleaning cloths. Feeding the five, one at a time, was an endless, recurring job. Cris got the situation under better control when he made a long feeding tray holding five shallow cans; we could feed all five at once.

Luckily there was one threat we did not have to face the first day or so. Trigger and Lady were away. When they returned, would they try to kill the puppies?

One morning just as the first spark of the sun burned over the dark ridge above him, Trigger's alert blond head came backlighted up over the edge of the mesa. The wolves were home.

"I'm going to show them the pups," said Cris. I begged for their safety. "No. It's a chance we've got to take sometime. It might as well be now." He set the puppies on the ground outside the Dutch door.

The big wolves shrank, then stepped toward the puppies, whining. Trigger bent his head, opened his great jaws and enclosed a pup's body. I looked away.

"You can look," Cris said. The wolf withdrew his teeth, closing them only on the puppy's fur.

Now an odd thing happened: Lady threw up. Only a little froth and water—the hunt must have been unsuccessful. I supposed she was emotionally upset by the pups.

Two more surprises hurried upon us, the first promising to be pretty serious. Trigger would not let us take the pups away. He was terribly excited. His eyes got black. He reared up and snatched Cris's arm. Cris expostulated with him in a quiet, friendly voice. Meanwhile I managed to smuggle the pups into the shed.

The next surprise was that as soon as Trigger was fed he wanted to enter the shed, where he lost his breakfast beside the puppies' box. So he too, I supposed, was "emotionally upset."

Trigger continued dangerously possessive and excited about the pups. It was apparent that our whole enterprise of photographing the pups could be shipwrecked. The wolves could easily prevent our even feeding them. Cris, to my admiration, patiently coaxed Trigger, sometimes yielding, sometimes firm. Gradually the wolves accepted us as part of the puppy situation. It was a happy relationship, precariously won.

With the Eskimos it was a different story. They came to lunch the day before their departure and the wolves, instead of vanishing as they would usually have done, stayed around the crackerbox, howling. They did not like those strangers so near the pups. On leaving, Jack and Jonas marched bravely down the hill, looking straight ahead. Trigger and Lady kept alongside. Trigger was uttering the same hoarse half-howls as when he had menaced the dogs. Cris hurried out and accompanied the Eskimos to their tent.

They broke camp the next morning. Their dog sled they cached upside down, with a grizzly hide roped over the dog harnesses. They would return for the sled after snow came. Followed by their troop of nine loaded pack dogs they set out across the tundra for Anaktuvuk Pass, two sleeps away. For the first time Jack carried a load—the radio, tied to a pack board. Cris had advised that it would do the radio no good to be submerged on the flank of a swimming dog.

And Cris brought the tenth dog, the forlorn, excited little red lead dog Tootch, up to the mesa.

He had bought her for a hundred dollars on the den hunt, hoping she would help to keep the wolves at home more often. He was unaware then, of course, that the wolves had rejected the dogs for good, even before the hunt party left the far bank of the river. Especially he did not know it was Tootch who had chased Lady.

Tootch was a vigorous personality. She was quarter wolf. Her long, curly, chestnut, black and cream-colored coat gleamed as if varnished. Her dark eyes were brilliant. Her hams bulged almost grotesquely with muscle, gained by hard labor. She was that remarkable combination, a slave lead dog.

As slave, she was accustomed to irrational beatings—to the solid tunk of a kick because, say, the traces fouled on a bush as she eagerly and correctly led a general trot-over ordered by Jonas. The conditions of a dog's life are hard where its master lives in the open with all his possessions, especially meat, on the ground. The dog must be severely disciplined.

However, seeing dogs kept for days without water, we felt they might have been less severely disciplined. Not until their howls could no longer be silenced by beating were they released to go to water. We never saw an Eskimo anywhere kind to dogs. Along the Bering Sea we had seen dogs in summer lying half dead with hunger. They were not working; why feed them? "We treat them fine," asserted one owner. "We give them water." Tootch, fortunately, had been fed because she worked summers as a pack dog.

The Eskimos apparently avoided any guilt or duty feelings by a convenient loophole: all things, even inanimate, have souls, except dogs; they have no souls.

The taboo above all taboos for a slave dog is meat. Tootch acted embarrassed to be caught even glancing at hung meat. The thought felt as guilty to her as the act. Cris had gone with the Ahgooks to bring in their first dead caribou. "I was naïve," he said. "I told them better tie the dogs and I would help bring the carcass over to the sled. They said, 'Oh no, we can go up to it.' Was I surprised! They drove the dogs right by it, bringing the sled alongside, and turned them around the head of the carcass. The dogs never even looked at the meat."

When packs replaced sleds, the saddled dogs lay around a kill, waiting for their loads of twenty or thirty pounds apiece of raw meat to pack to camp, and never gave a glance at the kill.

Slave dogs have one compensation: they are important. Above all, the lead dog is important. Among two hundred or so aggressive dogs at Anaktuvuk Pass, Tootch had fought and bluffed her way to the position of leader of a team, all of them bigger than herself. With dogs she was overbearing. With humans she was headstrong when she dared be, and slavish. She was the only dog I ever felt ambivalent toward— fond but at times resentfully hostile, as if she were an equal. Tootch cared about "face." She had an almost pathetic determination to save face.

Never did a small resolute dog suffer such a total reversal of life ways. She tried with all her being to maintain the continuity of her personality. She was known to herself only as a dog of authority and a dog who pleased her master. Confident of approval, she bared her teeth at Lady. We rebuked her. She "smiled" with tension and gazed steadily at us: where was reason? where was comprehensibility?

There was cold war between Lady and the dog. Lady thirsted to make it hot. Did she remember it was Tootch who had chased her savagely? She stood over Tootch. The dog crouched as if absorbed in more important, distant affairs, saving face and perhaps life by staring importantly at some distant object. Lady's bearing was the most arrogant imaginable in man or beast. She dared Tootch to offer one move. We switched her rigidly horizontal tail down, hoping it was hitched to her mood. "She's a different Lady," said Cris wonderingly.

Wolves are intensely jealous. If Lady started away over the tundra below the mesa, all we had to do to bring her flying back was to start toward the tied dog. In a matter of moments that black head came up over the mesa edge, its owner sure she would catch us petting Tootch and have her pretext for a fight.

"It shoots Lady full of adrenalin to see you even take water to Tootch," Cris said. Ruefully he added, "We sure have made little homebodies of the wolves!"

What surprised us was that Tootch did not understand even the tones of our voices. We spoke no Eskimo. The only English words she knew were useless—"Gee" and "Hah." We could not tell her to go or come. I tried to send her to meet Cris, coming on the tundra. She cowered just out of sight on the mesa side howling, convinced she was being banished from camp. But for her to misjudge our very tones—that was unexpected. We would be caressing her and suddenly she would flee terrified to the end of her rope. Had we uttered a threat in Eskimo? Or, more likely, was she aware that Eskimos sometimes spoke rage in smiling voices?

A building terrified her—she had never been in one. But I could not resist carrying her in. I laid her on the bunk, where she froze like a terrified fawn. Cris warned, "You're starting something."

It was two months before his warning was confirmed. He was away for a few days. As usual, I carried Tootch indoors and laid her on the bunk. Suddenly she became radiant. She spread her paws, laughed and played. Everything just all at once looked different to her. It was a canine conversion. From then on she slept on the foot of the bunk. But she was still a lead dog: she snarled authoritatively if we moved our feet.

A touching surprise happened on her first walk without a pack. She followed me—pack dogs are not allowed to run ahead. But things were kaleidoscoping in her brain. As I turned homeward, she suddenly went crazy with freedom and the wine of delight. She raced off—out of sight, to my anxiety—and tore back like crazy, then followed me sedately home.

Would human affection—so novel to her—ever make up to her for the loss of her importance in a world she knew, as boss dog in a canine social setting? Could she ever find a way to seem important to herself again? The question was serious. Were we doing right to keep her?

23   Living at a Wolf Den

It was on the evening of the day the Eskimos left that the most wonderful period of our life with wolves began. The "enabling factor" that started it was probably the den Cris dug in the pen for the pups. He finished it that afternoon and installed the gratified pups. It was U-shaped, having two entrances, and big enough for the adult wolves to enter. Cris also removed a top section of fencing at the corner of the pen so Trigger and Lady could leap in and out at will to visit the pups.

That night about eleven o'clock, when the sunlight was rosy on the mountains across the lake, Trigger and Lady came trotting over the shadowed tundra from a kill across the lake. At the foot of the mesa they paused. Trigger buzzed the male ptarmigan that hung out down there. Lady went to look at the wolverine. When I called she looked up and started up with surprising alacrity and speed. But at the top she looked at me as if she had forgotten I was there.

She evaded my hands and leaped into the pen, uttering the strong whine which we knew by now was the wolf "puppy call." I started into the cabin but Cris called me back in a soft urgent voice.

"Look there. She gave them her meat." All the puppies were in a bunch, eating. The long-legged young wolf whimpered gently to them. She lay down and the puppies toddled and climbed over her.

At this juncture Trigger arrived. He glanced the situation over. We did not wonder what he would do; we didn't know enough to suppose he would do anything. He stepped to Tootch, tied near the pen. Just out of reach of her bared fangs, with an expression of such bashful sweetness that it made us smile, he dumped before her his load, the contents of his stomach—about two or two and a half pounds of fresh red meat. I pushed it a foot closer so that the justly baffled dog could reach her present.

The wolves presently fell asleep near the recipients of their gifts, Trigger near Tootch, Lady near the pups. But Cris and I stood forgetting to move.

"Never underestimate little Lady," said Cris. "You said she wasn't mature as a parent and Trigger was, but she fed the pups."

What impressed Cris was wolf logistics. "They've got an ideal way of carrying their meat. In their stomachs. They can run and smell and chase things along the way, and nobody could tell they were taking meat to a den."

I was impressed by the good condition of the meat: it could have come from a market counter. Did wolves inhibit digestion? Later on, when Trigger must have brought his load eighteen miles, the last portion to come forth was tinged with brown but the rest was still fresh and red.

But it was not these points that held us motionless in the gray shadow of the mountain. Full and clear at last had been stated the great theme of feral generosity. Lady had given to pups no kin of hers, Trigger to a dog that more than once had bitten his muzzle.

"It makes me feel kind of awestruck," I said.

"It *is* an awesome little thing" agreed Cris. "It makes you feel as if you're on the inside of some of the little things of nature."

It always does us good, says Thoreau, "it even takes the stiffness out of our joints, and makes us supple and buoyant, when we knew not what ailed us, to recognize any generosity in man or Nature." From now on, for years to come, we were to see wolves concerned and eager to give the choicest food they could get not to wolf pups, for there were none, but to any indifferent dog pups they could reach. And always I felt a touch of wonder.

The next morning, preserving the sweet and wonderful stillness of the den, Lady slept in the sunshine, her head hanging into an entrance. The pups within were silent. Trigger was gone to the kill.

He circled the blue lake—ice was piled at one end. He paused to observe a sea gull floating near shore. At the kill he pulled the carcass farther out of water. With businesslike speed he tore off a load and started for home. But glancing back he saw the sea gulls settling on the kill. He ran back once to chase them away, then trotted on, stopping only once more to look back. They were settling again but some things can't be helped; you arrive at the tolerance of the wilderness. The nearer the wolf came toward home, the more bouncy and running he was.

Meanwhile I had made a mistake. I had a delicate role to learn in this extraordinary social situation—living with free wolves at a den in the wilderness. Officiously I fed the pups. Their noses were in their milk tray when here arrived Trigger, dripping from his necessary swim of the river, with his happy load. I snatched away the tray. Trigger stepped and looked around, sat down a minute, then in the willows he regurgitated.

Alas, the little stuffed puppies were not excitingly eager and squealing and attentive. But Trigger stepped to one and another and each followed the big damp legs to the flat pile of red meat. He licked it occasionally as the uneager pups gathered. When all were through he ate the remainder.

Was this the pattern? Lady baby-sat, Trigger brought the food. But the wolves were not bound by iron-clad instinct. They made changing adjustments to weather, food, distance and kind of kill, and not one but was a surprise to us. The first came that very evening.

This time Lady accompanied Trigger to the kill again. And on the way home she jumped to a wrong conclusion with almost human agility. She had gone downriver, looking for a better place to ford. Trigger swam at once and was nearly to the foot of the mesa before, looking back, he saw Lady on this side, coming. He ran back and she crouched like a playful cat and sprang at him. She had already made her error of judgment.

The wolves came on to the foot of the mesa and Trigger ascended, but Lady stopped and dug busily, humping her back. She made a quick disgorge and cached it by brushing duff over it with her nose; then she chose another spot, made a second disgorge and cached it.

When she arrived at the pen, Trigger's feeding of the pups

was at its height. Pups sallied around dragging pieces of entrail or chunks of red meat. They growled, rolled in them, essayed to bury them. Trigger lay watching them, head high, eyes benign, lips firmly curled. He looked content; this time he was reaping his full emotional reward.

Poor Lady was terribly jealous. She looked the situation over with sharp eyes, then crowded against Trigger and snapped and snarled at him, starting that almost unique thing for wolves, a spat. It was as if he had deceived her: meeting him apparently returning from the mesa, she must have supposed he had already fed the pups, so she cached her own load.

The next variation on the feeding pattern caused us anxiety about our future with the pups. Trigger alone went to the kill. As usual he returned briskly. We had no doubt he was bringing a load to the pups. Instead, at the foot of the mesa he, too, cached as Lady had done, but with a very different follow-up.

When he reached the pen we had the distinct impression that he had in mind taking the pups for a walk and "finding" some meat! He stepped to a pup, barely touched his long nose to it; it followed him. He came to the others, had them all at his heels, then went to the fence. To Cris's vexation, instead of jumping it he stepped onto it and sat down, mashing and nearly breaking down the wire. Then he stepped out. Obviously he wanted the pups to follow and was making it easy for them. They could not follow yet. But later would he and Lady lead them away from us for good?

At this same feeding there occurred another and pleasing variation in the pattern. Lady, who had baby-sat, stepped to Trigger's pile of meat and took bites for herself, abstracting each delicately, without greediness. You could almost see the social restraints on the wolf.

Trigger could fulfill the male role; Lady could not fulfill the female role. Was this why she did a charming little thing for the pups? She brought them their first toy. Lady was no martyr; it is laborious for a wolf to mouth-pack objects. At the kill she selected the lightest thing she could find—a lower leg and hoof. As food it was nothing. It was purely a toy.

The pups made a big thing of it. They romped and played with it. Watching them, Lady contentedly watching too, I thought with quiet marvel of that young wolf a mile away at the kill, mindful of the pups at the den and choosing a special trifle to bring home to them.

Wolves are terribly sensitive, jealous animals. And Lady's toy brought her jealousy again. That evening after the day's sleep, as the shadow of the mountain to the north grayed the mesa, Trigger arose, stretched luxuriously across the den mouth and uttered the "puppy call." Out from the den boiled the pups. Lady lay quiet outside the pen, watching what now ensued, the cajolery of wolf pups toward the adult wolf.

It is one of the gayest, prettiest sights in the world. The pups themselves are the softest and gentlest of creatures, blue-eyed, oddly leonine-looking at this stage, for their muzzles are short; above all, not quarrelsome among themselves as dog pups so often are, and brimming with adulation toward adults. The pups besieged their big meat-giver with feverish love pats and kisses. They thronged his head, sat on their haunches and threw both arms around his neck as far as they would go. They kissed his face and gave him love pats around the mouth with huge soft paws. They even kissed the inside of his mouth if he opened it. All their attentions were oriented to Trigger's head.

"Looks like they just tingle all over when they even touch him," said Cris. Their soft excitement reminded me of nothing so much as baby water ouzels, fluttering vibrissimo after being fed, so that the enchanted parent rushes for more food to repeat the delicious excitement. Tame babies have no such imperious drive to protect the continuity of their own feeding. But with the wild young, intensity and fervor begin early.

Lady watched until she could bear it no longer. She rose, leaped into the pen, went straight to her unregarded toy, about whose whereabouts she had not been in the least doubt, and snatched it. Holding it in her jaws and looking neither to right nor to left, the jealous wolf leaped out of the pen.

Perhaps the pups could not twist the big wolves around their paws but they came near doing it. Now, a wolf has control over his disgorge. He can lay out portions to cache here and there. And he can reserve part for himself. Trigger came home with a small load once. He laid out a small pile for the pups. A big chunk followed part way out but he swallowed it right back. "Figgahs he's given them enough," said Cris. "He wants that for himself." It was not coquetry but hunger, we were sure, that caused him to hold out on the pups. But the sharp-eyed pups had not failed to observe he had more. They gobbled their own meat, then applied themselves to coaxing out that reserved meat. They succeeded.

One thing that drove Trigger nearly wild was to be coaxed when his cupboard was bare. One morning too hot for a hunt, he was sleeping in the willows above the den when the pups began to coax. It was not a common thing; they must have been hungry. The wolf growled, lifted his lip, hustled from here to there, besieged by pups. Then he leaped from the pen, followed by Lady. They hurried from the mesa. Now what?

They parted. Trigger went to the Killik marshes, where he pounced as if hunting voles. Lady tried for a mother ptarmigan that temptingly played broken-wing. She never did try so hard for anything, but she failed. Trigger brought home a few voles in his stomach and gave them to the pups, then went back to sleep.

Is this puppyhood control a reason why adult wolves are such controlling animals?

The wolves carried some things in their mouths, others in

their stomachs, and some things in either. A ptarmigan was mouth-carried. Probably it would be hard to regurgitate. A parka squirrel might be carried either way. Trigger brought one home once, laid it out from his stomach, but, before I got the pups to it, swallowed it. When I turned back to him he had it out between his paws again, as he lay. "He's kind of proud of that squirrel," said Cris. "Lot of trouble to catch one." He gave it to the pups.

We came to think this mouth feeding had a profound, enduring effect on wolf personality. Humans have made only two biological inventions, according to J. B. S. Haldane: making cheese from maternal secretions, and taking a facing position in the sex embrace. The latter, he says, has made possible the human type of personality, other-regarding.

Wolves have made one biological invention—mouth feeding. It, too, leads to face orientation. Even in their courtship wolves are face-oriented. Wolf courtship is the opposite of a dog's terse, businesslike rump orientation. It is prolonged, lasting several months before actual heat. The wolves "French-kiss" the inside of each other's mouths as they formerly did to their parents. Perhaps their face orientation is what leads to their sensitive observations of each other, their quick social concern, as when Trigger observed that Lady was sick and instantly tried to help her. This social responsibility must help to hold wolf packs together. The basic face orientation may also help to make possible the tremendous gaiety and social zest of wolves.

One rather pleasing fact about the mouth feeding was that the wolves hated to give the pups stale meat but when they had choice fresh tidbits they could hardly wait to get to the pups and give up all they had; it gratified them to do that.

What did the wolves consider as tidbits? Thanks to two worried ravens we had a chance to find out. There was a kill in the draw back of the mesa and while the wolves were asleep we stole from the mesa with packboards to bring home meat for a rainy day for the pups.

A pair of ravens had their three young at the kill. The old birds flew up excitedly at Cris's approach, calling their young to come away. The young ravens could see no reason to leave all this meat. The old ones squawked. The young ones tore off bites, looked up and inquired briefly, "Quak?"

"Quork! Ork! Squa-ak!" yelled the old ones. They could not budge the babies so they tried to run Cris off, fluttering over him and shouting.

All this uproar did not pass unnoticed, you may be sure. Here came the wolves, tearing down the mesa side. Cris stepped back. Lady took no load but Trigger carefully selected a load for this off-hour feeding. And did he take the fresh red meat Cris had barely managed to uncover? It was unweathered, unpecked by birds.

Instead the wolf smelled all over the carcass till he located bits of connective tissue or sinew. These he tugged at, got back on his carnassials, or meat-chewing teeth, and chewed off. He ripped strings of fat from the intestines. He left the liver for the birds.

The pups preferred the meat the wolves brought them to that we sometimes gave. No wonder. Theirs was not stale muscle meat, it was tidbits, probably moistened from the wolf's stomach. The wolves sometimes brought small units, less, we were sure, as tidbits than as being handy to bite off— ears, penis, testicles, sometimes tongue.

Trigger betrayed another wolf preference one morning. He was nearing the foot of the mesa when he looked up and saw Cris standing on top, watching him. The wolf must have felt his approach to the den should be unobserved, for he veered and went around the mesa to come up from the back. He ran into me.

I was just shouldering my water pack at the spring when I

heard a squeak by my hand and looked down. Here was Trigger, not avoiding me but pleased at meeting me—I was not at the den so I was not disturbing to him. I knelt so he could jaw my face. We had a howl—I felt the departing vibrance and volume of the wolf's voice—then he spiraled to the ground in the full wolf greeting, to be petted.

But this visit was only an interlude. The wolf was homeward bound with a load of meat in his stomach for the pups. He could merely have walked away. But no. Wolflike he had to notify me: he uttered a brief sound and then hurried off up the mesa.

Cris for once expected him and was ready to film the delivery. It was not so easy as it seemed. Trigger stepped around in the pen and chose a spot. He got his load up on the step. Cris focused and stopped down. But the pups thronged Trigger. He stepped aside and before Cris could even swing the camera he had made his disgorge.

24   Silver-mane

The great seasons that attended our little occupations moved on. The June heat reached its climax on the nineteenth. That day was a turning point. By afternoon, though still hot, the weather was wild and lonely. The mountains were the color of Cris's dark-blue wool spinnaker shirt. There were sudden gusts of wind, a few drops of rain and the worst mosquitoes thus far. Three bulls passed, going north. We had been seeing almost no caribou. The herds, we believed, were out to the north of us. But some stir and movement was beginning.

That night the heat broke. In the morning there was fresh snow on the mountains, under crawling fog. A band of over two hundred caribou, mostly bulls, came out of the north, pausing on the mountainside back of the mesa to rest and graze. Trigger observed them, rose and stretched. Presently I noticed he was gone.

Up on the mountainside the scene was one of pastoral luxuriance. Among the green shrubs moved the bulls, with rich black antlers and white chests. Many were lying down; up toward the saddle where all had descended lay three or four who had not come down yet. All was peace and ampleness.

Suddenly half the caribou were in motion, banding for flight. I looked to their rear. Trigger!

The caribou traversed the mountainside, its rises and depressions, rough rocks and brush, with the speed of a fast-flowing river and that illusion of effortless flowing that caribou give when running. They "floated" across the mountainside. A couple of hundred yards behind floated a solitary tan figure, the wolf, drifting over the mountainside like a bird flying. But there would be no kill; there were no caribou falling behind. At a great dark rock outcropping the flow of caribou parted into strands, still flowing. It was a beautiful maneuver. The half above had not moved. I hoped they would go on up Easter Creek, their original direction. But now they, too, were in motion. They flowed, they fleeted back through the saddle, unpursued.

Thus began the June return of the caribou, the reversal of direction back into the mountains following the first intensely hot day of the year. We had observed it the previous year, on the northwest front of the Range.

On the following afternoon there occurred one of those

rare conjunctions of life and beauty that for a moment transport by their magic the toil-bound human. In a small way I
had had that feeling once in Thomasville, Georgia, riding
down a street where the foam of dogwood blossoms above
met the founting up of azalea blossoms from below. It made
a human feel gracious, stately and good.

The arctic magic was wild and stern. About twenty-five
hundred caribou passed during the late afternoon and evening. The air glowed from a rare humidity. Gray cumulus
clouds in the blue let down gray curtains of rain here and
there over the vast land, but never right here on Cris's thirst-
ing garden. There were rainbows, the most intense and glowing we had ever seen. Even the sunlight glowed, especially
toward ten in the evening, when all the hollows on the mountainside where the herds were passing were dark with shadows.

Cris and I sat on the north brink of the mesa watching
silently, warm enough in our parkas. On the uplifted stage
before us moved various bands of caribou. There was one
striking maneuver. Up on the sunlit saddle a band, rumps
white toward the sun, dropped over the crag into shadow.
Single file they angled down toward a sunlit shelf niched in
the shadowed mountainside. Toward it from the other side
came a band, reversing direction. The two files met and
passed noiselessly, as if in some ceremony, on the sunlit shelf
surrounded by darkness. Around the steep dark talus slide
appeared antlered bulls, filing with care in one another's steps.

It was not these stern wild scenes that most pleased Cris.
He likes tawny colors. And a tawny scene there was, on a
sunlit flat by a lake to the east of us. Scores of caribou were
idling there to graze. The tan of their bodies blended with the
tan tundra and warmly colored air in a magical evenness of
color that was like a vision of paradise.

The next morning this special humid beauty was gone. The
air was fresh and sweet and mild. For a few days caribou

passed, returning south into the mountains. We realized later that far larger numbers must have passed southward elsewhere.

Meanwhile I looked forward longingly to our first contact with the outside world since before breakup—the coming of the plane on July 3. Before that happened, two fantastic events nearly wiped it from our minds.

About ten o'clock one evening, when the tundra was lighted like a stage by the low sun, a strange wolf passed camp, uttering the mourning cry. The stranger stood on the spur east of camp and watched the mesa. Trigger and Lady ran to her. The stranger bit both on the flank. Wolves have their little ceremonies and reserves in meeting, and Trigger and Lady had omitted them. Afterward the wild wolf courted Trigger and Lady with endless retreats and advances.

She was the most strikingly handsome wolf we had ever seen, with a tan body and a wide silver cape edged with soot black. Cris gave her a name, Silver-mane. By night she hunted with Trigger and Lady. By day she lay on a knoll on the mountainside overlooking camp, a quarter of a mile away.

Meanwhile the second fantastic event occurred. About midnight one night we were awakened by Tootch, crying. She was on a yard wire beyond the pen. She gave a very cross yell, followed presently by peeved, self-pitying whimpers. Then silence.

Suddenly the wolf puppies shrieked. We realized instantly what was happening. Tootch was in the pen and trying to kill the pups. How many were already injured? Killed? In a flash I was out of bed and into the pen.

It was bedlam. Tootch was mauling a pup. Two others fought each other, screaming. From the den came savage yells. I yelled for Cris, who had stopped to dress. He came. He wrenched a switch from a willow. Tootch ran to escape. Out-

side the jump-out place in the fence stood Lady. Tootch
dared not jump out. Cris caught her across the open eye with
the switch. She screamed and jumped out. She fled down
the mesa side, followed by Cris and the wolves. I had never
seen Cris angry like this. For all we could tell, the dog had
destroyed the fruit of the den hunt and our hope of wolf-pup
pictures.

I had my hands and wits full. All the pups were fighting
insanely. Tootch had mauled the three in the yard. I could
not tell about those in the den. My first problem was to con-
fine each separately. I grabbed a wolf and carried it into the
cabin. I shut a second in the shed. I threw a Blazo box over
the third.

Screams of rage and pain were coming from the den. I
crawled in head first. It smelled suffocatingly of ammonia.
I could not see the wolves but they were fighting savagely. I
reached an arm ahead and grabbed the hind leg of one. Holding it fast, I wriggled backward out of the den and carried
the wolf into the cabin. I had to leave the fifth wolf in the
den. Whether it was injured or not I did not know.

It seemed to me that it must be the smell of the murderous
dog on their wet, mouthed fur that was driving the always-
gentle wolves mad. Hoping to rid them of that smell, I lighted
the gasoline stove and hurried to prepare a basin of warm
suds, meanwhile jumping to the bunk at every second to keep
one pup up there, the other on the floor.

Holding one wolf at a time on the bunk, I sponged, then
dried with a towel the three Tootch had mauled. Then I
set two on the floor. They flew at each other. Savage, in-
stantaneous, furious. Their tails quivered, their strength was
surprising.

Again I bathed each wolf. Again they fought. This was
no ordinary fighting. The wolves had gone berserk.

Perhaps if I could fill their stomachs with warm milk it

might quiet them. I prepared warm powdered milk and let each wolf drink all it would. Again I put two together. They fought! All I could do was keep them apart.

To my thankful relief Cris returned. He had caught Tootch.

"It was pitiful in a way," he said. I sensed that he felt ashamed of having struck her. "The only thing she could think of to do was to go down to the old Eskimo camp. Looked to her like there ought to be some kind of refuge there."

Tootch had swum the river four times before Cris caught her. "Lady swam right after her. She sure would have liked to help me punish Tootch for running away! Came up after I had her on the chain and was bringing her home and was going to jump on her. I had one heck of a time. Lady thought we had her now!"

Tootch's attack on the pups had been deliberate. For a little dog, she had put out considerable effort. She had climbed or jumped a six-foot fence. All that had saved her from strangling as she fell inside the fence and dangled by the neck on her short rope was the fact that it slipped off over her head.

A blood lust was in the pups for two hours. This was a unique occurrence. We never saw the like before or afterward. It was a berserk rage. One surprising fact was that the big wolves had not jumped into the pen to protect the pups.

Luckily no animal was seriously hurt. But the affair had one unhappy consequence: Cris put up the top wire again. He could not risk Tootch escaping again and this time killing the pups. This hampered the big wolves and cost us hours of sleep. The feedings were usually toward morning, in the small hours. When a big wolf arrived with a load, the frantically eager pups twanged the wire, awakening us. One of us had to stumble sleepily to open the gate and let the food bearer in. After a while Trigger learned of himself to whimper and waken us. Sometimes before we could reach the gate, the wolf miscarried and deposited its load outside the fence. Sometimes re-ate it. The pups might coax it out again. Or we might scoop the meat in a plate and rush meat and wolf to the pups. We sensed that contact with the excited happy pups was essential to keep the feedings going.

One more adventure, a minor one, befell us before the plane came. At a quarter of five on the morning of July 2, I stood on the brow of the mesa, watching with silent pleasure the three wolves on the green tundra just below, coming home from the night's hunt. Silver-mane was trying to play with Trigger. She held her head alert, put a paw on his shoulder and stood with bristle and hope. He tucked his tail under, turned and gnashed at her a little.

Suddenly I realized the wolves were not alone. A fourth animal was ambling near them. A brown animal—Tootch, of course. Always that first glimpse of an unexpected animal is hard to interpret: a fact that makes you realize how much of what you "see" is in your head, in the context. But it was not Tootch, it was the wolverine!

He must just have escaped. He was coming from the direction of the pen, moving hesitatingly, looking with interest into everything. He glanced at the wolves, they glanced at him. All went on with their own affairs. He placed his front feet on a stone to gain elevation and looked around with weasel-reared head. Then he saw me above, on the mesa rim. He stopped puttering and examining and loped away.

Of course the loss of the wolverine was a shock but it was not distressing. Cris had about finished with him. As to how he had got out, there was no break in the fence, no dig; he must have leaped and at last caught the overhang with his tool-paws.

I often wondered how the two wolverines fared on the

great arctic tundra. For the present they would make a go of
it, but when winter froze the land? I often thought sadly of
Sickie's wrecked tool-paw. (Of course the two wolverines
would go separate ways; Sickie must by now have gone far
away.)

A happier event signalized this day. Cris gathered the first
fruits of his arctic garden. Cris never disdains a small triumph.
Glowing with pride, he bore up to the cabin a bunch of
radishes, quite possibly the first ever grown outdoors north
of the Range. With respectful delight we ate them, tops and
all.

The day the plane was due was hazy and roughly blowing.
All day we watched the "gate" between the mountains up
Easter Creek, through which the plane must come. The gate
remained open but the plane did not come. Having no other
means of communication with the outside world, I asked Cris
hopefully if he had a hunch whether it would come.

He answered matter-of-factly, "It all depends on how the
mountains look from Bettles. And on the weather reports
from Umiat and Kotzebue."

I scrutinized the gate again. How would the Range look
from its south side? What were the weather reports? I ached
with a dead-steady longing for the letters lying right now at
Bettles.

About noon, when at any moment the plane might come
and one of us at least must run for the lake, Cris, to my
utter dismay, recklessly opened the gate and let the pups out
for the very first, number-one tundra walk of their lives.
They hurried down the mesa side, heading away as if never
coming back. As if they had not a thought of home or how to
get there in their gray-furry skulls.

"How are you going to get them back?" I inquired, in-
dignant with anxiety.

I don't believe Cris had given it a thought. "I don't know," he replied cheerfully. But he enlisted the best helpers in the world. He ran across the mesa to where Trigger and Lady slept out of the wind and returned with them. They took charge.

They watched the pups alertly. As the pups moved on they galloped to fresh vantage points and flopped down in the sun, watching. When the pups created a problem by splitting, two and three, the big wolves split too and followed them, feeling, apparently, that pups should not be unattended.

The pups plunged into the knee-high willows, leaped up to clear them and fell on their faces into them—or on their necks and chins. They flounced along absorbedly. Never again would they be so inexperienced about getting over vegetation.

The happy surprise was that finally they led back up the mesa of their own accord. Not where they had gone down but on the far side, and back to the pen. The little wolves had compasses in their heads! The big wolves did not lead; they followed the pups. The pups had made a sweeping, jiggling half-circle, a good third of a mile, and they knew right where home was.

Now all was well, and I resumed my longing for the plane, when things were again stirred up. Trigger and Lady had gone to the kill. As they trotted homeward on the tundra below, we were mystified by a peculiarly colored object sticking from Lady's mouth—a large, orange-pink object. Not till she neared the pen did we make it out—a caribou lung. She was bearing a present to the pups, and as usual it was the lightest thing she could find at the kill.

This gift led to turmoil and, as so often, to jealousy for Lady. She laid it beside the fence and we rushed to help her gain her emotional reward. For the second time this day Cris threw open the gate and the pups thronged out. Two made for the lung. But Trigger got the others. They turned and followed at the mere touch of that big nose bent near them. He was leading them away!

"Here, Trigger! Bring the puppies here, Trigger!" I beseeched with false, nervous seductiveness. Trigger glanced at me but kept going.

Cris caught on. "He's got meat!"

Trigger led the three pups to a fresh red disgorge.

Poor Lady! She left her two pups and hurried over, dark-eared and crying, to look at Trigger's grand success—the big donation, and all three pups strutting with pieces of meat, carrying them off, laying them down and running back to grab another piece.

As if this were not enough, Trigger led the three down off the mesa. Lady followed; anxiously we did too. He crawled under a willow thicket and brought forth another cache. The pups by this time were stretched wide across the middle. They moved on, exploring, followed by the big wolves, baby-sitting on the run.

Cris had a startling thought. "Tootch!" he yelled. "The other pups!" I sped up the mesa and threw pups and lung into the pen.

Now something happened that gave me a strange doubt. All this time up on her lookout knoll, Silver-mane had lain, nose on paws, watching, sometimes whimpering. Now she howled. Trigger and Lady—and the three pups!—gave a good howl right back. The doubt came to me, were these her pups?

The pups returned at last, again of their own accord.

In the evening the wind laid. I swallowed my disappointment. Andy was not coming. We took the camera, the big wolves and Tootch, who got on edgily with them, half scared, but also half gay at being free, and went down toward the river to try to film Silver-mane, who paced there, waiting for Trigger and Lady to go hunting.

Cris was huddled on the ground under a tarp, reloading, when he called, "Is that the plane?" I looked east. High and noiseless, through the gate drifted a silver sliver.

Cris ran ahead to launch the boat. Andy was circling to land. All at once I felt the pleasure, the great beauty of this evening. Soft sunshine and long shadows; golden plovers calling; white-rumped sandpipers perturbed about their nest as I passed; Tootch swimming alongside the boat as Cris shot it across the river hand over hand on the rope; the wolves swimming downstream from us. Silver-mane had vanished.

The sand bar on the other side was a paradise of flowers— orchid-colored vetch, as sweet-smelling as honeyclover, blue lupine, zones of greenish-white Indian paintbrush. A human was walking to meet us. It was like the Garden of Eden. Trigger trotted up to him and smelled his hand. Andy endured the ordeal impassively.

At the lake we climbed into the floating Norseman to escape the mosquitoes and sat on the floor in the back among mail sacks for Anaktuvuk Pass. For some reason our disappearance into the plane upset Tootch terribly. She ran shrieking on the bank, scanning each side of the plane. Had she seen people disappear forever in planes? She must have thought she was abandoned.

Ruthlessly we visited with our sleepy but courteous friend. He had flown until three A.M. the night before. We hung on his laconic words, jamming them with chatter. Cris arranged for him to return with supplies in a week. We could not know we should meet him then with somber hearts.

After he left we walked home lightheartedly with our backpacks of fruit and mail, while the wolves and the gay but wary dog trooped along or chased ptarmigan.

A triangle situation had developed among the wolves. Wolves do not breed until nearly two years old, but they court a long time ahead; they start choosing mates when a year old. Silver-mane, an older wolf, chose Trigger. But Lady wanted Trigger too. Perhaps if wild wolves had not been unnaturally scarce, she might already have found a potential mate among them.

When the three wolves joined company on the tundra each evening, Silver-mane courted Trigger. She pinned her ears together tall and slanting in the bewitching courting position. She bowed her chest and pivoted, her sinuous spine curved S-shaped. Trigger stood alert and tall, slowly wagging his tail.

Lady chased Silver-mane, her tail flying horizontally, an ominous battle flag. Silver-mane ran—at first. Then Lady played frantically with Trigger, leaping softly over him.

She baby-sat alone one afternoon. Trigger and Silver-mane left together for the hunt. Evening passed; they did not return. Lady howled lonesomely. The pups grew hungry and Lady asked Cris for food. She gave it to the pups. When Cris offered a pup some meat, Lady took it from him and gave it to the pup herself. I took her milk, but when I pushed away the pups she turned as if indifferent and walked away. She would not drink if they were rejected. Not until all were asleep in the den and Cris coaxed her again with a nice piece of meat would she eat for herself.

Trigger did not return that night. About ten-thirty the next morning, something—my conscience, I supposed—nagged me to go outdoors. There by the fence stood Trigger, silently looking in at the pups. He looked dilapidated. The lower half of his abdomen bulged as if sat on. I had a hunch, and, checking my first impulse to welcome him—he only looked around abstractedly at my pleased, "Why, Trigger!"—I opened the gate.

He went in, impeded by pups, and without the usual looking around for a spot, divulged a whole red heap. It vanished almost before Cris, imperiously called, could get there to glimpse the kind of animal. Cris hesitated almost a moment too long, greeting Trigger, who was now ready for amenities.

But he spotted an ear just as a puppy swallowed it. He had to ponder a moment at that; it wasn't caribou. The mass was practically gone, but I knew it had been no small animal.

"Calf!" said Cris.

Had Silver-mane guided Trigger far off to where the cows and fawns now were? Trigger had returned at an off hour; they must have gone a long distance. But instead of sleeping and returning later, he had wanted to bring this very choice load to the pups. As usual when a wolf has extra special tid-bits, he reserved none for himself.

We gave the empty wolf some of our scarce, moldy meat —Lady and Tootch expected and got a little, too—then he fell asleep instantly in his favorite pothole near the pen. Kneeling beside him I could not help feeling wonder and love for this generous, hair-clad stranger, our wild, forever-barriered-from-us friend.

Not again would Lady consent to baby-sit alone. About nine o'clock, as Trigger idled after the day's sleep, before departing for the hunt, Lady courted him. He rejected her roughly, as he had never done before. But they sang the deep hunting howl together. It turned out to be Lady's death song. Silver-mane answered from the ridge. Lady took the lead as she and Trigger left the mesa. She was running straight toward Silver-mane, waiting on the mountainside. That night Lady and Silver-mane fought. The next day Trigger and Silver-mane came home alone. Lady lay dead on the tundra, a nondescript patch of fading fur.

We had seen no caribou since the tide passed through, returning southward into the mountains in June, after the heat struck. Now a lone caribou passed, going south. The day was hot, the mosquitoes were bad. Exposed skin felt smarting and dirty from bites. Two days later two bands of two hundred each with fawns went south. It was stormy but still the mosquitoes were bad. Trigger, clad only in flat guard hairs, no wool undercoat now, winced and jumped and struck across his muzzle with a paw.

July 11 was a cold wonderful day, the wind cold, the storm of the past two days clearing on a big blue sky and white mists. New snow faded on the mountains. Twenty-five caribou—cows, half a dozen fawns, a bull—passed going north. Then ten cows with four fawns. Then twenty-five again, this time with only four fawns but eight bulls, half of them big fellows. All going north. It was the milling that precedes a big migration.

At one o'clock the next afternoon Cris called me outdoors. "Look!" he said. I looked south from the mesa at something so great and astounding that the first sight of it stopped words like a blow to the chest. It was impossible, but it was there. Up the Killik as far as the eye could see into the shimmer and haze of distance, the land was alive with black, moving dots —caribou.

They were coming toward us. Would they keep coming or turn aside? Nearing Easter Creek part of the wide, wavy front bulged to the left in a mighty pseudopod that flowed eastward. The main numbers came on. They were coming on a two-mile front, funneling down to half a mile to cross the river.

I had never seen this formation before, though Cris had seen it—a year ago almost to the day—when four thousand caribou had poured through the pass in the wake of a greater number. They had been going north. These caribou now were coming from the direction of the pass and also going north.

The formation was not a mass. The caribou were sprinkled apart. They were a multitude. They were not traveling at the migration trot but grazing as they came. This was the midsummer grazing formation—the bulls with the herds, the bands of spring joined, tiding together into the north on the second great northward pulse of migration for the season.

Cris went down to the river to film the crossing. I stayed on the mesa, baffled into a novel fury: this experience was outside of words.

Over the sunlit tundra, up on the mountainsides dimpling into rock outcroppings and crags, they came. Each was going where it pleased. Single ones sidled around crags. A hundred ran down an easy slope, hit green marsh, and white water flew up. Fast-flowing streams of movement passed among acres of slow movement. A thousand lay down, white in the sun, on the green marsh at the end of the cobalt-blue lake. Dark-shadowed caribou flowed past them.

Peace. Movement. Small counter-movements. Silence. A bird's pure call. And the ever-flow.

It did not hit your eye and stun you. It was a sector, a third only, of the 360 degrees that was filled with animals going someplace. Turn eastward: the mountains flow down in pyramids, white on top, greening on the sides. Shadows of clouds darken some, dapple another. The river rushes green. It is vast. Still. There are no animals.

The sun coasts lower, drifting north, and the mountains to the west go up in dark shadow obliterating form. But the tundra is still sunny. A movement down there to the west hurries—a little calf runs, catches up with a cow, one particular cow, who hurries obliviously.

Caribou swim the river constantly. The flowering of silver mist around them, shaking as they come out, makes a band of light along this side of the river. On the far side, bulls drop into the river in white explosions that make a zone of light over there, and a continual roar like a waterfall. A pair of big antlers sails downriver, swirls to a halt; a great gauze of light—the bull is shaking himself, emerging. One young cow drifts swiftly downriver, catches herself, trots fast—she must catch up with her own. Going someplace. But where?

Suddenly twenty are scared. Fifty are scared. They run reversing into the multitude. A cow makes a Paul Revere's ride, veering, scaring up hundreds. There is a barrage of hoofs. My God! will the whole thousand—thousand—thousand panic? The scare is muffled, quenched, lost, on the mountains, in the marsh.

The golden plover babies, the jaeger babies, the sandpiper babies, how about them? This is the hour that dooms them. The parent birds scream and hover and dive helplessly at the tan backs of the caribou.

A sudden three—a fawn, its mother and a young doe, perhaps her last year's fawn—appear right below me in the marsh, softly backlighted in the rich green, which is multitudinously shadowed now by the long shadows off each hummock. But they must hurry. They go.

The hills are alive, the mountain is sprinkled white. Each animal has its individual adventure. A slender-legged young cow with her alert, nimble calf comes onto a rise right by me. She stands and looks ahead and back. Thousands in sight. Where to go?

Down to the west the main movement proceeds in shadow now. Around each caribou as it comes from the river, white "steam" appears as if the animal merely by stopping gave off fog. The caribou leap, buck, shake themselves, playful and delighted on getting safely across.

A young bull dances teasingly behind three big bulls. One whirls, its high black antlers lower at him; he desists. A little white cow runs playfully at a big "black" bull, curves herself in a bow; he curvets back, ducking his antlered head at her.

The sun is behind the mountain, the light gray. Quak! Quawk! A multitude of calls here and there along the travel-ing congregation—cows and calves trying to keep together. In a big river crossing there is always confusion; caribou lose their own bunch. Some swim the river three times before straightening themselves out on course.

In the enormous gray land among the mountains, a little lost calf, bright tan, is in a chance empty place on the tundra, hordes going by on both sides. He jumps around in a circle, rearing on his hind legs, searching with his eyes for "her." So alert and pretty and desperate. He runs wildly alongside a running caribou for a few seconds—has he found her? But he takes off across the lone tundra beyond the multitude with mad frantic jet speed, stops and looks around, then runs frantically again. After a while he trots back alone along the river bar.

Cris came home about nine-thirty in the evening. We stayed out on the mesa watching. I told him my fury at words. He looked slowly around. "It's a kind of private experience," he murmured. "The caribou . . . and the beauty . . . and stillness . . . and clear pale sky . . . and that ruddy light on the mountains."

Now the wolves began their kills. First they stood at the foot of the mesa, watching the herds steadfastly. Then Trigger started toward the river; on the far side a great congregation grazed quietly. But Silver-mane observed the bright-tan lost calf. She chased it. The calf turned toward the lone tundra again and simply left her. She gave up and went to Trigger.

He was across the river now. He got a calf. He shook it. Silver-mane stood watching, then came up and both wolves stood over it a few minutes. I hoped it was dead. Then they sped on, putting the whole multitude by the river to flight.

There was a vast complex run from the wolves. With them, rather. For the wolves went into the midst of the caribou, and the outlying caribou fell in behind them and passed them. The wolves never changed their gait, probably could accelerate no faster.

In the herd a calf has less chance. There are too many things going on. He fails to sprint. He does not realize it is a wolf and not another caribou coming alongside until too late. Trigger killed four calves in a half hour. Silver-mane "let" him stalk, decide when to close in, let him make the kill. Then she approached and nosed the body.

At eleven-fifteen P.M., no more caribou were coming from the south. The sunlight was pink on the mountaintops. The caribou were gone, away to the north. That pseudopod to the east would swing back in a day or so and go northward too. Cris estimated that at least thirty thousand caribou had passed. And this had been only an afternoon and evening in their lives. They would go on, day after day, through different sorts of terrain.

The next morning Cris observed a cow haunting the place of the fourth kill. He suspected her fawn lay dead. We took

Tootch and went over. The dead fawn was there. Nearby were its mother, a young bull and two other cows, apparently looking for their fawns. The three cows came toward us eagerly, looking hopefully at Tootch.

"Quiet, Tootch," said Cris. "They think you're their little fawn."

The caribou fled, but first the one mother turned aside and went to her dead fawn. Surely now it would run.

We went to it. It had been bitten in two places. A bite on the back had wounded its liver, and there was a bite back of the ear. Apparently its neck was broken. It had the wonderfully soft light skin and fur of fawn caribou. It was only a yard long, each slender leg only a bone with fur on it. The head was no longer than that of a wolf pup at this same time. No fat. Muscular little shoulders. So perfectly, delicately made.

The bright-tan calf was still alone in about the same location as the evening before, hesitating, trotting up the hill, down the hill. A few cows hunted lost calves. One cow saw Trigger, and Silver-mane dancing by his shoulder, and hurried toward their calf-sized figures. They chased her. There were new black trails on tundra and mountain. Flowers were broken. Parent birds still cried.

As to the kills, were they wasted or used? We found that the first fawn had left its bloody bed in the sand, plunged into the river and drowned. The body drifted ashore on an island where later the wolves found and ate it. The second fawn, wounded, had also entered the river—anywhere away from the danger and terror. It must have drowned. The wolves had about eaten up the third fawn on the night of the kills. Later on we saw Tooch carrying a shoulder and leg, probably of the fourth fawn; we did not return to where it had lain. Many creatures stood to share the kills: foxes, wolverines, ravens, gulls, grizzlies, eagles.

Now there was an interval of quiet routine. We knew each morning when Trigger neared the mesa on his return from the night's hunt, for Silver-mane began to "mourn-howl." (It was not the full mourning howl.) She went off around the foot of the mesa and up to her lookout knolls. Would she have come up the mesa if Tootch had not been there? She and Tootch were hostile.

They had rolled together fighting for a second once but Cris was near and called Tootch away. Now whenever she passed below Silver-mane's knolls, she looked up at the wolf and uttered strange hoarse howls, as if we alone detained her from going up and killing that wolf.

On my daily walk with her—she still could not be trusted with the pups—we both watched for Silver-mane. The big wolves had no hard-and-fast routine: the night hunt was invariable but not the time of return; also the wolves sometimes made a daytime sortie.

Silver-mane did overtake us once. She and Trigger were coming home. Only Tootch's survival techniques—lead-dog techniques, perhaps—saved her. She pretended to be absorbed in something ahead. With life-and-death control she trotted, not ran, toward home as fast as she could without appearing to hurry, looking back over her shoulder now and then. Silver-mane would have killed her.

Trigger's morning return was ceremonious. First he greeted Tootch. He was the last four-footer friend in the ex-lead dog's life. She courted him elegantly for a dog, though woodenly compared with a wolf. Her eyes turned dark and brilliant. Trigger tolerated her in a lordly way.

Next he greeted us, savoring each joyous exclamation and caress. It all seemed to give him a happy, elevated feeling. Last he greeted the pups and gave them his load, large or small. Sometimes he had no load. (A hunt does not mean a kill; and old kills get used up. The wolf's glee over giving fresh meat shows how rare it is.) Then he was through; he did something else. You could greet a dog all day.

Usually now he came into the cabin. While I prepared his pint of warm milk, he tried to roll in the Ivory soap, the coffee, the bacon wrapper. Cris sprinkled Quelques Fleurs in his palm and the wolf rolled on that. He took his bowl of milk in his teeth and carried it out level to a safer place from his point of view to drink it.

"Trigger has the world by the tail," said Cris. "Silver-mane waits for him. We are glad to see him. Tootch is too. And the pups are wild about him. Looks like they tingle all over just to touch the tip of his tail."

He had a problem though. It was not the loss of Lady. On the day after her death he had given no sign of missing her. But the day after that he had done a touching thing. On returning home he smelled all their old resting places, then stood looking searchingly out over the tundra. Perhaps on the first day he was aware of what had happened, but on the next, taking a different route, on his return it may have seemed she might be at home.

His problem was that he could not get the human and animal parts of his family together. He wanted Cris to hunt with him. And as for me, in his complex family relationships, I had an extraordinary place: Silver-mane hated me. It gave me a wry exultation. "If a wild wolf feuds with you, you're in!" thought I.

I sometimes accompanied the wolves for a mile or two as they set out on the night's hunt. Trigger trotted ahead of me or waited for me. Silver-mane, without having come to him yet, stayed a hundred yards or so to the side. Whenever I stopped and looked at her, she scratched defiance at me with her hind legs.

At last I would go no farther. Then an old fabulous wish was gratified: I saw how wolves meet in the wilds. At first Trigger kept pausing and looking back at me; he expected me to come along. Silver-mane waited until she was sure he was coming, then trotted ahead of us both and waited again. The actual meeting was not carelessly impetuous but marked by the controls that give wolf demeanor its curious air of courtesy. When he was very close she took a few steps toward him and waited. When he came to her, she rose on her hind feet and dropped her arms across his shoulders, then jumped electrically from one standing position to another. Then Trigger, not Silver-mane, took the lead and off they went. Before they were out of sight though, they might pause briefly to play.

In play as nowhere else the elusive, basic difference between dog and wolf shows up. The dog is Jumper or Skippy. The basis of his life is dependence, therefore comparative triviality. There is no triviality about a wolf, even in play. The basis of his life is responsibility. For a wolf, play is merely interspersed in the serious business of making a living. Wolves are wonderfully gay animals but not frivolous.

Another elusive but basic difference is that his relation with the other wolf or wolves is not transitory and superficial; it is a life commitment. Dogs may pack and hunt together, but afterward each goes home. But to a wolf, the other wolf is mate—not playmate but pack mate or breeding mate. Their lives run together on the deep level of responsibility.

A curious trifle happened one evening that showed up the tensions in Trigger's extraordinary family. I deliberately teased Silver-mane, knowing I toyed with her life. No wilding should be tempted to trust the most treacherous and savage of species, the human.

I was coming home from a long walk with Tootch when I saw Trigger on the mesa rim, ahead to my left, watching me. Apparently he and Silver-mane had just returned from their own walk, for she had not lain down yet. She too watched me, standing on a low ridge to my right.

Trigger made no move until I gave our recognition sign, the half-lifted forearms. (Wolves like double confirmation from their senses.) At that he bounded down the mesa and trotted toward me, pausing to bridle by Tootch, then coming on happily, his ears making eaves, his eyes kind.

Silver-mane was watching intently. A mischievous impulse came over me. To mystify and astonish her, I gave Trigger the full wolf greeting: I lay flat on my back under his nose. It was the first time I had done this. Later, with other wolves, I found they instantly responded with the smile movements, showing pleasure, especially in the eyes; my pantomime was meaningful to them. But now Trigger stood motionless, looking not down at me but steadily up at Silver-mane. There was an odd bright look in his eyes like triumph.

The presence of all the passionate animals around us, two of them hostile, was bound sooner or later to lead to trouble.

On the dark stormy morning of July 21, about five A.M., a noise awakened me. Cris was up, standing at the Dutch door looking out. There were savage yells outside. Cris reported, with his usual interested but laissez-faire attitude, that Trigger was on the mesa, Tootch was going down the trail barking—"Telling Trigger not to worry about that wolf, she'll take care of it"—and Silver-mane was standing at the foot of the trail, advancing slowly to meet the dog. It looked, he said, like the showdown.

I jumped from bed and ran barefoot to try to save the dog's life.

Tootch rushed Silver-mane and jumped on her. The wolf pulled away and ran, Tootch right after her. Then Tootch stopped and started for home. Silver-mane stopped too, turned and advanced on Tootch, who turned back to meet her. Tootch either lay or was knocked down and Silver-mane shook her by the neck. But it wasn't long before Tootch had her on the run again.

What happened next was that Tootch again started for home. She could have made it, too, for Silver-mane circled to Trigger, who by now had arrived below. Instead, Tootch rushed the wolf again. This time Silver-mane got her down and had her by the throat. It was for the kill. Tootch was still fighting but she was screaming too.

So was I. I tottered down the rocky trail, barefoot and barehanded, screaming. Cris ran for Andy's gun, in the excitement forgot to loosen the case strap but got the gun out anyway and started shooting. He shot four times before Silver-mane broke the hold and ran. But a hundred yards away she started circling back. Cris shot again. This time Silver-mane ran away.

Tootch was slowly making her way up the trail. She dripped blood. She was afraid to come home. The Eskimos, Cris said, had "flailed the daylights out of her" if she fought. We laid her on the bunk. The damp fur of her neck gave off a strong peculiar smell—the metallic smell of wolf saliva. There was a deep puncture behind her left ear. Her throat was gashed so that the white corrugations of the windpipe showed. But she would heal.

The next thing that happened was that Trigger, who had followed Silver-mane, came home with deep blood on his neck fur but not quite to the skin. It looked as if it must have jetted from an artery to go so deep into his fur. Was it Silver-mane's blood?

"Are you sure you shot over her?" I questioned fiercely.

"I thought I did," Cris said. It was a sad turbulent feeling to think Silver-mane might be dead or dying. "Seems as if there's always *some*thing to make a person sad," Cris said.

To please Trigger we gave him a puppy to play with. It played, then the two started on a walk, so we released all the pups to go along. Bitter snow blinded and stung our eyes. There was a cold wind. But down in the hollow below Silver-mane's lookout, it was not too bad; we lingered there.

From up on the mountainside came a faint, infinitely sad moan. "It may have been her death cry," said Cris. "If it was, she would feel terribly sad that Trigger doesn't come to her."

Trigger did not answer her call—not audibly. But he did a nerve-racking thing: he tried to lead the pups toward her. Hastily we got them all headed up the mesa toward home, when Trigger gave a clear, quick, sizing-up glance at Cris and the pups. Then he played with, instead of snapping at, the pup closest to him. The next nearest one turned, he played gaily with both, the other three turned back and he led the string away.

If they once reached Silver-mane, we were through; we could never get them back. It was hopeless, I could not possibly return before they reached her, but I sped panting up the mesa for meat as a lure.

Returning with the meat, I beheld a beautiful sight. Cris was coming up the mesa side, followed by the whole troop of wolves. "I just thought of that old kill by the spring," he explained. "I grabbed a leg and waved it and the pups ran to see what I had. I let them smell, then I ran this way. Whenever they hesitated, I turned and showed it to them."

A couple of days after this, Cris made a fateful decision about the pups. I was away with Tootch on a walk. There was a mystic-arctic look that evening. The tundra lay wet and green under glowing low sunlight. The mountains stood shadowed and dark-blue. It was a thoughtful, painful beauty, as of death coming soon.

When I entered the crackerbox, Cris gave me a shy bright look. "Let's take the pups home to the States with us next fall," he said.

We had never discussed their fate because we knew it must be death. We could not abandon them on the tundra to starve; we could not afford to fly them out and somehow support them. But with Cris, as I have found, the impossible quite often becomes possible. We looked into each other's eyes with kindling recklessness and joy.

"Let's tell them!" I exclaimed. I had never let my heart out to these doomed young wolves.

We hurried to the pen and I "loved" them as never before. Even my voice, I realized, was different. Shy timid Miss Tundra responded, fearless for once: she yawned several times, a sign of wolf good feeling, and sat without shrinking for me to pet her.

But could we condition these free creatures for captivity? Cris tried. He put a rope around two of the free necks, Miss Alatna's and Mr. Barrow's. The wolves' reaction unnerved him. Miss Alatna looked at the thing following her, fled to Cris, sitting on the ground in the pen, and crept into his arms.

Mr. Barrow looked back at his rope. He tried to escape from it. Then he did the wisest thing he could think of: he dug a hole, gathered the rope into it and buried it. Confidently he started away. The thing resurrected itself and trailed after him.

Cris couldn't stand it. He took off the ropes. Somehow we must manage when the time came.

The evening of July 29 was a happy one. Trigger went with us and the pups for a walk on the sand bars, where he and Lady used to challenge each other to come to their digs. His presence made it easy for us because the wolf pups obeyed him instantly, obeyed his slightest whimper of command.

They followed him home. On the way up the mesa he seized a chance to give them a present: he caught a moulting bird and let them take it from his mouth.

After penning the pups, we put Mr. Barrow out alone to play with him. Trigger enjoyed one pup tremendously. He tolerated two or three. "But all five," said Cris, "and he thinks the devil is after him." He would hurry around the pen ahead of the loving mob, making a fiendish face and gnashing his teeth with harmless clicks.

Mr. Barrow lay on his back under Trigger's nose and urinated with helpless pleasure. He stood up and jumped over Trigger's shoulder as he lay—a wobbling puppy leap but a true wolf-play one. In the willow bushes he rolled on one of the old grizzly skulls. Trigger felt like doing something with it too; he lay down and gnawed on it. Mr. Barrow at once lay down side by side with him and essayed to gnaw too. Altogether it was the most companionable play Trigger had ever had with one of the pups.

But the time for his hunt neared; we were afraid he would lead Barrow off with him. We penned the pup. Trigger resented it. In fact we had to trick him with meat to get Barrow away from him. Afterward he lay looking off as if indifferent. Not till I had coaxed a long time did he turn and look at me. He looked straight into my eyes, not as usual for an instant, in a crossing glance, but for a full half minute. Then he licked my hand, cleaning the dried blood from a mean slice on my palm that I couldn't keep a Band-aid on. It was late when he left.

At two o'clock I got up from sleep, hearing whining and

thinking Trigger was home. It was only a ptarmigan mother coaxing her chicks. The sky was grand—pallid and bright to the north, swept here and there with reddened clouds. The world was empty.

At six, as I prepared breakfast, Cris came in. "Trigger's coming!" he said. I ran out to welcome the wolf.

Nearing the foot of the mesa came the dear familiar blond form. I ran back and set his milk to warm, then out to greet him. He stood on a flat rock near the top, looking down. I followed his glance. Silver-mane and three other wolves were bounding playfully toward the mesa, following him. At last the two had found companions and Trigger had brought them home.

The wolves saw us and froze. Then they sped westward, away across the vast bright tundra—Silver-mane too. We saw Trigger make his decision. He stood motionless, his side toward us, he jaw firm, choosing. Then he was gone, following the wild wolves. We never saw Trigger again.

27   Wolf Personalities

Summer is hardly a pause between the two great crescendos of the Arctic, spring and fall. On August 9 the everlasting whuff and scuffle and roar of wind around the crackerbox was stilled. For three days it was sunny and still, and cold at night. This was the turn of the year. The sea birds were gone. The arctic world was tilting in the void away from the sun-star. Far off, the terrible keening of the arctic night, never wholly stilled, sounded more plainly. When the wind and rain resumed, the tundra was yellowing: it was fall.

One evening Cris said suddenly, "The pups haven't had a howl since Trigger left." It was true: there had been two weeks of major silence. Just the soft little talking, protesting whines—girlish-voiced—as two wolves lay scuffling lazily over some plaything. Or the "conversational whimpers" when we were out walking. We hurried to the pen, knelt and started a howl.

Instantly there was gaiety. Alatna frisked to me. Like Lady, she loved a social howl. Limber tails began to swing. Wolves lying in the far corner hurried to join the group. All trotted fur to fur, a favorite formation we called "trooping." It was a happy occasion.

Afterward Mr. Arctic stood up back of Cris, paws on Cris's shoulders, and tried to take his cap. It was tied and he couldn't get it. He cried. Cris laughed. "I always know when it's Mr. Arctic. He's funny. When he has a problem he lets the world know about it." Wolves are great little talkers in a quiet way—this is apart from their howls. But Mr. Arctic talked more than most.

After supper he had a piece of meat left. He carried it around the pen, crying in a conversational way. He knew that anywhere he buried it, it would be dug up. Brushing another wolf in passing, he addressed his sweet mewing cries to it.

It was not a joyous occasion when we took the wolves into new territory one day. All seemed anxious and uncertain, especially when in the lead. But Mr. Arctic cried incessantly. He came up when I knelt, and leaned in my arms crying about it all. But he and the others were silent on re-entering familiar territory.

Mr. Arctic had a pleasing little habit new to me. He uttered conversational whimpers on the walks. I could see that the small social sounds wove the web of closeness about the pack, so I imitated them. I was whimpering socially once when Mr. Arctic ran past, wrapped up in his own affairs. It impressed me more deeply than many a big thing that the social wolf found time to utter a mouse squeak of response. Trigger used to utter that "social squeak" on coming across us unexpectedly.

Wind worried the wolves, as it used to worry Trigger and Lady when they were young. There was a day when the cabin thundered like a battle at sea. We could not hear, only see, lips moving in talk. The wind blew steadily as hard as it could, then increased. The floor throbbed, the pot on the stove danced.

A section of the pen fence leaned in and we went out to prop it. All the wolves were in the den crying. They came out to play with me, except Mr. Arctic. Peering from the depths, he cried on until I crouched and petted his head; then he fell silent. We could only guess what reassurance their parents would have given the wolves.

Now I had the heavenly relief of having an old longing, hopeless question answered. What other wolf personalities could there be besides those of Trigger and Lady? You cannot construct a wolf personality out of imagination. There was another question, but I never doubted I knew the answer to that: could any wolf be more wonderful than Lady?

Two of the wolves reminded us of Trigger and Lady. They were Mr. Arctic and Miss Alatna. Arctic, like Trigger, was the lordly type of wolf, yet also timid and luxury-loving. He often came up on walks, big wolf that he was, to be lifted and toted a minute, his hind leg dangling. We got ourselves into that by helping tired pups up the mesa and Arctic never forgot. He was the biggest and rangiest of the wolves.

Miss Alatna was the prettiest. She had a whorl in the soft fur of her forehead. She could leap a foot higher than the other wolves could. Like Lady she loved a sing. She even had a little dance; it grew out of a quaint habit she had from the time she was a pup until she was a great big wolf. She would barely gulp her own can of milk, then throw her milky mouth around the ear of the nearest wolf and contentedly suck off it her investment of milk. Every ear but her own was matted and mouthed. She was happiest if she could throw herself down and pat her forepaws evenly, but if necessary she would follow the irritated ear-owner around the pen. Her "nursing dance" came at the big happy moment each day when the gate was about to open. Then Alatna stood beside it and patted her forepaws evenly like a nursing kitten.

Out on the tundra, like Lady, she was fearless and gay, full of game and inventiveness, and she led.

Alatna and Arctic, the most happily endowed of the wolves, paired off, apparently as a matter of course. We wondered intently about whether their "engagement" would last clear through to the far-off mating time. At any rate, wolves do have remarkably long engagements. Wolves easily show affection but these two were especially affectionate. Returning one day from a long walk, Mr. Arctic lay down to rest on a flat rock. Wolves like elevations. At once Alatna snuggled beside him, presently reached up and kissed his face briefly.

The other wolves were all new to us in their personalities. Miss Killik was just a big, plain, hearty, affectionate wolf, unjealous, undemanding. In fact she was almost mysterious just because she had no knob of peculiarity to take hold of. She was the wolf who was one day to stand still and let me take porcupine quills out of her muzzle—and afterward run up to kiss me.

Mr. Barrow was entirely different from Mr. Arctic. Barrow

was not the lordly type. Stocky, broad-beamed, aggressive, at first he had ruled the roost. He would stand over Miss Tundra, his spiky tail straight out and quivering. After we evened thing up by feeding all alike with the milk tray, so that Miss Tundra was no longer the weakling and Barrow no longer the bully, then, oddly—or maybe naturally—he became a worried wolf.

The enigma among the wolves was Miss Tundra. She was sober, gentle and withdrawn. She had an odd expression, benignly quizzical, because of her gray "spectacles" and firmly curled mouth. If, in spite of her elusiveness and struggles, we carried her, she finally rode content or lifted a paw gently, showing she understood it was all in fun.

She had some kind of peculiar relation with the others. We even wondered whether she might have been killed if left in the wilds. She was the misfit. After we picked her up, or, rarely, took her into the now-dreaded cabin, when she returned she was jumped on ceremonially by the others, who rolled her down and smelled and bit her unanimously for several minutes, as if eating her experience off her fur. She seemed to enjoy it—at first. She was a puzzling wolf.

On August 23, Miss Tundra bloomed. In just five minutes she changed forever. I have no idea why. Cris said, "She just decided life was fun." It was a lupine conversion.

We were all down on the favorite sand bars. The other wolves had run ahead. Miss Tundra and I were alone. I pretended to dig a hole. She did not run away. She came up and looked intently into the hole and dug at the other side of it. I slapped the ground, then lifted my forearm sidewise, an old play gesture often used with Trigger and Lady. She caught on! This was play, this was a game. Her eyes sparkled, she lifted her own paw. She ran off—it's over now, I thought—but back she sailed and leaped right over me. I stood up and played "electric," jumping at her. She jumped backward, then jumped at me.

At all this commotion and laughter the other wolves came running back. And Miss Tundra for the first time in her life took on the whole pack. Her mane and hip fur bristled. She was all aroused. Cris came back too, surprised and amused. "Her face is beautiful when she's aroused," he said.

She puckered her nose and chopped her teeth at the others. She was electric. She was transfigured. She seized a bone and raced off, pursued by the whole pack.

From this day on, Miss Tundra was bold and merry and decisive. Alatna was the most lovable wolf we ever knew. Miss Tundra was to be the most wonderful.

28   Wild Shepherds of the Caribou

The crescendo of fall mounted: the tundra brightened with reds among its green and yellow. But there were no caribou. All through August only three lone bulls had passed, the first two in the velvet but the last with red antlers; his velvet was shed, except for a two-foot tatter hanging from the highest antler tip like a veil from a medieval headdress. Would the main fall migration pass this way as it had done last year? It seemed unlikely: the preliminary movements were beginning far up Easter Creek.

The wolves were coating up for fall. Black guard hairs, six inches long, rolled over deep, cream-colored fur and new wool undercoats. They were getting to be big wolves.

Daily the color on the tundra grew richer. Green disappeared. In the long arctic twilights, the red intensified, glowing upward from the yellow patches below the mesa so warmly it drew your eye as if to a light down there. On the long benches across the river, the tundra was tawny but underlaid with red like a warm live body under dead tan hair. And still the color deepened. At twilight the air itself seemed suffused with color. The bench tops were acres upon acres of crimson. Above them the mountaintops looked grim, hoary with snow over the black strata—grimmer now than they would look later, when pure white.

Perhaps it was Andy's last flight to us before freezeup that brought the note of sadness. Perhaps it was fall itself. That evening as we read our mail, rain ticked on the roof, the gas lantern dazzled and hissed by the head of the bunk.

An item in the mail saddened us, a review of a nature film, indicating that nature had been cutened up. Slowly Cris said, "I long sometimes for a no-doubt-boring truth and bigness."

It was an hour for sober review of our own life. "I failed you," I said, coaxing childishly for reassurance.

Cris smiled and took me in his arms. "Got greater things than I ever dreamed of. Way up here in the Brooks Range. not in a tent—a house! Oil heater, gasoline cook stove, peaches, grapes, tomatoes, meat!"

Wistfulness overwhelmed me in the next few days. It was pure woman-hunger, though I did not recognize it. It was months since I had seen a woman. My mother's birthday brought the feeling to a peak. A trifle never before recalled came to mind—because it was social and woman-filled I suppose. My mother and I on some trip had stopped overnight at a farmhouse. After our breakfast alone in the dining room, she had taken her cup to the friendly strangers, the women in the big clean kitchen, for one more cup of coffee. She was the sunny one—hair, face, eyes. It was a moment of ease and gaiety among women in their active work place. Leisured friendliness coming amidst activity. The moment when the fabric of hands to hands, of human kindness, gives unconsidered confidence. The moment as far as possible from that when one says, "Oh, I never thought I'd have to die this way."

And with this memory came a deep-forest one—for so memories mingle, the human never so far from the animal as we suppose—the death cry of some small animal in the night, "Oh, I don't want to die."

That evening I went out and stood alone back of the cabin. So still. There was the faint noise of the river, not heard in the uproar and commotion of August and the first week or two of September. An enormous moon, a quarter as big as the white mountains up Easter Creek, came around them into the sky, lighting it blue. At my feet the slopes of the cabin roof, flush with the tundra, were bright. Beyond them was the darkness below the mesa.

It was cold; you would suppose forbidding. But "nature" emerged—the nature so easy to love in the temperate zone, forgotten and out of mind here. Everything seemed propitious, amiable, giving delight, as if there were a towardness in things. It was the beginning of the "arctic euphoria."

The next morning the color was gone: mountains and tundra were the vast dun color of most of the year when out from under snow. The weather now was a gift, sunny and still. Ice flowed in the river and widened from the banks. The wolves were fascinated by the marginal ice on ponds. They stepped on it, broke through, pushed it with forepaws, carried pieces of it.

It was so cold the night of September 19 that I brushed

my teeth indoors, though I felt in my bones there would be "lights." Cris called me outdoors.

It took my breath. The lights were so close down overhead and the sky was full of them. Immense soft whiteness in a wide zone from east to west, the stars showing through it. Brightnesses to north and east, rooted in some great unseen light behind the mountains. The livingness of it! Aliveness and stir in the very texture.

The crescendo of fall mounted, and bang on top of it sounded forth the horns of the migration.

It was fourteen above zero the morning after the aurora, and Cris took the sleeping bags out to blow in the wind. There was a little sun, hazy clouds, wind from the northwest. I was starting breakfast.

"Lois!" he called. I ran out. "Take Tootch in." As I reached for her, I glanced west from the mesa edge. The caribou were coming.

They were coming from the northwest at the migration trot, swinging southeastward to cross the Range for winter. They were coming in the broken-column formation of the fall migration.

We took the wolves and camera and went down to the foot of the mesa to await them, Cris on one side of the rutted migration trails, I on the other, hidden by a knoll from the approaching caribou. The wolves crowded around my knees, crying a little from nervous tension.

From the other side of my knoll came the crush-crush of hoofs on frozen grass, the deep, reedy, quiet "Mah!" of a fawn—a pleasing sound, like part of the wind and the tundra. Around the knoll came the living, suède-soft gray bodies, personal, beautiful, each coated a little differently. An alert fawn prancing after its mother suddenly dived at her for milk. Two bulls had dazzling white antlers, dipped in water, then frozen. Others, cows too, had blood-red antlers. Some had tatters of velvet flying in the wind, blowing ahead of them, for the caribou were coming with the wind. They smelled nothing to alarm them, neither wolf nor human scent.

The scared wolves shrank against me or crouched into the brush. When a cow and calf came through alone, in a break in the column, and Alatna did lay chase, she quickly fled back to us. A band of big bulls was coming, their guard tines folded like huge brown leaves over their muzzles, their chests deep-furred and white.

After an hour I got worried: the wolves were becoming bored. If they went off I was not sure they would come home; they had never gone alone. But off they went, toward their favorite play place, the sand bars.

Hour after hour the caribou came on and streamed away into the distance toward the white-dusted mountains. Cripples passed. A "rocking-horse" bull, followed faithfully by by a small band of cows. He stopped in anxiety on seeing us, but limped on. A calf with a broken or dislocated shoulder which stuck out. A cow holding her hind leg stiff. A crippled cow making on alone, all others for the moment out of view.

This was not the main migration, though a mighty branch of it, and in dwindling numbers the stragglers would follow for days yet. But about four o'clock the main flow ceased. Cris packed his camera things. I started home, going straight up the steep mesa side.

All at once, from nowhere, here was Mr. Barrow at my side, crying and pleased to find me and be comforted for a moment, but anxious like me to find the other wolves.

On top of the mesa I howled. The wolves answered, from a direction we would never have searched in. They sat on the tan ridge side to the north, hardly visible in the tan brush. But they refused to start home. Cris arrived and we both howled and coaxed. But things had not been right and reassuring for the past few hours. Once as the caribou passed I had heard an anxious lost howl, probably from Mr. Barrow. The whole constellation of things has to feel right to a wolf; they observe and shrink from even a new bootlace mixing up the set of data that means "friend."

At last I went over crooning to them, with meat "bities," and the wolves followed me home. I crooned the singsong call we used at the end of the daily walk, "Let's go home and get some meat."

This had been a day filled with many moods of many animals, including our own pity for the laboring sick and injured. Many a time this day I had wished Cris had a gun to help some cripple die. Andy had long since taken his gun for moose hunting.

The next morning it was ten above zero. The lake rippled gray, but across the middle and at one end lay clear flat darkness. It was freezeup. The caribou had come with the freezeup, the ptarmigan would come with the snow.

"Slow" bulls, "rocking-horse" caribou, "tired" calves—these passed among the stragglers. A nimble antlered gray cow came through alone with a tired calf. She would speed ahead, her trotting hoofs meeting underneath her diagonally, her back limber and carried, her head turning a little, uncertainly. Then she would stop, look back and wait till the calf, slowly, doggedly trotting, was almost up to her, then she speeded ahead. She seemed eager to overtake other caribou. Were tired calves sick?

Two grimly revealing things happened. On September 29 the sky was darkly overcast, the tundra brown in the dark light. We were taking Tootch on the walk these days, and she and the wolves were ahead. We were walking by the willows alongside the migration trails scored in the tundra, backtracking the migration route. Suddenly we froze. Ahead on a rise between knolls stood two caribou, just come into view, watching us.

Tootch sped toward them. The five wolves followed doubtfully, emboldened by the dog. One cow fled. The other did an extraordinary thing: it stood still, looking down at Tootch baying it. Distrusting an animal that would not run, Tootch ran vainly after the fleeing caribou and out of our sight.

Meanwhile the young wolves made false starts toward the standing caribou—a yearling doe—first one ahead, then another, pausing, rearing their heads to look. Young wolves fear big animals. They hesitated. But they were instinctive caribou hands: they got behind the caribou. She fled toward us, coming along the migration trails.

An odd thing was happening: she was slipping a little on icy ponds. Lumbering after her came the pups, single file. It could not be. It was so. She was not flashing away from them. Still they could not have caught up with her. But fifty feet in front of us, she turned and faced them. She sank on one knee, then lay down. Still the wolves hesitated, wary about approaching. The tan throng surrounded her. Unharmed she got to her feet, turned and ran on. But only for a few yards. Untouched, she faced once more and lay down. The wolves did not leave her again.

"Kill it!" I said. "With your pocket knife. Anything."

I ran for the mesa to bring some kind of weapon. Starting back, I met Cris. "They had her throat slit already," he said.

We went to the carcass. The wolves' faces were dark red. We examined the body. The lungs had been only partly inflated. They contained eight abscesses, some as big as ping-pong balls, partly buried in the tissues. They looked like lung tapeworm cysts.

We backtracked the migration route again the next day. A lone caribou was coming toward us, and Tootch laid chase. We thought nothing of it, but just as they went behind a knoll I realized the impossible was going to happen. "She's going to catch it!" I said.

"It looks that way."

The barking neared. Cris set up the camera. They came back into view. Cautiously the wolves went toward them. Tootch caught and shook the caribou's hind leg. He sank to the tundra. He rose, struggling, arching his shoulders and bowing his head, but his hind legs could not obey. Tootch had hamstrung him.

He lay down, lay still, with no sign of anguish, deceivingly like a resting deer, while over him went on the things of all in the world most to be avoided: shouts, whistling, the furred animals coming about, smelling of death and horror. He held himself up again desperately and Tootch shook that hind leg fast, viciously. She took his throat. Hesitatingly the wolves closed in.

It was a sorrowful, hideous thing to have seen. My face, it seemed, would always be sterner for having looked upon it.

Not until the next day did we try to learn why this had been a slow caribou. We never found out, for the carcass had been practically eaten up by wild wolves. There were only a few gnaw-piles of bones along the edge of the willows where the wildies had dragged pieces of meat to eat near each other yet in partial seclusion from intruders.

As we were looking at these our wolves took off purposefully; they had caught a gust of wind. We hurried after them and came to two kills made by the wild wolves. Not surprisingly, neither had been much eaten on as yet. Undoubtedly the wildies would return to them; a kill is the same as a cache.

One was a bull and later Cris "stole" meat from it as a reserve for our wolves. The other was a fawn and it revealed to us at last the cause of "rocking-horse" caribou.

Ever since coming to the Arctic we had seen rocking-horse

caribou, only a very few each May; many by July. Apparently they could not winter over, handicapped in digging through the snow for food. So when wolves killed a rocking-horse caribou they killed a caribou that probably was not going to winter over anyway.

At first we had supposed these caribou had broken legs. But the calf had a swollen, diseased foot. Half the chiton was gone. The remaining chiton was tilted on the swollen foot, which was only a raw-red clump or lump. The hair was grown out long, showing the foot had not been used much. The foot was tangible evidence of hoof disease in caribou.

We found two more calf carcasses in the next few days. Or rather the wolves showed them to us. One was so hidden we never could have found it, dragged, perhaps by a fox, to the edge of a snowy brook in a willow thicket. The red rib cage remained but we could not find the legs. It seemed likely they would have shown evidence of hoof disease. The other calf, like our first one, had a swollen, diseased foot.

Kills are few. A band of about five wolves was operating in the wake of the migration, as a band had done the previous year. Yet in all our days of walking along the migration route, searching, aided by our own wolves, we found only those four kills made by wild wolves—three calves, two visibly crippled, and the bull. There could be little doubt that the latter, like Tootch's caribou, had been slow. Wolves simply cannot run as fast as healthy caribou.

In all our time in the Arctic the only healthy caribou we saw or found killed were fawns with big herds. We saw many chases. Silver-mane made a kill just around a knoll out of sight. But we knew she would make it. You can tell within a minute after a chase starts whether there will be a kill or not. The caribou that is killed is the caribou that slows down. It may slow down because of hoof disease or lung tapeworm or nostril-clogging by botflies. To a caribou herd it is no harm but rather a blessing for diseased members to be cleaned out.

On the other hand we observed caribou you would suppose handicapped outrun wolves with ease. For example, pregnant cows in May, just before fawning time. And fawns. One healthy fawn, fleeing with its band, had not even bothered itself to break into a run like the adults with it. As Cris said, "He paced. He reached out so far with his paws he seemed to be floating in the air and that action going on mechanically under him."

Even a rocking-horse fawn had kept up with its band once, when Tootch put them to flight.

Wolves appeared to be selective killers of caribou, selecting not the finest but the poorest, as they used to do with the buffalo in the old West. A shrewd observation was made in 1804 by Captain Clark of the Lewis and Clark expedition: "I observe near all large gangues of Buffalow wolves and when the buffalow move those animals follow, and feed on those that are killed by accident or those that are too pore or fat to keep up with the gangue."

But was it not bad for healthy calves to be killed? A classic answer was developing far to the south of the Arctic Circle, even as we walked the migration trails here on the cold tundra. Wolf "control" was started around the Nelchina herd of caribou in 1947, when the herd was estimated at 4,000. Ten years later it was estimated at an incredible 42,000. Census methods differ and the earlier figure perhaps was grossly low, and perhaps the latter high. But an "explosion" in numbers had definitely occurred.

The trouble was that the size of the winter range had not increased. Already in 1953 it looked heavily used, so Dr. A. Starker Leopold and Dr. F. Fraser Darling reported in their book, *Wildlife in Alaska*. By 1957, the lichens on that range were to be trampled, crushed, dug up; and the caribou would be tending to "yard," not going to the remaining areas of good lichen. And in that year the Fish and Wildlife Service was not only to reverse its policy regarding wolf control in the Nelchina area, but set it up as a "wolf management area," in which shooting of wolves would be prohibited. The wolf, in other words, would be given full protection on the Nelchina range, whereas before it was all-out control.

This reversal of policy was occasioned by a fear that the population of caribou was outstripping its winter food. After many years of control, the government agencies had begun to see the wolf as a useful and even necessary balance wheel in the life cycle of the caribou, and hence they ceased to aspire to a program of extermination. It was to be a tremendously important step forward in public understanding of real vs. mythical or "scapegoat" wilderness preservation.

A haunting thing happened one night. A big wolf came up the mesa. We found the tracks in fresh snow the next morning, coming up the old familiar trail to the crackerbox and pen. Was it Trigger's band that was operating hereabouts, and had Trigger, as the band passed near, come "home" for a little while? Once before we thought he had come in the night, but there had been no snow to show tracks.

On October 7, the last caribou passed through. For us, the migrations that beat like a pulse through our time in the Arctic were over.

Now that Tootch went along on the daily walks, new problems arose. She was half afraid of the wolves, wanted to dominate them and was wholly jealous of them. One day she did exactly what we had feared she might do: she took the wolves off and lost them. She returned so pleased with herself that we wondered whether she had done it on purpose.

Cris and I separated to hunt them. I was sitting despondent on a ridge when suddenly wolves surrounded me, crowding softly around, crying a little—a sign they had been worried at being lost.

They were quite capable of getting lost by themselves. They had done it before Tootch started going along. In unfamiliar territory once, seeing and hearing a river below in willows, they must have thought it was the river near home and that they knew where they were. They ran down and disappeared. When at last we all got together again, they were beside themselves with joy. The measure of their joy seemed the measure of their tension while lost. They stayed near us until really in sight of home, then ran ahead.

They had always wanted every one of the pack along on walks. If Cris let them out of the pen before I could start, they tore down the mesa after him, bethought themselves and tore right back up to find me. If he went ahead and I let them out later, they did not dream of starting until they had clustered around, each to be loved and hugged. Tails wagged. Claws innocently raked my cheek as wolves jumped to kiss me.

When Tootch started going along, we promptly saw we had two ridiculous duties. We had to protect the five big wolves from the dog. They longed to kiss her but she would bite their muzzles and hang on. Also one of us had to sit down and receive the overflow affection they dared not deliver to the dog. They brimmed with affection.

Tootch did not get along with "our" raven either. The eighteen ravens that had been around had gone off, perhaps to a dead caribou somewhere. But this raven elected to hang out on the mesa side, where he picked up scraps. He followed us on walks and, as ravens do, seemed to like the wolves near.

When we reached the open sand bars the raven prepared to play. He let the pups trot to within six feet of him, then rose and settled a few feet away to await them again. He played this raven tag for ten minutes at a time. If the wolves tired of it, he sat squawking till they came over to him again.

But he feuded with Tootch. She must have jumped him on the mesa side. He would hover just out of reach of her leaps and dive her, squawking.

He squawked at us too, but his tone differed. In his own mind he had some kind of relation with us, not hostile we were sure. He followed alongside us, winging slowly. Sometimes with amusingly nonchalant aerial competence he tipped his head and scratched it with a claw.

Tootch's pride and spirit were tremendous. In this situation where were only love and play, the ex-lead dog still strove for the only things that had given her life meaning: prestige and power. She and the wolves lived in different psychological worlds.

The dog was lonely. From the mesa rim she still watched

the empty tundra for Trigger. She looked up at Silver-mane's old knolls when passing. We were troubled over her predicament. We had taken her from a hard but exciting life of authority, useful work and socialness, and the storms of excitement when dog teams started on trips. We considered returning her to the Eskimos when we should leave the Arctic.

One thing decided us against it. She hated the very sight of her pack saddle, even empty. When she lay waiting for it to be loaded, her eyes turned pale and strained. We could not return the little dog to slavery. Soon we stopped packing her ourselves.

She knew only two things to do with the wolves, lead or bite. Play had been quenched out of her fierce life.

At first she got the wolves to follow by pretending to spy something far off. But infallibly she betrayed her pretense, stealing a glance to see if they were coming. They soon tired of rushing to nowhere, never stopping to smell or play.

To impress them she crossed the river one day. It was not simple or safe. The river, freezing later than the lake, was ugly now. Where the dog crossed, rapids rushed over blue ice. Two wolves followed, but when they slipped and fell to their shoulders they sensibly turned back. Tootch was committed; she went on.

She stayed out of sight on the far side for a long time. When she did try to join us, we were alongside deep swift current between ice shelves. She hurried up and down, started to let herself in, drew back. At last she shrieked. (Part wolf, she rarely barked.) She must have hated to do that. Cris in pity guided her back to the rapids.

Freezeup played into her hands. The wolves had often broken and carried marginal pond ice. Then one morning the ponds were hard clear across and greased with a film of snow. Innocently the wolves dashed onto the first one they came to. The ice knocked them flat. They scooted on their chins.

They scooted helplessly on their bellies. Spread-eagled, they shot across the pond. They tried just to stand still and their rumps glided aside and set them down.

But Tootch could even run on ice. It would take the wolves two weeks to learn to walk on it. Shrewdly they judged the degree of danger. They romped and skidded fearlessly on small ponds. But out where the big river chashed beyond its glistering ice shelf only Alatna, and she timorously, ventured near.

Tootch lost face cruelly one day. She had taken up enough of wolf play so that she was running circles on and off a frozen slough, carrying a trophy bone and followed by two wolves.

"Showin'm how agile and supple she is, where they slip and fall," said Cris.

She fell. Her trophy flew. She stood a minute, then retrieved the bone and retired behind the bushes, where she lay for the longest time. "Recuperatin' her self-esteem," said Cris sympathetically.

Miss Alatna made a singular gesture on catching sight of her once. A fractional gesture—a quick swing toss of the head. It was clear what the wolf wanted to do: tilt her head aside and lay an arm over the dog's neck. But it was too dangerous.

There was one wolf however that was devoting her life to winning Tootch. This was a truly remarkable affair. The wolf Tundra had a great power for loving; she directed it upon the dog.

I have known an affair like this to occur between a wolf dog and a human. It is rare and unlike usual dog devotion. The wolf dog—offspring of dog and wolf—is said to be liable to be more dangerous than either parent. That is easy to understand. Dogs have fierce hearts but are human-oriented; their fierceness shows toward animals, even their own kind. Wolves have gentle hearts but are not human-oriented. A human means no more to them than does a fox, but they are tolerant of other species, even of prey species when not hungry. If the combination occurred of a dog's fierce heart and a wolf's indifference toward man, the animal could be ruthless.

But the opposite combination is possible too: a wolf's solicitude and intensity, plus a dog's human orientation. Then you get an animal that has greatness. Courageous, untamable, serious yet gay, it has a genius for loving as Einstein had a genius for science. Its chosen beloved may learn love as few humans ever learn it, even from other humans.

Tundra, the wolf hound of heaven, pursued the loveless dog with relentless gentleness and undefeatable sweetness. She lay alone all day sometimes, crying a little from pain because her face was swollen where Tootch had bitten it. Then she courted the dog again. It was an epic contest.

The conclusion came months later, after we had left the Arctic. It came with that strange phenomenon, a lupine or canine conversion, of which we had already seen examples.

The timing of a conversion differs. It may be in slow motion, taking weeks, even a year or two. Or it may occur in a flash. Either way it is permanent. A slow-motion conversion had occurred when Trigger turned against the mean dog Weenok at Point Barrow. A flash conversion had occurred when Trigger and Lady were chased by the dogs released for the den hunt. Then there are masked slow-motion conversions. You don't notice the process; the culmination comes in a flash, looks like a flash conversion, as when Tootch suddenly saw the crackerbox as safe and fun; and when Tundra was converted on the sandbar.

It was a masked slow-motion conversion that climaxed Tundra's wooing of Tootch. One day Miss Tundra must suddenly have looked all different to Tootch. In one minute the dog changed. She laughed and played and delighted in the wolf's affection. Every morning from then on, she could hardly wait to get us up—she still slept on the bed—so that she could rush to the pen and be loved by Tundra. But toward the other wolves she never yielded.

After Tootch's conversion, Tundra continued to court her with infinite gentleness and social awareness. If Tootch guarded my glove, Tundra, who cared nothing for the glove, made the softest of gestures toward it with her head, her eyes beaming not at the glove but at Tootch's face. It was a kind of bow of wolf courtesy toward what the dog valued. One would have to see the movies of that to believe the wolf's soft courtesy. Tundra did another definite thing. Wolflike, she used her nose to push me away firmly though gently if I intruded to pet Tootch.

The wolves, our companions, were more mysterious and wonderful than we had dreamed. We had lost a sense of wolf-mystery on one level to find it on a deeper level. The mystery and uncertainty that had half veiled Trigger and Lady at first were replaced by the greater mysteries of nature. How trivial was our old question, would the wolves turn on us unpredictably! We discerned real questions now, not man-made ones concocted of fear and myth. There were answers we should never know; perhaps no one would. There were questions we should always wonder about. That dead wolf near the den, for instance.

Cris had come across it a hundred yards from the den where the pups were found. He had not examined it, except to note that it must have died that spring. In a mating duel? If so, was it male or female? The body answered one question merely by being there: are wolves cannibals? The dead wolf lay untouched.

The main fact about wolves had grown upon us slowly. Wolves have what it takes to live together in peace.

For one thing, they communicate lavishly. By gestures—the smile, for instance—and by sounds, from the big social howls to the conversational whimpers. They even seek to control by sounds first, not by biting. A full-grown wolf will plead with you not to take his possessions. And you in turn can plead with a wolf. He glances at your eyes, desists from what displeased you and walks off as if indifferent.

They have the big three peace enablers: social observingness (that wonderful wolf attentiveness turned upon social nuances), social concern, and what we used to call feral generosity. Now we realized it was deeper than that. It is social responsibility. We were to see more of it as our wolves grew older. But already we had seen wolves, both male and female, instantly take over responsibility for feeding and protecting from us pups not their own.

Wolves will do the same for dog pups. Disgorge for them too. Our male wolf Coonie, whom we reared later, kidnaped a dog pup, not to kill but to care for. Wolves are crazy about puppies.

Also they feel concern for an animal in trouble even when they cannot do anything for it. A dog got his nose full of porcupine quills on our walk one day. All the way home the wolf Alatna hovered anxious-eyed around his face, whimpering when the dog cried in trying to tramp the quills out. The other dogs with us ran along indifferently.

A new dog was chained and crying. All night a wolf stayed near him, whimpering a little when he cried. The other dogs slept.

A young dog wandered off, on our daily walk. The wolf with us ran to me, cried up to my face, then standing beside me looked searchingly around, call-howling again and again. When the dog sauntered into view the wolf bounded to him and kissed him, overjoyed.

Incidentally, as to this unexpected business of losing each

other, wolves are gazehounds and will eagerly overpass a trail and lose it. When Trigger and Tootch ran a caribou, the dog followed the zigzag scent trail. The wolf raised his head and ran straight toward the prey.

The hardest wolf behavior for humans to fathom is the "species quality." The wolf is gentlehearted. Not noble, not cowardly, just nonfighting. Trigger and Lady did not defend the wolf pups from Tootch. The pups' parents did not defend them from the men stealing them from the den. The first time Alatna witnessed a dog fight she was frantically upset. She would have jumped on any innocent bystander, but she did not, as a dog would have done, join the fight; she tried to end it. She did not know what to do; she stammered, as it were, in her actions. At last, incredibly, she pulled the aggressor off by the tail! (The socially observant wolf was never to err about who started a fight.)

The gentleness of wolves is often mentioned in early American accounts—gentleness both as nonbelligerence and as limited flight reaction. Captain Lewis of the Lewis and Clark expedition said that in the neighborhood of buffalo killed by Indians they saw a great many wolves: "they were fat and extreemly gentle." He added that Captain Clark killed one of them with a short staff, gentleness being, it would seem, no part of the Captain's own nature.

Gentleness may be appearing in our species. But the deadly words of Konrad Lorenz still characterize our species quality. "Latent in all mankind are the terrible drives of a very irascible ape."

It is almost as hard for us to sense our own species quality as it is to sense our species smell. We have an ape-fretfulness as well as irascibility. I caught a momentary glimpse of our species quality, so profoundly different from the species quality of wolves, the first time I returned to a city after living with wolves on the tundra. Suddenly, for just a little while, I was conscious of our species as a visitor from another planet might be conscious of it. The nervous faces; the fidgety, trifling, meaningless moves and objects; all the mincing paraphernalia of our weakly, thin-skinned, fetuslike species. I thought of the wide clean tundra, hundreds of miles of it, and the baggageless, purposeful, radiant pups that ranged that tundra with us.

In a reasonable world these peaceful predators would be the most cherished object of study by our race, trying to unlearn war. Why then do people hate wolves and seek to exterminate them? Probably for the same reasons as they do people. It takes a psychiatrist to say why. Lester Pearson in his Nobel Peace Prize lecture at Oslo quotes the Canadian psychiatrist, Dr. G. H. Stevenson, whose words apply equally well to our liking for war and for scapegoat programs of wolf extermination.

> People are so easily led into quarrelsome attitudes by national leaders. We men like war. . . . We like the excitement of it, its thrill and glamour, its freedom from restraint. *We like its opportunities for socially approved violence.* [The italics are mine.] . . . This psychological weakness is a constant menace to peaceful behavior. We need to be protected against this weakness, and against the leaders who capitalize on this weakness.

The ambivalent ape likes to be irascible but righteous. And professional wolf haters—Olaus Murie's phrase—capitalize on this weakness of ours. Wolves are not a menace to the wilds but orgies of wolf hate are. Wolves themselves are a balance wheel of nature.

Besides this basic flaw in ourselves, this orgiastic zeal, there are two minor reasons why we indulge in wolf hating. One is that wolves have had a bad press, from Red Riding Hood on. Automatically the museum information card by the fossil wolf skeletons from the La Brea pits in Los Angeles goes on to assert, "a savage creature," "these grim predators."

The other reason is that North American wolves have been tarred with the reputation of their European and Asiatic cousins, though American wolves have never normally been killers of man—perhaps because this continent was so rich in varied food supplies. There are authentic cases of unprovoked attack by wolves on man in America, but they are few.

One incident that is in all the books occurred back of our cabin in the Olympic Mountains. Down the steep slippery trail came a ranger, twenty feet at a jump in places, fleeing two wolves that had treed him twice. The male proved to have a broken jaw, perhaps kicked by an elk. His helplessness may have inclined him toward weakly prey. But the wolves had not closed in; they were wary.

Typical of the usual stories are these, of human and caribou kills.

The driver of a borrowed dog team was killed. By wolves, said the owner of the team. Investigation indicated that the dogs had killed the man and that the owner blamed wolves to avoid putting his dogs to death.

A myth-wolf tale can be made from real-wolf behaviorisms merely by suppressing a crucial fact. A wolf detaches himself from his pack—odd!—and follows a dog team home. That night he tangles with a male dog tied outside the shed housing the team. (Why tied outside?) A tale of menace. Until you learn there was a bitch in heat in the team.

In all sincerity a myth-wolf tale was made from observed facts when caribou wintered near Yellowknife, in 1953. Local people slaughtered about five thousand, butchering many on open lakes. Airplane passengers excitedly reported the lakes littered with "wolf kills."

To a human alone in the wilderness the question remains serious: will wolves attack? A month after our arrival in

Alaska, the answer was put into our hands as we stood by the frozen Yukon, partly surrounded by a pack of ten wolves. We were a little scared because the only wolves we knew then were myth wolves.

In the long, still, chill April twilight as we sat in the umbrella tent—new, then—there came a sound we had never heard before, the howl of a wolf. Thrilled, we stepped outdoors. Impulsively I imitated the sound, pouring out my wilderness loneliness.

I was answered. Not by one voice but by a wild weird pandemonium of deep-pitched voices. We stood awestruck. Each wolf opened up medium high. At once its voice broke with a yodel break to a low note which it held and held, a long, unvarying Oooo, while other wolves joined in, overlaid it with their own deep Oooo's, each on a different note. The wild deep medley of chords, broken by Wooo's entering, the absence of treble, made a strange, savage, heart stirring uproar. It was the hunting howl, as we know now.

It ended. We stole to the river bank. Trotting upriver toward us on the white ice came nine dark forms. In front of us they spread in a loose semicircle, watching us. One or two lay down, one or two trotted to touch noses with them. (Wolf socialness! We did not read it. And were the resting wolves pregnant? The other two their mates?)

Apprehensively I glanced into the black spruces at my left. A crush-crush of paws neared in there, a tenth wolf. The tent back of us seemed frail shelter.

"Should I throw them the meat?" I whispered. (Throw the baby from the troika.) The day before we had received a carton of raw meat in a supply drop from a bush pilot.

"No!" whispered Cris sternly. "Howl again."

This time I was too close, the wolves were not deceived. Besides—we did not understand it then—they had their howl out; wolves don't howl at random. One or two answered briefly but the main result of my howl was that the wolves rose and in desultory fashion trotted away upriver on their night's hunt. Not, of course, in the military file of myth.

But surely that tenth wolf had been after our meat? It would be easy to say he was. It is easy to misunderstand a wild animal's actions. The real story was told by his tracks in the snow. Coming up the wooded bank instead of the river, he was within thirty feet of us before he noticed us. He had backtracked hastily and joined the other wolves on the ice.

Myth wolves would have made a meal of us. For real wolves, humans weren't the dish.

30 *Leaving the Arctic*

The caribou migration had come through earlier than expected. When it was over Cris felt his work here was over too. He was impatient to get on to other projects. Andy was due to give us a drop the last of September. Could we get a message to him?

It would have to be brief, "written" on the mesa rim with empty Blazo cans. Cris thought carefully, then wrote, OUT 10 IF ICE. This meant that we wanted to leave the Killik on October 10 if the ice was thick enough for a safe landing.

Andy gave us the drop on September 26—with the wind, so there was more speed and smashage. It was a gray day of white mountain bases showing through cloud. Again and again he slowed, passing the mesa rim, evidently puzzled by the message. He flew away. Had he read it? We must prepare as if he had.

We had a heartbreaking decision to make—heartbreaking either way we made it. Should we take the wolves home with us to Colorado or kill them? No third course was open to us. If we deserted them they would starve. Young wolves require to be taught. Like that other great American predator, the cougar, the wolf has a long childhood. His parents run with him nearly a year. (The cougar runs two years with her kittens.) Our five were huge but they were puppies still. Not a day but some one of them, running heedlessly, took a tumble.

No parents had taught them what to hunt, and where and when to hunt it. They were still afraid of big animals, their normal winter prey, though doubtless with adult wolves they would have helped in the kill. Besides, there were no big animals here to kill. The caribou were gone south of the Range for winter. There would be only the few caribou ranging dark along the white arctic coast, utterly far away.

What was right to do in a situation unright from its beginning—the hour the pups were stolen from their den? "I took the responsibility for them then," said Cris mildly, "when I took them away from their parents."

One thing we could not do—betray them to their faces. I thought—ignorant of animal imperviousness to drugs—that I could put them to sleep with the Seconal and morphine that had been given to us, along with the sleeping pills not used at Barrow for Trigger and Lady, and then Cris could shoot them.

When Cris said we would take them, I felt joy and relief. When he said, "We'd better kill them," I felt relief in a different way. Long ago, in July, he had decided to take them along, but now we knew how they just lived for their daily walk in freedom.

It was a sorrowful problem. It haunted hours when we should have slept.

It was not a light thing to take them home. There would be an unbearable interval while Cris, working alone, would build a wolfproof pen and the freedom lovers would have to be chained. The pen would be such a huge labor and cost for us, so little for them when done. And Operation Heartbreak began in my mind when I thought of the wolves chained.

"All right," Cris said grimly. "You shoot Miss Alatna first."

I had a quiet little interview with fate—one of those when a question is asked (not, it seems, by oneself) and answered: Do you choose to do this thing—to take the wolves home? Yes, said I, knowing, though I could not foresee, what it might cost me emotionally. Just one item of the cost, and that the least, would be that for years Cris and I could not be absent overnight from home at the same time.

Cris measured the ice every day or two and changed his message on the mesa rim. ICE 7. ICE 11. Eighteen inches of ice are required to guarantee a safe landing for a Norseman.

Andy did not come on the tenth. Our message must have been unreadable. Nevertheless I prepared after each meal either for the next meal or to leave forever. I scoured the magnesium griddle and the stove free of salt grease so they would not corrode. We were leaving them and other things for the Ahgook brothers, who would come for their cache after the snow deepened.

As for the cabin, Andy had requested that we leave it, stocked with survival gear, as the only emergency shelter in hundreds of wilderness miles.

Would he come on the fifteenth, the day appointed before freezeup? Always I had an excited sad feeling in the pit of my stomach. And the unbearable memory of the pictures we should have got but didn't. I never thought of those Cris got.

There was a scene out on the high tundra one afternoon I should have liked to photograph. It symbolized our life in the Arctic. Yet what was there to show? The icy sun low to the south; the vast tan tundra; Cris in his old gray down jacket and hood belted by the webbing straps of his magazine holder, chopping at a frozen red carcass, the wolf-killed caribou bull; gray wolves slinking around him or lying with meat he tossed. At one side, the camera on the tripod pointing its black snout to the sky. And all around, the stern white mountains.

There was a "dog" around the hazy sun one morning. The temperature was twelve above zero and dropping fast. A ground mist dimmed the mountain bases. Gradually it sopped up the distance. Snow began—so fine it was imperceptible, just a quiver in the air if you looked the right way. Elsewhere there was only an illusive sense of movement in the air, as if your eyes were tired. Yet the ground whitened. This snow would not go. The hard glorious time was beginning.

October 11 was a great clarion memorable day. We walked for miles to the northwest. The wolves pounced in piles of leaves laid up by voles against the willows for winter food; the leaves were still green, harvested ahead of freezeup. Ptarmigan, white again now, rushed by in hundreds, streaming in off the arctic slope to winter here. A wolf hit my knee from behind and I nearly knelt. Salute!

At the limit of our walk Tootch sped on. Across the rise ahead, out of sight. The wolves followed.

"Meaties!" I shouted at the top of my voice. I always carried a small plastic sack of a dozen bites, finger-tip size.

The skyline broke. The wolves were coming back, Barrow in the lead. Laughing, holding a meat bit high, "Meat!" I yelled.

The wolf rose as he came. He hit me amidships and I rocked back laughing, my hand high. The pack hit me, leaping for meat.

"That was something!" said Cris after we were at home. "That little wolf packing that leg from way out there on the tundra, taking it into the pen!" Miss Tundra had picked up the bone half a mile from camp and packed it home. She rested her jaws often but she would not let me put the bone in my knapsack. At the pen she hurried in and laid it down, then ran to join the last romp before all were penned.

"She wasn't ready to go in yet," said Cris, "but she took that leg in, then came out."

He bore out their milk tray. The wolves finished drinking, then each went methodically down the line, licking every can. Mr. Barrow began his usual improbable routine. With businesslike speed he lifted each can from the frame, set it aside without looking—if it tipped back he held it aside with a paw —and licked the milk spilled on the framework. The other wolves licked down the line after him.

Now Cris picked up the cans, all but one. This was something Mr. Barrow never liked—Cris absconding with the "bones of the milk." He nudged Cris in the rear. A wolf feels safer to make aggressions from the rear. It was fun but it was half in earnest too. Cris used to wonder about it. Just how fierce did Mr. Barrow intend to be? Cris liked it now. "I like to feel'm sneakin' along, watchin' that leg."

Cris swung his leg smartly forward. Barrow's teeth clicked. On nothing.

As for that fifth pan, Tundra had it. Her once-sober eyes, quizzical in gray spectacles, were brilliant. Tundra had a lot of fun in her now. There was a stalking chase all over the pen. She eluded Cris. She went behind the willows. She sat to urinate. All the time she held the pan straight out and level in front of her and observed Cris over its rim.

The five were asleep at last, tired and fed. I went out to "love" them. In the sky twilight they opened into a dense, cream-colored fur rug, with little grunts, their eyes closed. Except Tundra, the least human-oriented of the five. She lay at the outside, curled against Arctic, keeping her eyes open, watching me pet the others. Jealous!

On the morning of October 14, the mountains to the west were carved against an orchid sky; the eastern sky was warm and clear. It was two below zero, the gradual, inexorable descent. Up on the crags, Dall sheep moved among the snow patches. They were hard to spot but plain when seen, for they were cream-colored. Tranquilly moving, the "high-behinds" presented heads to the rocks, eating, then lying together below the crags up there, on the south side of the mountains again after weeks of absence.

We took wolves and dog for their last long walk in freedom. Surely tomorrow the plane would come.

The wolves gloried. Where snow was drifted beside a lonely lake, they shoveled their noses in it, seized it up in careless bites. They leaped, spread their forepaws wide. They stood tall to each other and wrestled playfully.

Alatna tried to break the ice. She reared on hind legs and came down pushing, pushing with her front legs and looking at the ice gaily. She thumped it like a woman making bread.

The wolves ran up the hill south of the lake. After a brief absence they sailed down it. One took a tumble and fell on its head in a level-looking pothole of snow.

Alatna came down flying, throwing her paws madcap to each side, head low, changing directions as if crazy with joy and liberty, and feeling an impulse to go all ways at once. Powder snow puffed up.

The shadow of the Range was filling the valley down below us and the air was delicate, cold, wonderful to breathe. We went down into the shadow to follow the river home. I stopped breathing. The plane was coming.

We ran for an opening in the willows. The plane sped over us. We ran back and forth on the whiteness, waving our parkas.

Andy touched down on the clear glass at the far end of Tulialek Lake. For some reason we did not understand, the plane just sat there, not taxiing to our dunnage pile in that cove where I had camped alone once, long ago.

We hurried along the edge of the lake—drifts gave footing —and inched over glass out to the plane. So clear and dark the ice we could see every stone under water. Andy sat motionless in the plane. It looked as if any second it might break through. Because he had spotted our forms below, he had not flown to the mesa, where Cris's sign read, reassuringly, ICE 13.

Cris got a rope around the tail. We swung the plane to face the dunnage pile. Andy taxied toward it while Cris held the rope and kept the tail from slewing. It was almost uncontrollable on the glass.

The deep-furred wolves, cream and gray, gathered on the shore in a last rift of sunlight between peaks and watched.

Then—catching them. Their mouths bloody, biting the chains. Two crammed into the old box that Trigger and Lady had come here in. Three wolves staked. Freedom ending for the wolves.

While Andy waited, loading our dunnage, Cris and I hurried to the mesa for the last hasty, forgetful loads. We forgot to pick the precious green parsley, luxuriant in Cris's hot box. It had seemed too precious to eat; absurdly we had laid a plastic sack beside it, intending to take it out with us.

The sun was down as we reached the plane. Ten minutes more, Andy said, and he would have had to stay all night.

Cris sat in the back on the flight out. Mr. Barrow crept into his arms and hid his head in Cris's shoulder. Arctic leaned against his knees and put his head in Cris's lap. Tundra felt sick but did not throw up. She hid her head in the dunnage.

All the flight out through the Range, fading color burned in the west, the light going down on the Arctic for us. It was dark over the flat spruce lands when a tiny yellow oblong of lights showed Bettles Field below in the wilderness.

All was hustle—unloading the wolves, staking them so chains would not tangle. Roadhouse changed. Tile bathroom upstairs. Men from the States boarded here now. It was the beginning of influx for the deadly DEW line—Distant Early Warning line.

Now the confrontation implicit in our adventure from the start was coming to a head—wilderness and civilization. We were crushed against the very edge of it now. Taking wilderness animals from freedom to captivity. At sixes and sevens, for we knew wilderness and yet needed civilization. Back of us we left destruction.

Trigger would be killed soon for the bounty, fifty dollars. (Lady was lucky.) Slap-happy poisoning would kill wolves as wonderful as Miss Tundra. We were to learn to know her better in the months ahead. The DEW line, obsolete while on paper, would keep rolling, wiping out wild habitat and animals in the biggest, best-armed invasion of this fragile life zone, the Arctic, ever performed. Hardly a man of the thousands to come, on hundreds of planes and ships, but would want to kill. Kill a polar bear, a walrus, foxes, a wolf—everything in fact that moved. If the small plane could not land on the rough ice in twilight, shoot the polar bear anyway—there's that much accomplished, he drags away wounded.

The crackerbox we worked so hard to build would be a nest for wolf hunters. We would wish we had put a torch to it as we closed the door for the last time. But we could not have done that.

With the terrible stoicism of wolves recognizing odds too

great to fight, our five would endure planes and trains. Arctic lay quietly in the arms of our friend, Celia Hunter, while the needle went into him, the required injection for rabies.

There would be funny things but our hearts would break. The head nurse's Thule-white and stony horror when I offered to carry Mr. Arctic into the Denver hospital to see Dr. Olaus Murie, the famous wilderness biologist, then a patient there. The kind nervous proud old baggage master on the train: "I never took care of wolves before."

He kept open the door of the baggage car for coolness for these thick-furred creatures, each now in a separate box. He put paper across the front of each box: "I think I heard them eat a little then." As we led snarling Tootch past the cages at a long stop, we heard him explain authoritatively to train hands, "She's their nurse."

And Tootch, who wolflike had never come in heat in her two years, came in heat in our compartment on the train.

We would strain every nerve and achieve the Home Pen, then the Yard Pen, letting the wolves into Crag Cabin with us. Last, the Big Pen. And it all would be as nothing to the wolves but would keep us poor.

We should learn Buchenwald, for its makings are in our hearts, in the terrible "sweet" and "nice" ones too. Yet we should learn wolves as we had never learned them before.

Worth it? It would be vulgar to say yes, and egregious to say no. The vulgarity would be that incredible vulgarity of those who say it improves one's character to kill animals. The egregiousness would be in assuming a knowledge of the future we do not have.

In the cold dawn of October 23 we set the cages off our jeep pickup beside the cabin in the Tarryall Mountains, staked the wolves out and after a few hours' sleep began building the first pen for them.